D0209616

Psychotherapeutic Change

AN ALTERNATIVE APPROACH TO MEANING AND MEASUREMENT

Psychotherapeutic Change

AN ALTERNATIVE APPROACH TO MEANING AND MEASUREMENT

Alvin R. Mahrer, Ph.D.

Professor of Psychology
School of Psychology,
University of Ottawa

W · W · NORTON & COMPANY
New York   London

Copyright © 1985 by Alvin R. Mahrer

Published simultaneously in Canada by Penguin Books Canada Ltd,
2801 John Street, Markham, Ontario L3R 1B4

Printed in the United States of America

First Edition

Library of Congress Cataloging in Publication Data

Mahrer, Alvin R.
  Psychotherapeutic change.

  Bibliography: p.
  Includes index.
  1. Psychotherapy.   2. Personality change.
3. Psychotherapy—Research.   4. Personality
change—Research.   I. Title.
RC480.M334   1985   616.89'14   85-588

ISBN 0-393-70007-0

W. W. Norton & Company, Inc., 500 Fifth Avenue, New York, N. Y. 10110

W. W. Norton & Company Ltd., 37 Great Russell Street, London WC1B 3NU

1 2 3 4 5 6 7 8 9 0

CONTENTS

FOREWORD

This book is a sophisticated and iconoclastic presentation of one experiential psychotherapy's stance towards the meaning and measurement of psychotherapeutic change. It has much to offer both humanistic therapists and anyone interested in the challenges of psychotherapy research. Applying theory from his two earlier volumes on experiential therapy, Mahrer attacks traditional outcome research strategy as an inappropriate and outmoded conception which has derailed efforts to identify and measure the effective ingredients of therapy. The basic deficiency is that "in the process-outcome paradigm, the real change occurs outside, in the patient's extra-therapy world. In our paradigm, the real change occurs in the therapy session itself." Accordingly, the basic task is to determine causal relations between the operations and methods of the therapist and the changes in the patient *during the session!* The heart of his book is a detailed rational and empirical explication of three new experiential meanings of psychotherapeutic change, all of which require observational measurement of in-session events.

Mahrer is a self-described "clinician researcher" whose credentials justify both designations and who makes no apologies for placing "clinician" first. Indeed, he asserts that to conduct meaningful research within the new in-therapy change paradigm, one must be "a master of the theories [and applications] of psychotherapy used by therapists whose work is studied." Throughout Mahrer offers nontraditional statements which initially bewilder or frustrate, inevitably challenge, and ultimately illuminate the reader. Further, his new paradigm mirrors the best recent thought in psychotherapy process research. Anyone interested in psychotherapy deserves an encounter with this intriguing volume.

Donald J. Kiesler, Ph.D.
Professor of Psychology,
Virginia Commonwealth University

INTRODUCTION

I am a practitioner of psychotherapy. For thirty years I have been doing psychotherapy, reading books and articles about psychotherapy, training predoctoral and postdoctoral students in psychotherapy. I also work with a few other professors and a fair number of graduate students in doing psychotherapy research.

If there is one issue where practitioners and psychotherapy researchers join together, it is in the issue of what we mean by "psychotherapeutic change" and how we see whether it is occurring. This book is all about psychotherapeutic change, and it speaks to the practitioner and to the psychotherapy researcher.

Intended Contributions

What are the purposes of the book? What are its intended contributions?

To introduce three new meanings of "psychotherapeutic change." These three meanings come mainly from psychotherapeutic practice, and especially from an experiential theory of psychotherapeutic practice. But the actual three meanings are useful for many practitioners and many clinical researchers. I am calling them "new" because the purpose is to organize smatterings and pieces here and there in both the psychotherapy and research literatures, and to package them in a way that is respectable and useful for both clinical work and clinical research.

First, one begins with a careful study of the individual patient. On the basis of your own grasp and understanding of this person, frame out some ideas of what this particular person is capable of being and becoming. This is discussed in chapter 2 (Directions of Potential Change). I show how this can be done for therapists who follow an experiential approach, and I also discuss how therapists and researchers following other approaches can adapt and use their own versions of this method.

A second consists of identifying moments in psychotherapy sessions where something good is happening. By "something good" I mean instances when there is genuine and significant psychotherapeutic change, movement, progress, improvement, or good process. This is discussed in chapter 3 (Indices of Psychotherapeutic Movement). The purpose of that chapter is to assemble a list of these moments of psychotherapeutic movement from most therapeutic approaches, including experiential psychotherapy. Many practitioners know when something good happens in their sessions, but researchers are just beginning to look at these moments. I believe that there is an exciting future in studying therapy sessions this way.

A third consists of what is termed "therapist statements as prescriptions-for-change." This is the title of chapter 4. The idea is that a large proportion of what therapists say and do contains an incredible yield of prescriptions for how patients are to be, behave, and become. From this perspective, psychotherapeutic change means being, behaving, and becoming the ways contained in the bulk of statements made by therapists. This way of looking at therapist statements is proposed as making a difference in how and what therapists say to their patients. It also is proposed as a new way of studying the process of psychotherapeutic change by researchers.

To provide ways of assessing and measuring these three proposed meanings of psychotherapeutic change. The business of psychotherapy researchers requires that meanings be assessed and measured. Therapists are also entitled to be concerned with such questions as, "How do I know that some change is occurring? What are the cues and indications that changes are taking place?" Both researchers and therapists have their own concerns with matters of assessment and measurement of psychotherapeutic change, whether or not they agree with each other on the actual methods and on the criteria of the methods they use.

To study psychotherapeutic change by studying what occurs in the sessions rather than outside the sessions. The three proposed meanings and measures of psychotherapeutic change pertain to what occurs in the actual sessions themselves. Studying psychotherapeutic change means studying the events of the actual sessions. Most psychotherapists already know and do this. Most psychotherapy researchers do not. They traditionally use meanings and measures of psychotherapy change which call for extra-therapy measures. They study "outcomes" which are assessed outside of therapy, generally after therapy is over. While this makes sense for the more traditional meanings of psychotherapeutic change, the argument presented here (chapter 5) is that the proposed three meanings of change call for measures of what goes on in the actual therapy sessions themselves. The intended contribution is to introduce "in-therapy outcomes" as an alternative to the standard research strategy of extra-therapy outcomes.

These are the three main intended contributions. In addition, there are a few personal convictions about the study of psychotherapeutic change.

The Study of Psychotherapeutic Change: Some Convictions

I expect that I am typical of most psychotherapists. Nearly everything I have learned about psychotherapeutic change has come from reading what psychotherapists have written and from listening to tapes of what other psychotherapists actually do in actual therapy sessions. Precious little has come from the research literature. I believe that many practitioners have a great deal to contribute to the study of psychotherapeutic change. The invitation offered by this book is for practitioners to add their wisdom and knowledge to the research study of psychotherapeutic change by being with researchers, working with researchers, and being researchers.

I believe that one of the major contributions of Carl Rogers and the client-centered school was to pioneer the way for clinicians to study what goes on in psychotherapy. Rogers and his colleagues showed how a client-centered theory of human beings and of psychotherapy could open the way for a solid and continuing program of psychotherapy research. I am convinced that an existential-humanistic theory of human beings and its experiential theory of psychotherapy are ready to offer a great deal to the study of psychotherapeutic change. The invitation to others in the existential-experiential family is to consider psychotherapy research as part of what they might do.

I know that most students in clinical psychology, psychiatry, psychoanalysis, and the other psychotherapeutic professions have justification for a rather unfriendly attitude toward "research." Their eagerness for learning psychotherapy is typically bracketed from acerbic requirements to learn about traditional research strategy, research design, research methods and procedures, statistics and quantitative methods. My conviction is that a great deal of traditional research approaches and methods are ill-suited to the study of psychotherapeutic change, and that the alternative approach proposed in this book can make this kind of psychotherapeutic research relevant, cordial to the learning of psychotherapeutic practice, and almost fun.

Respected reviews of psychotherapy research seem to confirm that the bulk of psychotherapy research aims at answering two questions. One is: Which psychotherapies are more effective with what kinds of patients with what kinds of problems? (E.g., Fiske, 1977; Goldstein, Heller, & Sechrest, 1966; Kiesler, 1966, 1971a; Strupp, 1963; Strupp & Bergin, 1969.) Another is: What are the effective ingredients or components of psychotherapy? (E.g., Burton, 1976; Frank, 1974; Goldfried, 1982; Gomes-Schwartz, 1978; Prochaska, 1979; Rogers, 1957; Strupp, 1973; Yalom, 1975.) Both of these questions leave obscure, implicit, and unanswered the heart of the matter, viz., What constitutes 'improvement' in psychotherapy? (See Strupp & Bloxom, 1975.) My conviction is that both psychotherapy practice and psychotherapy research would profit from a careful study of the meaning and measurement of psychotherapy change.

Walking Together Through the Book

Chapter 1 answers two questions. The first is: What are the current meanings and measures of psychotherapeutic change? A brief overview is given of what most researchers, as well as a few clinicians, accept as the meanings of psychotherapeutic change and the ways of gauging these changes. The second question is: What are some of the issues upon which a researcher or clinician will either accept the current meanings and measures of psychotherapeutic change or move toward an alternative approach? The aim is to frame some of the issues and to show the position taken by those who would espouse an alternative approach. In other words, the aim is to give some of the theoretical bases for an alternative approach to the whole meaning of psychotherapeutic change.

Chapters 2–4 answer the following question: If you accept an alternative approach to the meaning of psychotherapeutic change, what meanings and measures would you use? Chapter 2 gives a set of principles, used in an experiential psychotherapy, whereby the researcher or practitioner can start with information about the individual patient and generate predictions of what the person can be or become. It is the individual patient's own directions of potential change. This is one measure of psychotherapeutic change from an alternative approach.

Chapter 3 reviews the indices of psychotherapeutic movement during a session, emphasizing those used by researchers and including the perspective of an experiential theory of psychotherapy. This is the second measure of psychotherapeutic change.

Chapter 4 gives the final meaning and measure of psychotherapeutic change. It consists of using therapists' statements as containing prescriptions-for-change. The background and researchability of this method are described, and the method itself is discussed. While appropriate for experiential psychotherapy, this method is also quite useable in many other approaches.

Chapter 5 argues that using these three meanings and measures calls for in-therapy data. Two paradigms are proposed for research on the real pay-off in psychotherapy. One is the traditional process-outcome paradigm; the other is an "in-therapy change" paradigm. The alternative approach and the three proposed measures favor the "in-therapy change" paradigm rather than the traditional process-outcome paradigm.

Psychotherapy Research Teams

This book was generated from experiences as a practicing psychotherapist who does psychotherapy research. Four streams of experience should be noted. One involves weekly meetings with my own psychotherapy research team. While all the members deserve some acknowledgment, there are several who earn special thanks, and among these are Dr. Patricia Gervaize, Dr. Gary M. Durak, Irit Sterner, Kerry C. Lawson, Despina J. Nifakis, Olga Kersten-Matwin, Wayne Nadler, Richard Markow, André Brunette, and Marvin Zemell. I am the boss of one research team. I am a member of another which is bossed by Professor Henry P. Edwards. This book was in part an expression of his diplomatic tolerance of alternative meanings and measurements of psychotherapy change.

Both of our psychotherapy research teams required audiotapes and videotapes of actual psychotherapy conducted by professional psychotherapists. Spearheaded by the efforts of Dr. Patricia Gervaize, we have developed a rich library of such tapes, thanks to many professional psychotherapists, largely from the United States. This book depended on hours of careful listening to these tapes, screened and confidentiality-protected above and beyond the standards of professional bodies responsible for the legal-professional-ethical codes on these matters.

My psychotherapy research team is comprised of graduate students, usually seven to ten, who come together once a week to do work and discuss matters. The team is invaluable. Pat Gervaize and I seem to chat about psychotherapy research just about any time. A great deal of this book came from all those talkings together. These were invaluable, and precious.

Psychotherapeutic Change

AN ALTERNATIVE APPROACH
TO MEANING AND MEASUREMENT

1
An Alternative Approach to the Meaning of Psychotherapeutic Change

Our purpose here is to answer two questions: 1) What are the current meanings and measures of psychotherapeutic change? 2) What are some of the issues upon which a researcher or clinician will either accept the current meanings and measures of psychotherapeutic change or move toward an alternative approach to its meaning and measurement? Answering the second question introduces an alternative approach to the meaning of psychotherapeutic change.

A BRIEF OVERVIEW OF CURRENT MEANINGS AND MEASURES OF PSYCHOTHERAPEUTIC CHANGE

With regard to the *measures* of psychotherapeutic change, researchers generally are flexible and accepting. They acknowledge multidimensionality, omnibus measures, multiple levels of assessment, different ways of measuring varying indications of change (e.g., Bergin & Lambert, 1978; Berzins, Bednar, & Severy, 1975; Mintz, Luborsky, & Christoph, 1979; Strupp & Hadley, 1977). In other words, there are very few agreed-upon measures of psychotherapeutic change, and a fair degree of flexibility.

But the picture is not the same with regard to the *meanings* of psychotherapeutic change. Most researchers and most clinicians tend to use only a few meanings. Just what are the current meanings? There are lots of ways of classifying them. What follows is just one way. Whatever classification is used, the moral is that there are only a few meanings of psychotherapeutic change used by researchers, while there are loads of measures available for any meaning the researcher uses.

Changes in Psychopathological Condition

One general meaning is that psychotherapeutic change refers to something called "psychopathology." Variations on this word include sickness, maladjustment, psychodiagnostic condition, mental or emotional illness, intrapsychic state, psychodynamic conflicts, pathology. Whatever term is used, the idea is that it is an unwholesome condition. The patient is described as being schizophrenic, in a borderline state, having a psychosis, being severely maladjusted, being emotionally ill, having a psychiatric disease or mental illness, having certain kinds and degrees of psychodynamic conflicts, being pathological.

Psychotherapeutic change means that there is less psychopathology. The condition is alleviated, improved, cured, reduced, resolved. The patient is no longer sick, has less maladjustment; the psychodiagnostic condition is improved. The patient is no longer schizophrenic or borderline or psychotic. The degree of maladjustment is reduced. The severity of the intrapsychic, psychodynamic conflicts is ameliorated.

This is a common meaning of psychotherapeutic change. But how does the researcher or clinician measure the kind and amount of change in the psychopathological condition? There are all sorts of measures designed to do this. There are lots of test batteries, diagnostic interviews, psychometric devices, projective devices, measures of all aspects of maladjustment, intrapsychic conflicts, emotional illness, pathology. There are methods of measuring these conditions and states in regard to work, fantasy life, family, self, community relations, peer relations, social relations, sexual relations, cognitive and thinking processes, perceptual processes, mental status.

Furthermore, all of this information can be gathered from many different perspectives. There are self-reports by the patient, scores on all kinds of tests and instruments, observations and descriptions from the therapist, data from the perspective of the spouse or family, measures from the perspective of research observers, material from other clinicians and therapists, data from significant others such as neighbors and friends and people at work, records from the social community, referral sources, and agencies.

All of this comprises one meaning and one set of measures of psychotherapeutic change. It is quite common for many researchers and clinicians.

Changes in Problems

A second meaning of psychotherapeutic change is in regard to "problems." Instead of seeing patients in terms of "psychopathological condition," the clinician or researcher sees them as changing in regard to some sort of identified problems.

There are typically three different meanings of "problems," depending on the perspective from which the problems are defined. One perspective is that of the patient. The patient defines the problem as nail-biting, or not getting along with a spouse, or being depressed, or stuttering. Often the patient and therapist go through a process of deciding upon and defining the problem which is to be the target of their therapeutic work (e.g., Kanfer & Phillips, 1970; Krasner, 1975; Mischel, 1968). Nevertheless, the patient has a large hand in defining just what the problem is defined to be.

A second perspective is from that of a referral agency. This may be a social agency, social worker, physician, court, spouse, family, school psychologist. From that perspective, the problem is defined as the patient's alcoholism, abusing the daughter, lack of attention, slow reading, borderline personality, stealing, dominance, refusal to be reasonable, disturbing the other patients, fighting the medication, bothering other students, and so on and on. When there is a referring agency, the patient generally has much less of a direct hand in defining just what the problem is.

A third perspective is that of the therapist. While the therapist may accept the framing of the problem as defined by the patient or by the referral agency, frequently the connection is loose. The therapist's version of the problem may be much "deeper" than the patient's, may be much broader than the patient's, and may have little to do with the patient's version of the problem. Where the patient may define his problem as being depressed, feeling low, not having much energy, the therapist may essentially overlook what the patient says and frame another version. Accordingly, the therapist may define the problem as that of an anal fixation, or as problems of aggression, or as having problems with authority figures, or as oedipal problems, or as being immature, or as being obese, withdrawn, alcoholic, irresponsible, or out of work.

What is the meaning of psychotherapeutic *change*? It means that the problem is gone, improved, ameliorated, reduced, less bothersome. However the problem is identified before or during therapy, someone looks at it later and judges that some change has occurred. Who are the ones to make these judgments? This may depend upon who defined the problem in the first place. The patient may or may not play a role here. The referral source may or may not play a role here. The therapist generally does play a role here. The researcher almost always plays a role here, if only in selecting which of the perspectives is or are to be used in defining the problem in the first place. Accordingly, the change in problems is measured from the perspective of the patient, the therapist, persons who are positioned to witness changes, the referral agency, other observing clinicians, the researcher, the complainants, and "objective observers."

The measures which are used to assess change depend upon the meaningful perspective(s) from which the problem is defined in the first place. There is a full selection. These include symptom and problem inventories and checklists, behavioral assessments, self-reports, clinical interviews, projective tests, psychometric devices, interviews with significant others, clinical impressions, observation forms.

All of this comprises a second meaning and ways of measuring psychotherapeutic change, typically quite different from the first. But there is a third.

Changes in Personality Dimensions

A third meaning of psychotherapeutic change is in regard to some kind of personality dimension, rather than problems or psychopathological condition. It starts with the idea that there are personality dimensions which apply to just about every patient. Some of these include ego strength, impulse control, reality contact, assertiveness, internal-external control, dependence-independence, social responsibility, support systems, conformity, stress management, cognitive development, sex-role identification, flexibility-rigidity, passivity-activity, detachment-involvement. Each of these personality dimensions has a pole which is considered bad (unhealthy, abnormal, immature, regressed, pathological, maladjustive, disturbed, problematical), and another pole or midrange which is considered good (healthy, mature, adult, normal, adjusted).

Once the researcher selects which personality dimensions are to be used with the patient, personality change means that the patient is to move toward the good pole or toward the midrange. For example, patients are to move toward increased ego strength, from low reality contact to greater reality contact, from strong external control to internal control.

The researcher has to select which personality dimensions to use. But once the selection is made, then there are all sorts of measures to assess where the patient stands on the personality dimensions. Each of these dimensions has a number of measuring scales and inventories, tests and interview methods, behavioral and observational instruments. Each of these personality dimensions can be assessed from the perspective of the patient, the therapist, other clinicians, objective observers, and significant others.

There are many other ways of classifying the meanings of psychotherapeutic change, but it makes some sense to classify them into changes in psychopathological condition, problems, and personality dimensions. In terms of meanings, these three classes are common. That is, most meanings of psychotherapeutic change fall under one or more of these three classes.

But none of this really applies to researchers or clinicians whose theory of human beings is existential-humanistic and whose theory of psychotherapy is experiential. Other theoretical approaches also find rather alien the common meanings of change as psychopathological condition, problems, or personality dimensions. While these common meanings make a good deal of sense for psychoanalytic-psychodynamic approaches, for behavioral approaches, for many of our traditional psychotherapeutic approaches, they are far from universally fitting for all approaches. And that means that the whole library of measures also has little or no goodness-of-fit for these alternative approaches.

TOWARD AN ALTERNATIVE
CONCEPTUALIZATION OF
THE MEANINGS OF
PSYCHOTHERAPEUTIC CHANGE

The purpose of the present section is to present an alternative conceptualization to the meaning of psychotherapeutic change, one which comes from an existential-humanistic theory of human beings and its experiential theory of psychotherapy. The question is: What are some of the issues upon which a researcher or clinician will either accept the current meanings and measures of psychotherapeutic change or move toward an alternative approach to the meaning of psychotherapeutic change? I intend to identify four issues having to do with personality, psychotherapy, and psychotherapeutic change. The argument is that there is a commonly accepted position on each of these four issues, that if the researcher or clinician accepts the common position it follows that the common meanings and measures of psychotherapeutic change will be accepted. However, if the researcher or clinician accepts an alternative position on these four issues, then the common meanings and measures of psychotherapeutic change will be rejected in favor of an alternative set.

The Meaning of Psychotherapeutic Change:
Theory-Specific Versus Common Across
Most Theories

The question is: Are there meanings of psychotherapeutic change which are accepted by most approaches to psychotherapy or does each theory have distinctive meanings of psychotherapeutic change? In much of the clinical and research literature, some meaning of psychotherapeutic change is used with a kind of tacit understanding that most approaches would accept that meaning. The idea is that we can frame rigorous meanings of psychotherapeutic change which would be acceptable to virtually all approaches. The experiential theory of psychotherapy rejects this idea. It holds that meanings of psychotherapeutic change are tied to particular theories of psychotherapy, i.e., are theory-specific. While some meanings of psychotherapeutic change may be cordial to a fair proportion of theories, most theories have their own useable set of actual meanings of psychotherapeutic change. Meanings are theory-specific rather than common across most approaches.

If we ask, Are there some meanings of psychotherapeutic change which a fair proportion of approaches would accept? the answer is yes. For example, a fair proportion would tend to accept that psychotherapeutic change means change in psychopathological condition, in problems, or in personality dimensions. Perhaps 60% to 80% of clinicians and researchers may agree to that. Experiential therapists would tend to agree that there are some meanings of psychotherapeutic change which a fair proportion of other approaches would accept. But this is an assessment of the current state of the field. It is not a question of whether meanings of psychotherapeutic change are theory-specific or cut across all or most theories of psychotherapy.

Experiential psychotherapy's meanings of psychotherapeutic change do not include change in psychopathological condition, problems, or personality dimensions. Our existential-humanistic theory of human beings and our experiential theory of psychotherapy have no place for the concept of psychopathology, for the concept of common dimensions of personality, or for the practice of self-reported problems by the patient or patient-problems as defined by the therapist or external observers. So we do not accept the popular meanings of psychotherapeutic change.

What is more, our theory of human beings and of psychotherapy holds that each theory of psychotherapy has its own meanings of psychotherapeutic change. To the extent that the theories differ, the meanings of psychotherapeutic change will differ. In other words, each theory of psychotherapy is free to identify its own meanings of psychotherapeutic change. If meanings are held as theory-specific, then each theory is free to accept or decline the common meanings of psychotherapeutic change. We decline.

If we think of psychotherapeutic change as involving psychopathological condition, problems, or dimensions of personality, at that general level many therapeutic approaches would nod agreement with one another. But once these approaches get down to the level of actual practice, the agreement washes away and the theory-specific differences appear. At the actual working level, theories differ significantly in the explicit and concrete meanings of psychopathology, problems, and personality dimensions. What is more, at the actual level of measures used, each theory's specific meanings of psychotherapeutic change display a singular uniqueness.

Experiential psychotherapy solidly endorses the theory-specific position on this issue. Other approaches and psychotherapy researchers also agree that the meanings of psychotherapeutic change (or "outcome") are manifold, and are limited only by such factors as the number of approaches and the ingenuity of the researcher:

> In other words, there is no one answer to the criterion problem. There are as many answers as our theoretical and research ingenuity can establish. There are no best measures that one can recommend for evaluating the outcome of psychotherapy. There are as many measures as are relevant and required by the theoretically specific constructs of patient change involved. (Kiesler, 1971a, p. 45; see also Kiesler, 1966; Goldstein, Heller, & Sechrest, 1966)

Experiential psychotherapy is not the only approach which declines the common meanings and measures of psychotherapeutic change. Kanfer (1975) likewise asserts that the meanings and measures of psychotherapeutic change are theory-specific and, on that basis, declines to accept the common meanings and measures. According to Kanfer, behavior therapies decline change as change in psychopathological condition, in personality dimensions, and even as problems in the ordinary sense. The behavioral learning theory of human beings and the theory of behavior therapy frame out a distinctive set of meanings and measures of psychotherapeutic change:

> A distinguishing feature of behavior modification techniques is the belief that the target of treatment is a specific, observable class of behaviors rather than a change in the personality structure of the patient. From this basic tenet follows the rejection of traditional broad-gauge test instruments which purport to assign a person to a psychiatric diagnosis, or to reveal essential personality mechanisms or the interpersonal organization of personality components. . . . As a consequence of the assumptions

about the task of behavior therapy, outcome criteria for the effectiveness of a technique and associated measurement procedures differ radically from previously established assessment methods. (Kanfer, 1975, p. 75)

I support the position that the meaning of psychotherapeutic change is theory-specific, and that many approaches do indeed have their own sharply different meanings of psychotherapeutic change. However they are grouped and classed and categorized, neither the idea of nor the actual common meanings of psychotherapeutic change apply to experiential psychotherapy or to many other psychotherapies as well. What then? It means that experiential psychotherapists and other dissidents respectfully decline to accept the meaning of psychotherapy change as change in psychopathological condition, in personality dimensions, in problems — or in anything else which is held as common across most or all psychotherapies. That is the negative part. The constructive part is that experiential psychotherapies, as well as other psychotherapies, are free to define their own meanings of psychotherapeutic change. With regard to the so-called common meaning of psychotherapeutic change, these psychotherapies hold to alternate conceptualizations.

The Basic Definition of What Psychotherapy Is and What It Does

There are commonly accepted definitions of what psychotherapy is and what it does. Even though psychotherapies differ in many ways, it is possible to frame out a few standard definitions of what psychotherapy is and what it does. What is more, these definitions have high goodness-of-fit with the common meanings and measures of psychotherapeutic change. If you tend to accept the common definitions of psychotherapy, then you will tend to accept the common meanings and measures of psychotherapeutic change. However, the other side of this coin is that if you do not accept these common definitions of psychotherapy, if you accept a different definition of what psychotherapy is and what it does, then you may be inclined toward an alternative conceptualization of the meanings of psychotherapeutic change. Experiential psychotherapy is one of those which decline the common definitions of psychotherapy and the meanings of psychotherapy change which go with them; we are quite inclined toward an alternative conceptualization.

There are many definitions of what psychotherapy is and what it does. Of these, I believe that the following is not only representative, but also perhaps an exemplar of careful thinking and articulation:

> In all forms of psychotherapy (including such diverse variants as orthodox psychoanalysis and behavior modification) a psychological influence is brought to bear upon the person who has enlisted an expert's help in effecting change. . . . In broadest terms, the enterprise called "psychotherapy" encompasses a person who has recognized that he is in need of help, an expert who has agreed to provide that help, and a series of human interactions, frequently of highly intricate, subtle, and prolonged character, designed to bring about beneficial changes in the patient's feelings and behavior that the participants and society at large will view as therapeutic. (Strupp, 1977, p. 3)

If we accept this as a definition of what psychotherapy is and what it does, the question is whether this definition fits our theory of practice. For experiential psychotherapy the answer is no. Very little of this definition would fit. What does it mean if some psychotherapies do not accept this definition? It is more than a matter of cosmetics, more than a matter of tolerating a little sloppiness in a given definition, more than a matter of looking for a definition which fits virtually all approaches. It means that the declining psychotherapies would fall outside the meaning of psychotherapeutic change which is contained in that definition. Experiential psychotherapy rejects each substantive part of the above common definition, and that in turn means that experiential psychotherapy is on its way toward an alternative conceptualization of psychotherapeutic change. If other psychotherapies likewise reject all or most of the substantive parts of this definition, they likewise are inclined toward their own meaning of psychotherapeutic change.

What would be the experiential psychotherapy definition of its psychotherapy? This is a definition of experiential psychotherapy, and not psychotherapy in general. However, the proposed definition will try to match the format of that given by Strupp. Here is the symmetrical definition of experiential psychotherapy:

> In experiential psychotherapy, a method is followed by therapist and patient who choose to work together. . . . In broadest terms, the enterprise called "experiential psychotherapy" encompasses a person who follows the method and a therapist who is skilled in using the method. The method is designed to open the way toward integrating and actualizing changes in the person who follows the method.

There are serious and significant differences between our definition of experiential psychotherapy and the earlier definition of psychotherapy in general. The general definition regards psychotherapy as an influence brought to bear upon the patient. In contrast, experiential psychotherapy understands change as occurring through a method, one which is not described in terms of some sort of "influence" of therapist upon patient. The general definition sees the patient as enlisting an expert's help in effecting change, and as being a person who has recognized that he is in need of help. Not so in experiential psychotherapy. Patients are understood as undertaking psychotherapy on the basis of as great a spectrum of reasons (motives, psychodynamics, personality processes) as persons undertake just about most enterprises. But very few of the reasons would have to do with enlisting an expert's help, or seeking to effect change, or recognizing that he is in need of help. Those reasons for undertaking psychotherapy simply make little sense from the perspective of experiential psychotherapy.

In the general definition of psychotherapy, change comes about by means of the interactions between therapist and patient. In contrast, experiential psychotherapy explicitly rejects the patient-therapist interactive relationship as the major ingredient of psychotherapeutic change (Mahrer, 1978a, 1978b, 1980, 1983; Mahrer & Gervaize, 1983). In the general definition, the goal is to bring about changes that the participant and society at large will view as therapeutic. In contrast, experiential psychotherapy emphasizes integrating and actualizing changes in the person who follows the method; there is no place for "society" as a judge of what is therapeutic in the patient.

All in all, a definition of experiential psychotherapy differs in just about every substantive way from the general definition which is offered as applying across psychotherapies. Now let us turn the tables.

Would experiential psychotherapy offer a definition of psychotherapy which applies to most psychotherapies? Our serious answer is no. At the definitional level of what psychotherapy is and what it does, the theory of experiential psychotherapy holds that too many psychotherapies differ too significantly from one another to have one "basic definition" which is to apply to all or to most. That is the serious answer. There is also a tongue-in-cheek answer. From the perspective of the theory of experiential psychotherapy, many therapies are little more than therapists and patients negotiating and fulfilling roles, and relating to one another in ways which are consistent with these roles (Mahrer, 1983). In other words, psychotherapy is little more than role relationships. Accordingly, using the structure of Strupp's earlier basic definition of psychotherapy, our "basic definition" of most (other) psychotherapies would read as follows:

> In most therapeutic approaches, the enterprise called "psychotherapy" encompasses the construction and playing out of role relationships conjointly constructed and played out by the therapist and the patient. Each of the participants defines a role for oneself, a role for the other, and an appropriate role relationship between the two. The changes which ensue are befitting whatever role-relationships are co-constructed by the two participants.

This "basic definition" of psychotherapy would be branded unfair and objectionable by many psychotherapies. Yet I believe it is a fitting definition of many psychotherapies. In the same way, many proposed "basic definitions" of psychotherapy are unfair and objectionable to experiential psychotherapy, and perhaps to a fair number of other approaches as well. The point is that the substantive contents of many "basic definitions" of psychotherapy apply to some psychotherapies only, and not to all psychotherapies or even most psychotherapies. Basic definitions of what psychotherapy is and what it does carry a load of conceptual baggage coming from particular approaches. Psychotherapies falling outside the basic definition of psychotherapy represent significantly different approaches, and experiential psychotherapy is one of these.

Once you have a basic definition of what psychotherapy is and what it does, you also have a definition of how to measure psychotherapeutic change. Definitions include how to measure that which is defined. Let us return to Strupp's basic definition of psychotherapy. If we accept that definition, then how do we measure psychotherapeutic change? On the basis of the definition, " . . . it is necessary to stipulate that 1) change must be demonstrable; 2) it must be relatively permanent; and 3) it must be attributable to the interpersonal transactions between patient and therapist" (Strupp, 1977, p. 3). This makes sense if one accepts Strupp's basic definition of psychotherapy. It is not what must be done to demonstrate that psychotherapeutic change has occurred; it is what must be done *only* if you accept Strupp's basic definition of psychotherapy.

We do not accept Strupp's definition of psychotherapy, and therefore we do not accept all of Strupp's criteria of how to demonstrate psychotherapeutic change. However, we do accept the first one, namely that change must be demonstrable. The other two we do not accept. Where Strupp holds that change must be relatively permanent, experiential psychotherapy is concerned with the occurrence of substantive and significant change in the session itself; it is outside the boundaries of the experiential therapist to be concerned with whether the change occurs in the patient's extra-therapy life one week later or a year later or for a decade or so. Where Strupp holds that changes must be attributable to the interpersonal transactions between patient and therapist, experiential psychotherapy attributes change more to the following of a method of therapy which does not count so much on the therapist-patient interactional relationships. Therefore, if we decline Strupp's criteria, the symmetrical statement for experiential psychotherapy would be as follows: On the basis of a definition of experiential psychotherapy, in order to measure or demonstrate that psychotherapy change has occurred, it is necessary to stipulate that 1) change must be demonstrable; 2) it must occur in the session itself; 3) it must be a change which experiential psychotherapy would accept as a change in the patient's integrating and actualizing ways of being and behaving; and 4) it must be attributable to the methods and procedures of experiential psychotherapy.

The upshot is that experiential psychotherapy is representative of those therapies which decline the common definitions of what psychotherapy is, what it does, and how those meanings of psychotherapeutic change are to be demonstrated and measured. We elect to frame our own definition of what experiential psychotherapy is, what it does, and how our meaning of psychotherapeutic change is to be measured and demonstrated. And this in turn means that experiential psychotherapy joins with those therapies which likewise decline the common meaning of psychotherapeutic change and instead look to an alternative conceptualization of the meaning of psychotherapeutic change. This, then, is the second large issue upon which a researcher or clinician will either accept the common current meaning of psychotherapeutic change or move toward an alternative one. We now turn to a third large issue.

The Core Meaning of Personality: Static Versus Evolving

The common meaning of psychotherapeutic change includes some change in the patient's psychopathological condition, the patient's problems, or the patient's personality dimensions. The change is typically shown by contrasting the way the patient seems to be in or near the beginning of therapy with the way the patient seems to be later on, e.g., at the end of therapy or after some months or years.

If the researcher studies change in the patient's psychopathological condition, the idea is that there is a more or less continuing person, a core meaning of personality, who is there throughout. While there is change in the continuing person's psychopathological condition, there is a continuing core whose psychopathological condition changed from pre to post. If the researcher likes the idea of change as change in the patient's problems, then there is likewise a core meaning of personality which continues over the course of psychotherapy. "When I started therapy I felt low and sluggish all the time; therapy is over now, and I feel alive and happy." The "I" who defines and evaluates and reports the change in problems comes from the continuing substantive core meaning of personality. If the researcher favors change in terms of personality dimensions, what continues from pre to post is the core meaning of the personality who has those personality dimensions. There is a continuing core personality who changes in its dimension of assertiveness or masculinity-femininity or some other dimension.

In other words, the conceptualization is of a static, inner, continuing personality core which persists over the course of therapy while changes occur in and to its problems, its personality dimensions, or its psychopathological condition. Change occurs in the problems, in the personality dimension, in the psychopathological condition, but not in the core meaning of the person who has these. In this sense, many different approaches to psychotherapy share the idea of an enduring, continuing personality core which is unchanging, while changes occur a little further away—in its problems or personality dimensions or psychopathological condition. The enduring inner core is that which continues from pre to post, the continuing entity to whom the changes occur. No matter how different these approaches are in other respects, they share the idea of this continuing, enduring, static inner core, no matter how it is described or understood. It is that continuing inner core which allows the researcher to compare pre and post, for the pre-post changes occur around a recognizable persistent inner core.

Experiential psychotherapy is one of those approaches which declines the idea of a continuing, enduring, substantive inner core. What can change is much more than the person's distal problems or personality dimension or psychopathological condition. What can change is the person herself or himself, the very inner core of personality. In the beginning of therapy I was a cowardly wimp, and now I do not have that problem any longer. One explanation is that I am the same person, but I no longer am that way. Experiential psychotherapy is representative of another explanation, i.e., I am no longer that person who began therapy. Change can occur in the very inner core of personality, an entity which is assumed to be enduring in most common approaches to the meaning of psychotherapeutic change. Change can occur in the very inner core which, in experiential psychotherapy, is understood as evolving, as capable of evolving, as capable of evolving so that the person is really no longer the same person. This is much more than poetry. It means that pre and post measures are replaced by measures of an evolving inner core, and it means that change can be deeper and more profound than changes in problems, in personality dimensions, and in psychopathological condition:

> As currently constituted, outcome research seeks to control enough variables to allow predictions about which therapies applied to which people will provide a given result. But this involves a transformation of those therapies which claim to enhance the freedom, spontaneity, and well-being of their clients into something very different. The struggle is between control for prediction and support for individual development. (Budge, 1983, p. 303)

Although psychoanalysis considers itself as a deep and profound therapy, it tends to accept the idea of a continuing, enduring personality core removed from the changes which can occur in problems, personality dimensions, and psychopathological condition. In contrast, experiential psychotherapy holds to a conceptualization of personality in which change can even include development and evolution in the inner core of personality itself.

What all this means is that those approaches, such as experiential psychotherapy, which hold to the notion of an evolving, changing inner core to personality (rather than a continuing, enduring inner core) would not be satisfied with the meaning of psychotherapeutic change as change in problems, in personality dimensions, or in psychopathological condition. These three common meanings of psychotherapeutic change fit well with a conceptualization of personality which includes the idea of a continuing, enduring inner core which is there pre and is there post. They fit well with most behavioral and psychoanalytic/psychodynamic conceptualizations which share a notion of an enduring identity, personhood, sense of self, ego. But if change reaches further down into the realm of the very inner identity, includes a change in the very heart of who and what the person is, then the meaning of psychotherapeutic change is by no means limited to more distal changes in problems, personality dimensions, and psychopathological condition. We are getting ready for an alternative conceptualization of psychotherapeutic change.

The Meaning of Psychotherapeutic Methods: Big, General, and Loose Versus Concretely Specific

The point of this section may be framed as a proposition: The more the researcher understands psychotherapeutic methods as general classes, big categories, large operations, the more the researcher will tend to accept the meaning of psychotherapeutic change as changes in problems, in personality dimensions, in psychopathological condition; on the other hand, the more the researcher understands psychotherapeutic methods as concretely specific, the more the researcher will tend to decline those common meanings of psychotherapeutic change and lean toward alternative meanings of psychotherapeutic change.

What is the independent variable? If we are interested in psychotherapeutic change, what is the functional unit which brings about the change? When we think of psychotherapeutic methods (procedures, techniques, operations), are we thinking of categories which are rather large or rather small, programmatic or specific, molar or molecular? Answers to these questions determine the meanings and the measures of psychotherapeutic change. If psychotherapeutic methods include the smaller functional units, then these approaches are freer to decline the common meanings and measures of psychotherapeutic change.

The method may be as large as psychotherapy itself. At this gross level, its meaning may be contrasted with such other gross categories as chemotherapy, milieu therapy, surgery, incarceration. When the meaning of psychotherapeutic method is so very large, it makes sense to accept psychotherapeutic change as change in such big outcomes as problems, personality dimensions, psychopathological condition. Reasonable questions are along these lines: For habitual criminals (or homeless people or those who are depressed or alcoholic), which treatment is more effective: psychotherapy, chemotherapy, or milieu therapy?

Psychotherapeutic method may refer to defined approaches such as client-centered therapy, experiential psychotherapy, behavior therapy, psychodynamic therapy, rational-emotive therapy. Then it is appropriate to ask such questions as: What are the long-term effects of behavior therapy as compared with client-centered therapy? For problems of situational anxiety, what is the comparative effectiveness of experiential psychotherapy and psychoanalytic therapy? For such a molar meaning of psychotherapeutic method, it is fitting to accept psychotherapeutic change as change in problems, in personality dimensions, and in psychopathological condition.

Psychotherapeutic method may refer to some large feature of the approach. For example, one method may be individual therapy, another may be couples therapy; there are family therapy, brief therapy, crisis therapy, network therapy, long-term therapy. For this large meaning of psychotherapeutic method, fitting questions may include: What is the cost-effectiveness of individual versus family therapy? Is brief therapy just as good as long-term therapy for certain kinds of "psychotic" patients? Again, for such molar meanings of psychotherapeutic method, it is sensible to accept psychotherapeutic change as meaning change in problems, personality dimensions, or psychopathological condition.

Psychotherapeutic method may refer to particular kinds of therapeutic programs such as assertiveness training, parent effectiveness training, relaxation programs, desensitization programs, conflict resolution training, information feedback programs, stress reduction programs. In general, these include packages of treatment procedures expressly designed for designated kinds of difficulties and problems. It is understandable that such programs are quite well suited to the meaning of psychotherapeutic change in terms of problems, personality dimensions, and psychopathological condition.

As the meaning of psychotherapeutic method moves from molar to molecular, from general to specific, we come down to such specific methods as reflection, self-disclosure, restatement, interpretation, exaggerating the feeling, focusing, saying it directly to the designated referent, repetition of affect-laden words, and similar specific techniques and procedures of the concretely operating therapist. At this molecular level, when "psychotherapeutic methods" refer to such concretely specific operations, the common outcome meanings of "psychotherapeutic change" do not fit. When the patient seems concerned with the kind of person the therapist is, and when the therapist then discloses something about herself (or interprets or reflects), it makes little sense to look for consequences in terms of changes in the patient's psychopathological condition, personality dimensions, or problems. Those bigger outcome meanings of psychotherapeutic change are better fitted to the bigger meanings of psychotherapeutic methods, e.g., relaxation programs, brief therapy, individual psychotherapy, or Gestalt therapy.

For experiential psychotherapy, psychotherapeutic methods include the more molecular, specifically concrete, interchange-to-interchange, in-session therapeutic step to next therapeutic step. By being at that level of meaning of psychotherapeutic method, we find it rather useless to consider the common meanings of psychotherapeutic change. Indeed, the principle seems to be that the more the clinician or researcher accepts the concretely specific meanings of psychotherapeutic methods, the more the clinician or researcher will tend to decline psychotherapeutic change as changes in problems, personality dimensions, or psychopathological condition, and instead to incline toward an alternative conceptualization of psychotherapeutic change.

CONCLUSIONS

Here are four issues on which clinicians and researchers explicitly or implicitly take some position:

1) What is the meaning of psychotherapeutic change? Is the meaning specific to given theories of psychotherapy or is there a set of meanings which are more or less common across most approaches?
2) What is the definition of what psychotherapy is and what it does? Would the clinician or researcher accept psychotherapy as an influence brought to bear upon the patient, as the patient enlisting an expert's help in effecting change, as the patient recognizing that he is in need of help, as change occurring by means of a complex series of interactions between therapist and patient, as aiming at the goal of bringing about changes that the participant and society at large will view as therapeutic?
3) Is the meaning of "personality" one in which there is a static, en-

during "core" or does psychotherapeutic change permeate into and include an evolving changing "core"?
4) What is the meaning of "psychotherapeutic methods"? Is the meaning big, general, and loose, or concretely specific and func-
tionally operational?

If the clinician and researcher accept the more common positions
on these four issues, then they would tend to accept the more common meanings of psychotherapeutic change as changes in problems,
in personality dimensions, and in psychopathological condition. They
would tend to accept standardized omnibus sets of measures of outcome, improvement, cure, change (cf. Bergin & Lambert, 1978; Berzins, Bednar & Severy, 1975; Goldfried, 1980; Gruen, 1980; Parloff,
1979; Waskow & Parloff, 1975).

On the other hand, if the clinician and researcher decline the common positions on the above four issues, if they accept alternative positions on these four issues, then they would be ready for alternative
conceptualizations of the meaning (and measures) of psychotherapeutic change. Experiential clinicians and researchers quite definitely
decline the common positions on these issues. We are representative
of those psychotherapies which accept qualitatively different meanings of psychotherapeutic change, definitions of what psychotherapy
is and what it does, the nature of the core meaning of personality,
and the referential meaning of psychotherapeutic methods. Accordingly, we accept alternative meanings and measures of psychotherapeutic change.

The balance of this book is dedicated to a description of the meanings and measures of psychotherapeutic change from the perspective
of experiential psychotherapy and as illustrative of how one alternative conceptualization deals with the basic issue of the meaning and
measurement of psychotherapeutic change.

Directions of Potential Change 2

Chapters 2–4 address the question: What are the meanings and measurements of psychotherapeutic change from the perspective of experiential psychotherapy? This therapy declines the common conceptualizations of personality, psychotherapy, and psychotherapeutic change. It is representative of those approaches which accept an alternative conceptualization coupled with its own meanings and measurements of psychotherapeutic change. There are three meanings used by experiential psychotherapy, and each is presented in this and the subsequent two chapters. The more specific purpose of this chapter is to answer the question: How may we predict the directions of potential change for the particular patient?

Psychotherapeutic Change as the Individual
Patient's Directions of Potential Change

There are three parts to this meaning of psychotherapeutic change. One is that we are dealing with directions of *potential* change. It answers questions such as: What is this person capable of becoming? What are the potential or possible ways that this person can be? What are the directions of potential change for this particular individual? As we know more and more about this person, it should be possible to see what this person can become. While these directions of potential change may well include the ordinary meanings of problems, dimensions of personality, and psychopathological condition, much more is usually included in the directions of potential change. They typically include the actualization or realization of the personality resources in this person, new ways of being and behaving and experiencing, new worlds in which to exist and be.

A second part highlights this very *particular* person. The directions of potential change are singularly descriptive of the highly individual patient. The more we learn of this particular person, the more the directions of change are of and for this particular person. One may frame general directions of change which are coupled with experiential psychotherapy, but the working meaning of psychotherapeutic change requires that we get down to the level of the kind of person this specific individual can become.

The third part consists of general *principles* to enable the research clinician to go from this particular patient to this particular patient's directions of potential change. Knowledge about this particular person is useful only when we can apply some general principles to go from this individual person to the directions of change for the person. Given the right knowledge about this person, these principles can generate a picture of what this particular person can become, i.e., this particular person's directions of potential change.

The therapy session as the window upon the directions of potential change. When we think about research predictions of what this particular person can become, it is easy to think about situations outside therapy, in the patient's actual world, and it is easy to think in terms of the end of therapy, and even some time after therapy is over. These terms of reference are not totally excluded by our meaning of psychotherapeutic change, but those places are not where we look for changes to occur.

Experiential psychotherapy is organized around the idea that changes are expected to occur in the session itself. Indeed, the therapeutic process may be regarded as a flow of opportunities to allow oneself to engage in actual changes. When we speak of the directions of potential change for this patient, we are referring to what this person can be within the next moment or two, and certainly within this session and the next sessions to come. While the changes may of course include what happens later and outside the session, the actual research predictions apply to what happens in the session and in the sessions to come.

The final step in each experiential session looks to the external world, the world of the patient's life outside the therapy room, the world of tomorrow and next week and 13 years from now. In this final phase of each session, the patient and therapist taste and sample potential changes as they can occur within this unfolding real world outside the therapy room. The situational context is that world out there, and the task consists of dipping into new ways of being and behaving. In effect, the patient and therapist taste and sample, try out and consider what it is like to be a new and different person, being and behaving in new and different ways, within the context of the actual life which is potential, which can occur.

Accordingly, the meaning and measurement of directions of potential change for the individual patient refer to here-and-now events of the therapy session itself. What occurs later and outside the therapy session is not excluded. But the window is located in the therapy session itself. This whole matter is discussed in more depth in chapter 5. Suffice it to say for now that the clinical research predictions *can include* the traditional meaning of "outcome," but for us it is the therapy session which is the window upon the directions of potential change.

Each Theory of Psychotherapy Is Invited
to Develop Its Own Meanings and
Measures of Psychotherapeutic Change
for the Individual Patient

Experiential psychotherapy has its own way of defining and measuring psychotherapeutic change for the individual patient. Indeed, for purposes of actual measurement, the specific meaning of psychotherapeutic change will vary significantly from one patient to another. But our meaning is suited to experiential psychotherapy. For the research clinician, the invitation is to spell out the meanings and measures of psychotherapeutic change for the individual patient on the understanding that each theory of psychotherapy is entitled to have its own. In this connection, many researchers have called for such particularized treatment goals outfitted to the individual patient (e.g., Bergin & Lambert, 1978; Kiresuk & Sherman, 1968; Klonoff & Cox, 1975; Weed, 1968):

> Little systematic consideration has been given to the design and analysis of studies oriented toward testing whether therapy produces particular effects designated as desirable for the individual patient. Such methodological work is needed. (Fiske et al., 1970, p. 30)

Generating individualized therapeutic predictions has been done in psychotherapy research. One of the large-scale attempts was the long-term psychotherapy project of the Menninger Foundation (Robbins & Wallerstein, 1959; Wallerstein, 1966; Wallerstein, Robbins, Sargent, & Luborsky, 1956) in which a mass of assessment data on each subject patient was used to " . . . generate individual clinical predictions about the anticipated course and outcome of the recommended therapy for that patient . . . " (Wallerstein, 1968, p. 588).

A central problem is whether some single omnibus set of outcome measures can be used for most therapeutic approaches, or whether each approach would have to develop its own. If we want to get down to the level of the particular patient, and if we wanted to generate statements about what this particular patient can become or treatment goals for this patient, it seems to me that each therapeutic approach would have to have its own way of doing this. Below are the considerations which lead me to this conclusion.

1) The more you apply general meanings and measures of psychotherapeutic change to the individual patient, the greater will be the dispersion in interpretations from different approaches. For example, a number of clinical researchers may agree that patients in general should have "remission of target symptoms," and they should show gains in "predetermined areas of functioning." Even the individual patient should show change in these domains:

> It had been argued that the changes sought in therapy are highly specific to the individual patient. Thus, we should not expect all patients to improve on every dependent variable, but should determine whether each patient achieves remission of his target symptoms, or perhaps whether he gains in those areas for which the therapist or the pretreatment assessment determines that his condition is most favorable. (Fiske et al., 1970, p. 30)

How do we determine the "target symptoms" for this particular patient? How do we determine changes in "predetermined areas of functioning"? One clinical researcher brings her meaning and measures to the first few sessions and concludes that the target symptoms include some cognitive slippage, and that the areas of functioning most favorable for this particular patient are those in which there is excessive external stimulus input. A second clinical researcher, operating out of another theory, concludes that the central target symptoms include stuttering and excessive perspiration, and the areas of functioning most favorable for this particular patient include interpersonal communication in authority situations. They agree at the general level, but differ immensely when they get down to the work of specific individual predictions.

At the general level, many meanings of psychotherapeutic change make apparent sense to clinical researchers from different therapeutic approaches. At the level of the specific individual patient, genuine differences come into clear focus. In fact, these differences are magnified. The moral is that each therapeutic approach would seem to need to develop its own meanings and measures of psychotherapeutic change down at the level of the individual patient.

2) The more the clinical researcher comes to know about a given, individual patient, the less fitting and useful are the common general meanings and measures of psychotherapeutic change. This is compounded when we take into account different therapeutic approaches for understanding this individual patient. Then the more an experiential therapist or a client-centered therapist or a classical psychoanalytic therapist knows about this particular patient, the more ill-fitting become the common general meanings and measures of psychotherapeutic change.

If psychotherapeutic change is taken to refer to "problems," it would seem that measures of problems would be tailored to the individual patient. Self-report measures, scales, inventories, all sorts of problem checklists — all of these would seem to capture the particular patient right now. But this is not the case. To begin with, inventories and checklists of problems tend to cater to certain theoretical orientations. One which is eminently suited to psychoanalytic theory would not be equally fitting for experiential theory or for communications theory. Also, however concretely the problems are described, they can only point toward general classes of problems rather than the exact nuances, conditions, and meanings which fit the statement to this particular patient, especially as we come to know more and more about this individual patient's specific problem. Furthermore, self-report inventories typically consist of a limited number of problems which are grouped into a much smaller number of factors and clusters, such as tension anxiety, depression, obsession, and so on (e.g., Derogatis et al., 1974; McNair, Lorr, & Droppleman, 1971). Even with self-report measures, it seems that each approach would benefit by developing its own measures for the individual patient.

What about large-scale, omnibus batteries? The serious problem here is that the more one knows about this specific patient, especially as one comes to know this particular patient from within one approach rather than another, the more such omnibus test batteries emerge as ill-fitting. Almost without exception, such large-scale, omnibus batteries confine psychotherapeutic change to a few general personality dimensions and measures of psychopathological condition which are derived from some common, but single, theoretical approach. Within these strict limitations, it is hoped that the omnibus patterns of change could accommodate the individual patient. For example:

> Using such a battery acknowledges that there are many patterns of change. That is, amelioration may diminish or augment some aspects of functioning. For example, in rigid, compulsive people, some loosening of affect control may be regarded as salutary, while a tightening of controls over affect would be regarded as an improvement for patients with problems reflecting fluid regulation of action. (Holzman, 1975, p. 133)

Neither client-centered therapy nor experiential therapy nor many other therapies accept as salient the basic notions of rigid, compulsive personalities, or notions of either loosening or tightening of affect controls as truly significant avenues of psychotherapeutic change. All in all, it seems as if much more work has to be done, especially by each therapeutic approach, to develop measures which capture a fair amount of knowledge and understanding of a very particular patient.

3) The more a particular theoretical orientation sheds its own light of understanding on a particular patient, the less useful are standard, common meanings and measures of psychotherapeutic change.

For example, as an experiential psychotherapist comes to know and understand a given patient, the more will that therapist see what this person can become in terms of changes which make sense from within that therapeutic approach. The patient may be described as changing toward increasing integration and actualization, terms which make sense within experiential psychotherapy, but not within desensitization therapy or cognitive behavior therapy. The patient may be described as having possibilities for certain kinds of experiencings, for constructing and existing in certain kinds of external worlds, for certain kinds of experience-enhancing behaviors. While these directions of potential change make sense within the theory of experiential psychotherapy, they do not lend themselves to measurement by means of the MMPI, California Personality Inventory, or the 16 Personality Factor Questionnaire.

Since the same reasoning holds true for most theories of psychotherapy, the more a given theory comes to understand a given patient within its own conceptual system, the more useful it would be for that approach to develop its own meanings and measures of change as applied to the specific particular patient.

4) Some theories of psychotherapy accept the idea of a progressive unfolding, a process of change in who and what this particular patient is and can become. For these theories, the standard meanings and measures of psychotherapeutic change are unsuited for the individualized patient, and these theories are encouraged to develop their own meanings and measures of psychotherapeutic change for the individualized patient.

What seem to be meaningful directions of change for the given patient in the initial sessions are revised as the therapeutic process moves along. Indeed, for these theories, the framing of directions of change is itself a progressive process as therapeutic change moves along from session to session. Experiential psychotherapy is representative of those approaches which accept the idea of such progressively unfolding possibilities for directions of change. On the other hand, most meanings and measures of psychotherapeutic change accept a different paradigm in which the meaning and measurement of change, even for this particular patient, starts with the initial, baseline picture at the beginning of therapy. This is the traditional pre-post paradigm, and it fits theories which understand personality change in terms of pre-therapy measures and post-therapy measures. For example:

> What is needed (as is well understood in the concept of the necessity for follow-up) is clear and present demonstration that the patients were steadily sick before they entered treatment, and were steadily well (or at least better) afterwards. (Cartwright, 1975, p. 60)

Most existential-humanistic psychotherapies would not accept the concept of patients as sick or well. But, more importantly, the traditional pre-post notion of personality does not fit conceptualizations in which what is "pre" is understood as free to change into another "pre" and to continue changing into a progressive series of "pre's" which are the "posts" for the preceding "pre's." Again, the solution, for these therapies, is to develop their own meanings and measures of psychotherapeutic change for the individualized patient.

5) In experiential psychotherapy, we gain an increasingly idiosyncratic grasp of this particular person's own capacities and resources for experiencing. Not only do we look for potentials for experiencing, but we look for this particular person's own array of specific potentials for experiencing. Suppose that the clinical researcher were to turn to the standard meanings and measures of psychotherapeutic change and to ask which of these are designed not only to capture potentials for experiencing but also to capture precisely what this particular patient's own array of potentials are and can become. The standard meanings and measures would have precious little to offer. If this is the case for experiential psychotherapy's work with a specific patient, it is likely that the same holds true for some other therapies which likewise have their own meaning of psychotherapeutic change at the level of the concrete specific person. The same conclusion looms again, namely that these psychotherapies are best served by developing their own meanings and measures of psychotherapeutic change.

In general, the conclusion is that therapies which highlight work with the individualized patient must decide whether the common meanings and measures of psychotherapeutic change do an adequate job in both the meaning and the measurement of psychotherapeutic change at the level of the individual patient. Experiential psychotherapy says no. Indeed, I suspect that many psychotherapists and many therapies would likewise say no. Accordingly, these psychotherapists and these therapies are invited to develop their own meanings and measures of psychotherapeutic change for the individual patient.

A Topographical Map of the Individual Patient's Directions of Potential Change

On what basis does the clinical researcher figure out the kinds of changes (goals, outcomes) for this particular patient? In order to answer this question, the clinical researcher uses some implicit or explicit schema or model or conceptualization or topographical map of what patients are like and what constitutes psychotherapeutic change. This schema or topographical map is applied to the specific patient, and change becomes sensible and clear. Then the clinical researcher can say, for example, that this patient's self-reported excessive smoking is to be reduced to two cigarettes a day, or that the patient's refusal to use cars, together with the daily routines which support this refusal, are no longer there, and the patient now uses cars with ease. Every approach has its own explicit or implicit map of psychotherapeutic change. The one used by experiential psychotherapy is given in Figure 1. Applied to the individualized patient, the clinical researcher can make experiential sense of this particular patient and can generate statements about what this particular patient can become, i.e., the directions of potential change for the individualized patient.

The clinical researcher begins by filling in the schema given at the left in Figure 1. To do this, the clinical researcher must ask a number of questions which make sense in the context of the experiential theory of psychotherapy:

(a) What are the operating potentials for experiencing? Each patient functions, behaves, operates on the basis of several potentials for experiencing. The task is one of increasing grasp and precision

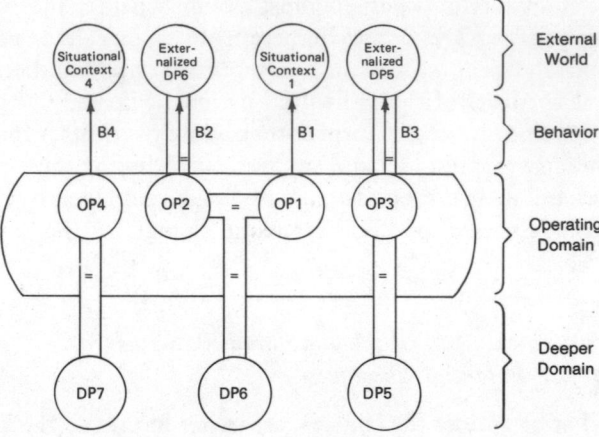

Figure 1. Topography of the Individual Patient's Directions of Potential Change (left).

in identifying exactly what these operating potentials are in this patient (OP1–4, Figure 1).

(b) What is the nature of the external world in which this person exists, and which this person constructs? The clinical researcher understands that this person selects out, exists in, organizes and builds her own external worlds. What are these external worlds? They consist of quite particular situational contexts, such as a third husband who gets drunk and beats up the patient every so often, or tense and antagonistic executive committee meetings in the department of chemistry of which the patient is chair. External worlds are also comprised of figures who are externalizations of the patient's own deeper potentials. For example, if the patient's own deeper potential consists of harsh and calculated ambition (e.g., DP5 in Figure 1), the external world may be constructed so as to include a figure who is harshly and calculatingly ambitious (e.g., Externalized DP5, in Figure 1). The clinical researcher's task is to be accurately descriptive of this particular person's own external world as it relates to the patient's own potentials for experiencing.

(c) What are the behaviors used by this patient in constructing the external world and in enabling the experiencing of the patient's own

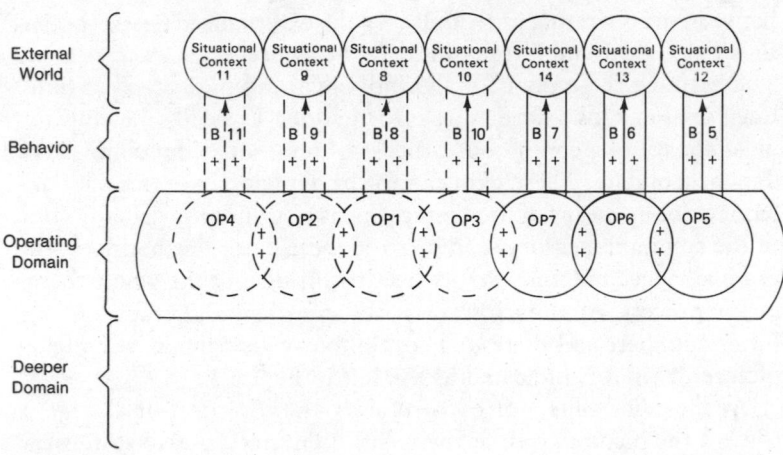

Figure 1. Topography of the Individual Patient's Directions of Potential Change (right).

potentials? Of all the possible meanings and categories of behavior, the clinical researcher is attuned only to these two. There are explicit behavioral ways of being which construct and maintain the specific involvements, relationships, situations, parts of the external world which are meaningful for the patient's own potentials for experiencing. There are also explicit behavioral ways of being which quite specifically enable the patient to experience what this person has available to experience. It is the clinical researcher's task to define accurately what these behaviors are.

(d) What are the patient's deeper potentials for experiencing? In Figure 1, these are indicated as DP5–7. They refer to those potentials for experiencing which are not directly experienced, which are not linked to actual behavioral ways of being, which are not a part of the patient's way of functioning and operating. They are deeper. Typically, relationships between operating and deeper potentials are negative (problematic, unpleasant, hurtful, pained, distanced, disintegrative), and this is indicated by the two negative signs in the channels of relationship between the operating and the deeper potentials. These negative relationships are also reflected in the relationship channels between operating potentials (e.g., OP1 and OP2), and between the operating potentials and the externalized deeper potentials (e.g., OP3 and Externalized DP5, Figure 1).

Obtaining these data for the individualized patient takes time. Each session adds a little more information. Typically the clinician must engage in a continuous process of revision as more and more data accumulate. These data cannot be gathered in pre-therapy interviews or by means of pre-therapy measures. Indeed, virtually none of the common measures can provide these data. Furthermore, the gradually accumulating picture occurs throughout the whole therapeutic process. After each session, the experiential therapist adds a bit of data here and there to a continuously growing and changing picture of what is indicated at the left in Figure 1.

At the same time, for each session, the direction of change is toward the picture given at the right in Figure 1. Always, in every session and throughout the course of therapy, this is the direction of change. The more data we have about the way the patient is on the left, the more we can generate and refine specific statements about the directions of change for this individual patient.

But how do we do this? With some data about the patient, experientially relevant data, how do we generate specific statements about his directions of potential change? The answer is that these statements are generated by means of a set of principles. In other words, by using the topographical map and by using the right principles, the clinical researcher can see the directions of change for this individual patient. This is done at the end of each session, whether it is the initial, middle, or final session. The principles for experiential therapy will be discussed shortly, but first we come to the matter of a new role for the clinician or the traditional researcher.

A New Role: The Clinical Researcher

In order to investigate the directions of potential change or to do psychotherapy research based upon the alternative conceptualization discussed in chapter 1, the researcher must be a clinical researcher. Knowledge of research methods and design, measurement methods and statistics, computers and instruments, is insufficient to do this kind of research. Even a passing knowledge of psychotherapeutic approaches is insufficient. Knowledge of the psychotherapy research literature is insufficient. In order to do research on individual patients' directions of potential change, the researcher must be a master of the theories of psychotherapy used by the therapists whose work is studied. This is a breed of the *clinical researcher.*

The clinical researcher who studies the directions of potential change of the individual patient in experiential psychotherapy must be quite knowledgeable in the theory of experiential psychotherapy. The topographical map in Figure 1 must make conceptual sense before the clinical researcher can be effective. The clinical researcher must be knowledgeable about operating potentials, deeper potentials, relationships between potentials, and constructed worlds. The clinical researcher must understand the existential-humanistic theory of human beings and the experiential theory of psychotherapy.

In the same way, to investigate the directions of change of the individualized patient in rational-emotive therapy, ego psychoanalytic therapy, transactional analysis, or client-centered therapy, the clinical researcher is to be quite knowledgeable of the theory of that psychotherapy. A researcher who studies individualized changes of patients in cognitive behavioral therapy is a clinical researcher to the extent that the researcher is knowledgeable of cognitive behavioral therapy.

Training of the clinical researcher who investigates psychotherapeutic change at the level of the individual patient requires substantive knowledge of the particular theories of psychotherapy with which the clinical researcher will be involved. Without this in-depth clinical knowledge, the researcher is essentially handicapped in studying psychotherapeutic change at the individual level.

The balance of this chapter, then, is for the clinical researcher who grasps the existential-humanistic theory of human beings and the theory of experiential psychotherapy. The balance of the chapter answers the question: How does the experiential researcher predict the directions of potential change for the individual patient? Given the data needed by the experiential researcher, what are the principles for generating the individual patient's own directions of potential change? There are 12 principles. They are used by the experiential psychotherapist, and they are the ones used by the clinical researcher. The balance of this chapter, then, illustrates how experiential psychotherapy answers the above questions and constitutes a kind of manual for the clinical researcher studying the directions of change within an experiental perspective. The invitation is for other therapies to frame their own principles for specifying individual patients' directions of potential change.

ACTUALIZATION OF THE GOOD FORM
OF THE OPERATING DOMAIN

As given in Figure 1, the "operating domain" includes the substantive personality which is directly related to the way the patient functions, behaves, feels, operates. It is comprised of the operating potentials (OP1–4, Figure 1) which directly determine how the patient functions. What happens to the operating domain over the course of the session(s)? In general, it tends to undergo two interrelated kinds of changes. One is that its "form" moves from one in which the person feels bad, unpleasant, anxious, in turmoil, constricted, to one accompanied with good feelings of inner peace, wholeness, togetherness, harmony, and oneness. The nature of the experiencing changes from its bad face to its good face, from its bad form to its good form. The second interrelated direction of change is from partial, truncated experiencing toward a state in which experiencing is heightened, moves toward greater amplitude and saturation. This is referred to as actualization. In general, then, the direction of change is toward actualization of the good form of the operating domain.

The general prediction is that the individual patient will change in the direction of actualization of the good form of that person's operating potentials. But this general prediction is of little use to the clinical researcher. Accordingly, the following three principles are designed to enable the clinical researcher to frame specific predictions which can be assessed.

1) There Will Be Heightened Experiencing of the Good, Integrated Form of the Operating Potentials

The clinical researcher begins by a careful description of the current immediate nature of the operating experiencing as it is on the left in Figure 1. Suppose that this is described as the experiencing of separation and withdrawal, being at a distance from people. Knowing just this, what is the direction of potential change? On the basis of the first principle, the clinical researcher reasons (and predicts) as follows:

This potential for experiencing will move toward its good, integrated form. If the patient felt good in undergoing this experiencing, what would be the nature of the experiencing? What would "separation, withdrawal, being at a distance from people" look like if it were accompanied with feelings of wholeness, oneness, inner peace and harmony, togetherness? What can it become in its integrated form? The clinical researcher may envisage an image of the experiencing of intact independence, autonomy, being able to move to a safe distance at times. By allowing oneself to enter into an integrative state, the clinical researcher can get a picture of what the potential for experiencing can become, were it to move in the direction of its good, integrated form. On the left, in Figure 1, relationships between operating and other potentials are signified by negative signs. On the right, the direction of change toward the good, integrated form is indicated by the two positive signs in the relationships among and between the operating potentials.

This potential will also move in the direction of heightened *experiencing*. In other words, the integrated good form (e.g., intact independence, autonomy, being able to move to a safe distance at times) will be experienced in greater depth and breadth, greater amplitude and saturation. This direction of change is indicated by the change from smaller circles (OP1–4) on the left, to the larger circles on the right (Figure 1).

How does the clinical researcher take the problematic (had-feelinged, disintegrative) operating potential and extrapolate the direction of change toward its good, integrative form? This is a two-step process. First, the clinical researcher must allow the operating potential to be experienced within an encompassing context of good feelings, of inner harmony and oneness, inner wholeness and peace. Then, within the context of these integrative feelings, the clinical researcher must allow the potential to take its integrative form, to occur in its good form, to take form and shape in this integrative manner. It transmutes; it transforms. It occurs in its good, integrated form. Here is where the clinical researcher benefits from training in experiential psychotherapy, both its theory and its methods. Here is where the researcher must also be a clinician, i.e., a clinical researcher.

The clinical researcher can understand how an operating potential can transform into its good, integrated form. The experiencing of chaos, lack of organization and direction, structurelessness, can move in the direction of becoming, for example, an experiencing of impulsiveness, openness, freedom, spontaneity. What starts out as the experiencing of guarded attraction to persons of one's own sex may transform into highly sexual relationships, or into newfound closeness and intimacy with all sorts of persons. The experiencing of controlling superiority may move into the good, integrative form of powerful leadership. As the clinical researcher gains more and more descriptive data of the nature of the operating potential, and as the therapeutic process rumbles along, the clinical researcher is ready to receive the good, integrative form of the operating potential.

There are two special cases. One is when the operating potential is already more or less in its integrative form. That is, it is already accompanied with relatively good, integrative relationships with other potentials, and it therefore is accompanied with good feelings of wholeness and oneness, peacefulness and inner harmony. What is the direction of change? Whereas little change in form may take place, the direction of change is toward heightened experiencing, undergoing it in greater amplitude and saturation so that there is a deeper and fuller sense of whatever it is.

Another special case is when the patient moves back and forth between two operating potentials. For example, consider the painful experiencing of attacking, hurting, being mean to (OP1, Figure 1) and also the painful experiencing of being mistreated, maligned, injured (OP2, Figure 1). The patient moves from one to the other across a relationship which is disintegrative so that the experiencing of each is painful, turmoiled, and bothersome. This is the person whose painful experiencing of one of the potentials is potentiated by the disintegrative relationship with the other, and whose experiencing of either is constricted and truncated by the other. Accordingly, the person typically undergoes a measure of unhappy experiencing of the sense of attacking, hurting, being mean to, and then moves away from this and into a measure of unhappy experiencing of being mistreated, maligned, injured.

The direction of change is toward the fuller, deeper experiencing of the good, integrated form of both potentials. For example, the disintegrative bad form of attacking, hurting, being mean to moves toward its integrated good form of perhaps resolute toughness and forthrightness. The disintegrative bad form of being mistreated, maligned, injured may take the integrative good form of being passive, pleasantly vulnerable, and openly receiving. In short, both of these "yoked" operating potentials yield heightened experiencing of their good integrative form.

On the basis of this first principle, the direction of potential change is both qualitative and quantitative. Qualitatively, the change is toward the good integrative form of the potential. Quantitatively, the change is toward the fuller and deeper experiencing of the potential.

2) There Will Be an Increase in Good-Feelinged, Bodily Sensations of Actualization

There is a direction of change in a particular class of bodily sensations. The referent is the body, and more specifically certain kinds of bodily sensations which can be identified, pointed to, felt, and measured. According to experiential theory, the direction of change consists of the heightening of bodily sensations of actualization: tingling, energy, excitement, lightness, buoyancy, vibrancy, aliveness, and vitality.

In general, these bodily sensations increase. But the increase occurs in several ways. One is in terms of sheer intensity. The patient moves from lower to higher levels of these bodily sensations. Whereas the patient may have had moderate levels of bodily felt excitement, the direction is toward more intense excitement. It is simply felt more strongly, more extremely. Secondly, the sensations occur over more of the body. From having sensations of lightness in the chest or some other bodily zone of such good feelings, the person has these good sensations over more and more of the whole body. Perhaps the parallel is moving from bodily felt sensations of climax confined to the genital area to a state in which climax is felt throughout the entire body.

Third, the sheer length of time stretches out. While the person may have had a few seconds of good-feelinged tingling over the course of a week or so, the direction is toward having such bodily sensation perhaps most of the time. Finally, these good bodily sensations of actualization spread over more and more of the person's potentials for experiencing. Whereas there may be some good sensations accompanying the experiencing of playful sexuality, the direction of change is toward having such sensations in conjunction with all the experiencings which comprise the operating domain. All or most of whatever the patient experiences can be accompanied with good bodily sensations.

This change to bodily sensations of actualization allows the patient to "wake up" from the earlier state. Now the patient can look back upon what it was like to exist in a bodily state of relative deadness, unaliveness, numbness, frozen feelings, unfeeling. This earlier state of un-actualization is seen when the patient achieves the new state of actualization. All of this is an indirect way of describing this change as including a decrease in bodily sensations of deadness, unaliveness, numbness, frozen feelings, and unfeeling.

The change toward heightened bodily sensations of actualization is independent of the nature of the operating potential. It can be predicted without knowing the nature of the individual patient's operating potentials. It is for everyone, compliments of the experiential process of change.

3) There Will Occur New Behaviors for the Good Form of the Operating Domain

The clinical researcher can predict that the direction of potential change includes new behaviors which provide for the actualized good form of the operating domain. These are new ways of being and behaving. They fall into two categories, each of which will be discussed in turn.

New behaviors which construct new external worlds. Experiencing does not just happen; it needs appropriate situational contexts, the right external world. This is true of every operating potential, regardless of its nature. On the left in Figure 1, each of the operating potentials needs some sort of particular external world in order for experiencing to occur. In order to experience separation and withdrawal, being at a distance from people, there must be some kind of appropriate situational context. In order to experience a sense of failure and worthlessness, some proper kind of situational context is called for. Furthermore, these situational contexts do not just appear. The patient must behave in effective ways to shape, select, build, mould, create the right situational context, and also to maintain and preserve it. All of this takes behavioral skill. As the patient then moves toward actualization of the good form of the operating domain, as the operating potentials move toward heightened experiencing of their good, integrated form, this newly emerging experiencing calls for new situational contexts, new external worlds, and this is accomplished by means of new behaviors. Accordingly, the third principle is that there will occur new behaviors which construct new external worlds appropriate for the heightened experiencing of the more integrated good form of the operating potentials. On the right in Figure 1, these new external worlds are indicated as situational contexts 8–11, and the new behaviors are indicated as B8–B11.

The actual research prediction goes something like this: Given this operating potential, and given these behavioral means of constructing these appropriate situational contexts, it is predicted that the patient will use new behaviors to construct new situational contexts appropriate for the more actualized good form of that potential. This is still not very specific. The clinical researcher will be unable to identify the specific new behaviors or the specific new situational contexts. But the clinical researcher will be able to predict that new behaviors and situational contexts will occur, and to recognize them as they do occur.

Consider the woman whose operating potential includes the painful experiencing of separation, withdrawal, being at a distance from people. There are at least two specific situations in which this experiencing occurs, each of which calls for quite particular behaviors to construct and maintain these situational contexts. One occurs when her father awakes in the morning, comes into the kitchen, and angrily snaps at her for being "a self-centered little bitch! Don't you ever think of anyone else?" He then gives her a fiercely hateful look and she knows he won't talk to her the rest of the day. She constructs this situation by living at home, getting up daily at 6:30 a.m., turning the radio in the kitchen loud enough to wake her parents, arranging to take their dog for a morning walk at 6:45 a.m., hurrying around in the kitchen so that the dog barks incessantly to get going on his walk, looking vacantly out the kitchen window when her father enters the room, and sighing in an aggressively provocative manner as her father starts to talk.

A second behaviorally arranged situation is when several of her fellow graduate students have coffee in the lounge. She envelops herself in a moat of silence, seldom faces any of them, generally takes her coffee and exits, deftly steers interchanges into one-sided complaints about the program and away from whatever the other person is inviting her to talk about. The consequence is the occurrence of a painful experiencing of separation, withdrawal, being at a distance from people.

Suppose that this experiencing (OP1, Figure 1) moved toward its more integrated form and became an experiencing of good-feelinged independence, intactness, and autonomy. What kinds of new behaviors (B8) might construct what kinds of new situational contexts and external worlds (Situational Context 8) appropriate for this new form of the operating potential? The clinical researcher identified several new behaviorally arranged situational contexts. One consisted of graduation from her masters program, acceptance of a job as a consultant to a number of social agencies, a job requiring that she function independently, arrange her own schedule, and serve as a responsible organizer of her own programs. The change would include moving out of her parents' home and into an apartment on her own, having a few companions with whom she shared such independent activities as camping, bicycle touring, and cross-country skiing. Here were new situational contexts, brought about and maintained by many new behaviors, all serving the heightened experiencing of the good, integrative form of the potential for experiencing. These new external worlds would not just happen. They would be brought about by sets of new behaviors which built the successful completion of the graduate program, architected the seeking and finding of a very particular kind of professional position, constructed quite specific new external worlds in which she would be existing and experiencing. By using this third principle, the clinical researcher can predict the directions of change toward specific new behaviors and behaviorally constructed new situational contexts.

Consider the patient whose operating potential (OP4, Figure 1) consists of the tight, painful twisted experiencing of sexuality. He constructs the right situational contexts by specializing his medical practice so that he deals with young women, by getting them to give him some object from their purse (e.g., matches, a stamp, pencil), by winding a sexual fantasy around that item, and by masturbating to the tune of that fantasy as he sits in his car, parked far away from his home. If this experiencing, in its integrative form, consists of the experiencing of sexuality which is wanton, wicked, dangerous and thrilling, the predictive question for the clinical researcher is: What are the situational contexts or external worlds in which this new experiencing can occur, and what kinds of behaviors might construct these situational contexts and external worlds?

The directions of potential change yielded possibilities of mutual dyadic masturbation where the patient and his wife started in the bedroom and sinewed their way throughout the home and out into the countryside. The behaviorally constructed new situations also included soft and hard pornographic videotapes for the couple's entertainment, followed by wickedly delightful new intercourse styles in dangerously tempting surroundings. He could entertain, playfully consider, and reject the devilish possibility of doing all this before a mixed audience of selected neighbors and colleagues as well as his younger sister, favorite aunt, and taut parents. Constructing these new situational contexts requires new behaviors. Pornographic videotapes must be obtained, he and his wife must acquire knowledge of rich new intercourse styles. Each new situational context calls for new behaviors which arrange for its presence in the patient's life.

All in all, once the clinical researcher has a picture of the good-feelinged, integrative form of the potential, the direction of change is the occurrence of new situational contexts, new external worlds, constructed by new behaviors and designed to provide for the heightened experiencing of the integrative form of that potential for experiencing.

New behaviors to carry forward the heightened experiencings. Actualization of the good form of the operating potential requires new and appropriate situational contexts. One set of behaviors acts upon the external world, fashioning the appropriate new situational contexts. These behaviors are described above under principle 3. But these behaviors are not enough to enable the experiencing to occur. That requires the right set of new behaviors which actually open up the experiencing, which provide for and enable its carrying forward within the context of the new situation. In Figure 1, B8–B11 signify both the new behaviors which construct the new external worlds, and also the new behaviors which carry forward the experiencing within the context of those new external worlds. As far as the carrying forward of experiencing is concerned, these are the payoff behaviors.

Generally these behaviors have at least two characteristic features. One is that they are self-initiated; the patient does something, gets it started. This feature contrasts with that of being reactive, responsive, activated by others, initiated by the demands of some situation. Second, there is an openness, directness, expressiveness, immediacy, rather than hesitancy, incompleteness, nonspecificity, abortiveness.

The experiencing of gentle tenderness may be readied by constructing the right partner, but the actual experiencing occurs when the patient reaches out and touches, places his head on her lap, says the right words, allows the right look to happen, permits tears to occur. The experiencing of warm appreciation toward parents calls for a situation where the patient is with one's parents, perhaps in the same room, but the actual experiencing is brought forth when the patient does something, says the right words, carries out the right actions.

The experiencing of wickedly dangerous sexuality may be readied through constructing a situation in which the right person or persons are watching a pornographic videotape, but the actual experiencing calls for specific behaviors in that situation. These may include allowing oneself to have sexual bodily sensations, replaying the juicy parts, engaging in mutual sexual touchings and arousals, allowing oneself to be excitedly guilty. The experiencing of independent autonomy may call for leaving the parental house, but the actual experiencing tends to occur when the patient gets herself an apartment, writes out a check for the rent, makes herself a salad in her very own kitchen, hangs the right picture in the right place, and enjoys the apartment with the right companion.

The main job of the clinical researcher is that of being able to frame out the good, integrated form of the operating potential, and to see what it can look like as this experiencing heightens (principle 1) and occurs with good-feelinged bodily sensations (principle 2). The clinical researcher must be able to envision this, to have a picture of what this is like. Then the clinical researcher must be able to see the kinds of situations or external worlds which this particular patient can construct with explicit behaviors, situations and external worlds which are appropriate for this new, good-feelinged, integrated form of the experiencing, and the clinical researcher must envision highly concrete, highly individualized behaviors in those situations, behaviors designed to carry forward the experiencing (principle 3).

In order to do all of this, in order to frame these predictions, the clinical researcher must know more than these three principles. In addition, the clinical researcher must have an understanding of the concept: "actualization of the good form of the operating domain." If the concept makes sense, the principles can be used; if the concept makes little or no sense, the clinical researcher will have trouble using these three principles. Secondly, the clinical researcher must know this particular, individual patient quite well. While these principles enable prediction from each session of experiential therapy, the more the clinical researcher knows this particular patient, the better are the predictions generated by these three principles. Finally, the clinical researcher must be inventive, creative, loose, able to allow possibilities to occur. Given these characteristics, the clinical researcher is nicely able to use these principles in generating directions of potential change with regard to the actualization of the good form of the operating domain.

INTEGRATIVE RELATIONSHIPS WITH DEEPER POTENTIALS

The above three principles involved actualization of the good form of the operating domain. We now turn to principles which involve the relationships between the patient or operating domain and deeper potentials. According to existential-humanistic theory, these relationships are typically disintegrative. That is, their relationships are characterized by distance, separation, avoidance, opposition, resistance, pulling back from, denial, pushing away; there are feelings of distrust, hatred, tension, anxiety, turmoil, fragmentation, being in pieces. These disintegrative relationships are indicted by the two negative signs in the channel of the relationships between the operation potentials and the deeper potentials (Figure 1).

Both the existential-humanistic theory of human beings and the theory of experiential psychotherapy hold that the direction of potential change is toward integrative relationships between the operating and deeper potentials. This means that operating and deeper potentials intermingle with one another, welcome each other, accept and love one another. Relationships are closer, more intimate, friendly. There is no separation or distance; instead, the patient can gracefully ease into and out of the operating and the deeper potentials. Relationships are softened, eased, and accompanied with feelings of inner harmony and togetherness, oneness and wholeness, peace and tranquility. The change toward integrative relationships is indicated by the positive signs in the overlap between potentials on the right in Figure 1.

This overall direction of change has specific implications for concretely predictable changes used by the clinical researcher. Although this is an internal change, there are concretely predictable changes in the patient's actual ways of being and behaving, and in the patient's external world. The balance of this section includes principles 4–8, which the clinical researcher can use to define and predict the directions of potential change which occur as relationships with deeper potentials move from disintegrative to integrative.

4) Disintegrative Feelings Will Be Replaced by Integrative Feelings

Bodily-felt feelings of disintegration will be replaced with bodily-felt feelings of integration. The patient starts with feelings of tension, anxiety, disjointedness, disharmony, being in pieces, being fragmented and torn apart, inner turmoil and disjunctiveness. These disintegrative feelings tend to go away and to be replaced with feelings of inner peace, harmony, wholeness, oneness, inner togetherness, intactness. Independent of the nature of the potentials, the direction of potential change is away from disintegrative feelings and toward integrative feelings.

The disintegrative feelings may occur as such bodily sensations as a persistent throbbing ache in the forehead and behind the eyes, low back pain, aches in the joints, searing pains across the chest wall, muscular crampings, shakings and tremblings, burning sensations in the stomach, hot flashes over the face, perspiration on the back. The direction of change is toward their extinction and replacement with sensations of bodily soundness and intactness. To the extent that these bodily sensations express the disintegrative relationships between the patient and the deeper potentials, the process of integrating these relationships carries with it such palpable changes in distressing bodily sensations. In general, as internal integration occurs, dramatic changes may occur in these associated bodily hurts, aches, and pains.

There is also the special case of disintegrative feelings of being caught, stuck, impassed, trapped between two operating potentials (e.g., OP1 and OP2, Figure 1). One may consist of the experiencing of greed, grasping, owning, possessing, and the other the experiencing of giving, providing, sharing, offering. It may be the middle ground between being loyally devoted to one's family and being freely autonomous, between heterosexual and homosexual relations, between self-concern and loving intimacy, between group participation and being the lonely solitary figure, being radical and conservative, the experiencing of organized concentration and directionless drifting. Regardless of the nature of the potentials, the patient is rigidly confined to the painful middle ground, with its attendant feelings of being caught and stuck, confined and imprisoned. The clinical researcher can predict that such disintegrative feelings will wash away, and instead there will be integrative feelings of inner freedom and harmony, space and openness, unity and oneness. In general, the direction is from disintegrative feelings toward a state of integrative feelings.

5) Externalized and Internalized Forms of the Deeper Potentials Will Extinguish

Suppose that the deeper potential consisted of the experiencing of nasty anger, aggressive jabbing and poking, always getting in the way and making trouble, incessantly striking out in anger. If the relationships with this deeper potential are intensely disintegrative, there may be someone in her world who serves as the externalized form of this deeper potential. Her husband or her older sister may then fulfill this role, incessantly jabbing at her, saying nasty and cutting remarks, hurting her with angry shots. If the deeper potential is DP5 (Figure

1), the husband or older sister is indicated as Externalized DP5. The patient's relationships with both the deeper potential and the externalized deeper potential are sharply disintegrative.

On the other hand, if relationships with this deeper potential are intensely disintegrative, the deeper potential may take the form of some internalized bodily phenomenon, something in the body which expresses the deeper potential. It may occur as sharp jabbing pains in the stomach, and the bodily phenomenon is an ulcer.

The principle is that the internalized and externalized forms of the deeper potentials will extinguish. As relationships between the patient and the deeper potential become increasingly integrative, there is less and less basis for the disintegrative form of the deeper potential to occur as some individual in the patient's external world or as some physical phenomenon within the patient's body. Whether internalized or externalized, it tends to fade out of existence. The jabbing pains of the ulcer go away, together with the bodily phenomenon which was the internalized deeper potential. There is no further need for the husband as the person with angry shots, or for the sister as the one whose remarks were so cutting. It is as if this form of husband or sister fades away, no longer plays a role in the patient's world.

If the disintegrative relationships are with a deeper potential for unfeeling coldness, then perhaps some key figure in the patient's world fulfills that role. It is the patient's aunt, the one who has always been cold and unfeeling toward the patient and with whom relationships have always been disintegrative. The patient knows the aunt as being that way, can present evidence to confirm that she is that way, and is sure that the aunt is really a cold and unfeelinged person. Yet the aunt also serves as the externalization of the patient's own coldness and unfeeling. As relationships with this deeper potential move toward integration, the structural basis for constructing and maintaining the cold and unfeelinged aunt tends to wash away, and the change is toward the receding away of the cold and unfeelinged aunt.

In a similar way, the patient has never gotten along with his younger brother who plays the role of the useless one, the substanceless nonentity, the one without value or worth, never to be taken seriously. This is the externalization of the patient's own deeper potential. The patient regards the younger brother this way, treats him this way, criticizes him for being this way, and hates him for being this way. Yet the younger brother is always in the patient's world, radiating the patient's own deeper potential for uselessness and substancelessness. The change occurs as the patient undergoes movement toward integrative relationships with his own deeper potential. As this occurs, the whole basis for constructing and maintaining the brother in this role tends to fade away. No longer is the brother constructed and maintained into being that person. There is an extinguishing of the role of such a person in the patient's external world.

Internalized bodily forms of the deeper potential will tend to wash away, and this includes the actual, tangible, physical nature of the bodily phenomenon. In its disintegrative form, there is a bodily manifestation of an aliveness, a deadly vitality which acts upon, does to, is a vigorous life-force. It occurs as a cancer, deep within the body, eating away, consuming, spreading. However, as the disintegrative relationships with this deeper potential move toward integration, the very foundation of the cancer softens, eases, and moves toward extinction. As a consequence, the change is toward the actual washing away of the bodily physical presence of the cancer; it goes away. In the same way, the disintegrative deeper form of a potential for the experiencing of unwilling resistance, defiant uselessness may take the physical bodily form of ineffectual muscles around an eye. The consequence is a "lazy eye" so that the right eye essentially does no work, will not function. As relationships shift in the direction of integration, the whole basis for the "lazy eye" eases and diminishes, and the "lazy eye" is no longer a lazy eye. All manner of bodily physical phenomena tend to wash away when they exist as the disintegrative form of the deeper potential and when relationships move in the direction of integration.

Clinical research predictions about these internalized bodily phenomena are rather simple: They extinguish. Clinical research predictions about the externalized forms of the deeper potentials are somewhat more complicated. The patient will move in the direction of no longer imposing roles upon the other individual. The patient will move in the direction of neither constructing nor maintaining the other individual as the externalization. The older sister will no longer be constructed and maintained as incessantly jabbing, hurting with angry shots. The aunt will no longer be forced to be the cold and unfeeling one. No longer will the patient impose upon the younger brother the role of being the useless nonentity.

This may mean relationships with these figures extinguish. As there is no further basis for constructing and maintaining the older sister as the externalized agency for incessantly jabbing and hurting with angry shots, the patient may let the older sister go. There may be no further relationships with the older sister.

Secondly, this change may mean relationships are different. Whereas before the aunt was perceived, constructed, and maintained as the cold and unfeelinged one, the direction of change is toward allowing new kinds of relationships to develop. The two may work out a different kind of relationship on the basis of other potentials in both patient and aunt. They may be better or worse, full of pleasure or pain. The patient and the aunt are still with one another, only she is no longer the cold and unfeeling one; she has been allowed to be different.

Thirdly, the patient may have a new relationship with the other individual who proves to be "really" the way the patient has constructed and maintained him as being. No longer does the patient impose upon the younger brother the role of being the useless nonentity. Yet, as the patient allows the younger brother to be, lets him be whatever he is, the younger brother exudes his own genuine uselessness. The clinical prediction holds. As the patient no longer constructs and maintains the brother as the useless nonentity, and as the younger brother nevertheless stands present as his own, genuine uselessness, relationships are qualitatively different. The patient may remain with the brother, but differently. Now the patient can welcome, play with, allow integrative relationships to emerge with his useless younger brother. On the other hand, the patient may have little to do with his younger brother, but the letting go will occur easily, gracefully, integratively.

All in all, the clinical researcher predicts that externalized and internalized forms of the deeper potential will move in the direction of extinguishing.

6) Disintegrative Relationships With the External World Will Extinguish, and Integrative Relationships Will Occur

The heart of the problem lies in the disintegrative relationships between the patient and the deeper potential. As the clinical researcher gains understanding of the nature of these internal relationships, it will become clearer that relationships with this particular deeper potential are characterized by avoidance, distance, separation, tension, fear, anxiety, being torn apart, being fragmented, in pieces. Then, as the clinical researcher looks at the patient's external world, there can be three kinds of disintegrative relationships between the patient and the external world. Each of these can be predicted to extinguish and to be replaced with integrative external relationships.

(a) As indicated in principle 5, the external world may be populated with an externalization of the deeper potential. If this is the case, the clinical researcher predicts that the direction of change is from disintegrative relationship to integrative relationship with the externalized deeper potential. If the patient avoids, pushes down, is bothered by the deeper potential for experiencing hurting others, incessantly jabbing at others, and if the older sister is constructed and maintained as the externalization of this deeper potential, then relationships with the older sister will be disintegrative. The patient will be tight and constrained with her. There will be disharmony and tension between them. As given in principle 6, the direction of change is toward the washing away of these relationships and the emerging of integrative relationships. The patient will feel a sense of oneness and harmony with the older sister, a sense of letting be, a freedom and openness, a sense of togetherness and peace, a welcoming and acceptance.

If the mother has disintegrative relationships with her own deeper potential for closed-in aloneness, she may construct and maintain her young daughter into being its externalization, and the mother duplicates with the young daughter the same disintegrative relationships. She is troubled and bothered by her daughter. They pick at and hurt one another. There is distance and separation between the two. Being together means hating one another. The mother recoils against and rails at the daughter's closed-in aloneness, criticizes her for being that way, hates her being that way. As the mother gains integrative relationships with her own deeper potential, the clinical research prediction is that relationships between mother and daughter will likewise soften and move toward integration. The mother will be welcoming and accepting with her daughter, will enable closeness to occur, will have feelings of oneness and harmony with the daughter, and relationships will be characterized by peacefulness and tranquility.

In the first kind of disintegrative relationship, some figure in the external world is constructed and maintained as the externalization of the deeper potential. We now turn to the second kind of disintegrative relationship in which the external figure is a complicit partner of the operating potential.

(b) The operating potential bears a disintegrative relation toward the deeper potential. Given this condition, the patient constructs and maintains some figure in the external world who bears this same relationship to the patient. The formula works like this: If I hate this deeper potential in me, then you are likewise to hate me for being this deeper potential. Suppose that the deeper potential is the awful experiencing of being an unwelcomed intruder. With disintegrative relationships toward this deeper potential, the patient may construct an external world containing a person, who maintains the same disintegrative relationship toward the patient. That is, someone distastefully regards the patient as an unwelcome intruder, recoils from the patient as an unwelcomed intruder, has charged distance from the patient as an unwelcomed intruder. It is as if the patient constructs someone who has the same disintegrative relationships toward the patient as the patient has toward what is deeper.

Then the change occurs. There is now an integrative relationship between the patient and the deeper potential. Accordingly, relationships with the external world become less disintegrative and more integrative. Instead of recoiling from the patient, others welcome him with friendliness. Relationships between the patient and others become easy, softer, marked by mutuality and give and take. In short, relationships become more integrative.

Once the patient hates and fears what is within, it is common that the patient will fashion someone who hates and fears the patient. If the patient is disgusted at the deeper potential, then there is someone who is disgusted with the patient. When the patient draws back from his insides in rigid anger, there is someone who draws back from the patient in rigid anger. The direction of change is toward softening, easing toward integration. The patient can welcome and play with the other one, can be comfortably close and friendly with the other one.

(c) The third kind of a disintegrative relationship with the external world is a general one. It refers to the patient's relationships in general. When relationships with the deeper potentials are sharply disintegrative, the patient's relationships with the external world in general tend to be disintegrative. There is general avoidance and distance, separation and charged space, clashing and grating, tightness and tension, disharmony and fragmentation. The clinical researcher predicts that these relationships will move in the direction of integration, with its welcoming and acceptance, friendly playfulness and closeness, letting be and giving freedom to be, interpenetration and harmony.

Once the clinical researcher can identify how the external world is used to fashion disintegrative relationships, the principle enables the researcher to predict that these will tend to wash away and to be replaced with more integrative relationships.

7) There Will Be a Decrease in Disintegrative Behaviors

As relationships between the patient and the deeper potentials become integrated, the clinical researcher can predict changes in the patient's feelings (principle 4), in bodily phenomena (principle 5), in certain parts of the patient's external world (principle 5), and in the relationships between the patient and parts of the external world (principle 6). We now turn to the patient's behavior. As relationships between the patient and the deeper potentials become more integrated, the clinical researcher predicts that there will be a decrease in disintegrative behavior. There are two classes of disintegrative behavior, and each will be discussed in turn.

Behaviors which construct and maintain the externalized deeper potential. First we examine the nature of the deeper potential. Next we look into the patient's external world, and ask if it contains some externalization of the deeper potential, perhaps an individual or agency as the externalized form of the deeper potential. Finally, we identify the behaviors the patient uses to construct this externalization into the external world, and to keep it alive, to maintain its presence. These are the behaviors which principle 7 predicts will wash away.

These behaviors may consist of merely selecting the right figures. With a deeper potential for domination and control, he selects out a world populated by dominating individuals. In quite painful ways, he is made to feel rotten by sets of dominating and controlling figures in his world. Yet the behaviors he uses are merely those of carefully selecting the right kind of dominating and controlling others. He does not make them that way. He does little to mold them into being so dominating and controlling. All he does is select them out of all possible people to be with. Indeed, he is highly sensitive in ferreting out those who are dominating and controlling. These behaviors are finely honed. His friends are all dominating and controlling individuals. Each of his wives was superbly dominating and controlling. He is drawn toward a series of supervisors and bosses who are dominating and controlling. Almost without trying, only by behavioral selection, he manages to locate and be with individuals who are excellent externalizations of his deeper potential. The clinical prediction is that he will move in the direction of no longer selecting such persons, no longer behaving in ways which pick out these readymade dominators and controllers. That is one class of behaviors which decrease.

A second class is comprised of ways in which the patient actively molds the other, fashions and defines the other into being the externalization. Consider the mother whose deeper potential consists of a voracious consuming, a pulling from the world, a drawing of everything into her. Externalized out into the world is her daughter, whom the mother actively fashions into being so voraciously all-consuming. The daughter is now nine years old. Mother has succeeded in making the daughter painfully thin, rejecting just about all food so that mother must dedicate her daily life to finding the proper nutriment, taking her to clinics, observing her for aches and pains evidencing the child's wretched physical condition. Also, mother is tormented by the possibility of the child's having her own thoughts, so mother incessantly probes what the child is thinking in order to search for alien ideas. Mother is ever vigilant against contaminating relationships so that she assesses the child's every outside contact, whether peers or menacing outsiders. Having constructed the situation with professional skill, mother rails at the daughter's taking all of her time, preventing her from being with her own acquaintances, blocking her relationship with her own parents, and altogether consuming the poor mother.

A third class of behaviors requires cooperation between the patient and the other person. The patient behaves in a way which invites the other individual to be the externalized deeper potential. Here is the critical first step. If the other individual takes up the game and starts playing, then the patient can continue behaving in just the right way. It is a matter of two people working with one another, each behaving in just the right ways, until the patient and the other succeed in constructing and molding the other individual into being the externalization. It is as if the patient says, "You seem to be a likely candidate. If I do this to you, will you respond in just the right way?" Doing all of this requires the right behaviors in partnership with the right playmate.

She has a deeper potential for being a bully, a powerful victimizer, one who tramples on others. How does she construct and maintain others into fulfilling this role? She locates a likely candidate in her husband, and engages in the appropriate behaviors to build that role. When she and he are in the presence of a third person, she speaks so as to have precisely timed pauses which invite the husband to intrude and cut her off. She also describes something which is challengingly inaccurate so that the husband is invited to correct her. If the husband intrudes or corrects her, she defers, look pitiable, and casts a hurt glance at the other party. By working in an effective partnership, the patient has succeeded in constructing her own deeper potential in the bullying husband.

As integration occurs between the patient and the deeper potential, all of these behaviors wash away. No longer does the patient behave in ways which fill the external world with externalizations of the patient's own deeper potentials.

Behaviors which construct and maintain disintegrative relationships with the externalized deeper potential. Some behaviors serve to build the externalized deeper potential in the external world. Other behaviors then proceed to build disintegrative relationships between the patient and the externalized deeper potential. Not only will patients have externalized deeper potentials in their worlds, but relationships with these externalized deeper potentials will also be disintegrative. If the patient's deeper potential consists of the experiencing of bullying and victimizing, relationships are to be characterized by tension and fear, intransigence and disharmony, hatred and warfare, antinomy and avoidance, clashings and attacks. Building these relationships calls for the right class of behaviors.

If the deeper potential consists of the experiencing of a self-centered narcissism, an overweening self-interest, the patient may cultivate an acquaintance into being that way. But that is not enough. Relationships with that person are to be disintegrative. Accordingly, the patient arranges to have her acquaintance come over to her house whenever the patient is busy with some project such as making a dress for her daughter or transplanting a bed of flowers. Then the patient deftly inquires into the acquaintance's own life. Grabbing the bait, the acquaintance plunges into a celebration of self-interest which the patient builds upon with further questions. The net result is a disintegrative relationship in which the patient is frustrated with the acquaintance, silently angry at her, made to feel used and intruded upon, separated and distanced from the acquaintance.

He is a staid and conservative owner of a small neighborhood restaurant, and he hires an attractive young waitress whom he constructs into being the externalization of his own disintegrative deeper potential for sexual wildness and lascivity. Whenever she is a few minutes late in the morning, he alludes to her sleeping with some other guy, and does so with a deft innuendo which obviously bothers her. He frequently touches her on the shoulder and upper back in ways where are suggestive and inviting, and she draws away. In front of others, he stares at her body in ways which invite the customers to share in aggressive snickers. When she is clearly bothered by his behavior, he surrounds himself in a superior coldness which bespeaks of his threat to fire her if she openly protests. All of these ways of behaving establish a disintegrative relationship in which he is distant and painfully separated, tight and tense around her, and in which relationships are aggressively charged. As his own relationships with the deeper potential move toward integration, all of these relationship-maintaining behaviors tend to wash away.

He knew his father as a cold and unfeeling martinet with whom the patient's relationships were always disintegratively hurtful and painful. As the externalization of the patient's own deeper coldness and withdrawal, the father was a fitting figure, yet the patient behaved in subtle ways which perpetuated these disintegrative relationships. He never failed to remind his father about times when the father proved how cold and unfeeling he really was. When the patient lost his job some time ago, father never said anything. When the patient's son had a serious accident and nearly lost two fingers, father never visited the son or showed any sign of concern. When the patient bought a new home, everyone came and celebrated the new home, but father stayed away. The patient engineered little clashing arguments with his father, complained to his mother how bad father was, offered to make up with father in an artfully removed way which proved father's awful coldness. The patient never revealed anything weak or flawed to his father, and then complained of father's being distant and removed. All of these behaviors deftly maintained the relationship as disintegratively hurtful and painful. When, however, the patient's relationships with his own deeper coldness and unfeelingness moved toward integration, then the remarkable change occurred, and all of these behaviors washed away.

In Figure 1, these relationship-building disintegrative behaviors are indicated as B2 and B3, and the disintegrative relationships are indicated by the two negative signs in the channels between the patient and the externalized deeper potentials. The clinical researcher predicts that these behaviors will extinguish. More specifically, the prediction is the extinguishing of specific behaviors which this patient uses to build disintegrative relationships with those parts of the external world which serve as the externalization of the patient's own deeper potentials. Once the researcher knows these behaviors, the seventh principle predicts their extinction.

8) There Will Be an Increase in Integrative Behaviors

The general change is toward an increase in what may be described as "integrative behaviors." For purposes of clinical research prediction, however, this principle must be applied a little more rigorously and to the particular patient.

There will be an increase in the skill of using bodily sensations to monitor behavior. As relationships between the patient and the deeper potential become integrated, the patient comes into closer and closer touch with a whole spectrum of bodily sensations. Right now, in the chest or legs or face, there is a trembling or a surge of warmth or a tightening of the muscles. The patient becomes much more sensitive to what is occurring right now in the body. This includes pleasant and unpleasant bodily sensations; it includes subtle little sensations and big strong ones; it includes those which are momentary and those which are enduring. But more important than just becoming increasingly aware of these bodily sensations is the skill of using these to monitor behavior.

One skill is using bodily sensations as danger signals, as indications of immediate threat. It is as if the patient learns to use the bodily sensations as signals: "Watch out, something is wrong!" This is the first skill. The patient learns, for example, that his particular danger signals include dizziness and a slight headache. Another patient learns that her bodily danger signals include a tightening across the chest or butterflies in the stomach. Another patient learns that there is a threat when there is a hot ball of pressure filling up the whole chest cavity. Each patient learns the specific and individualized bodily signals of threat or danger.

Once this skill is learned, the associated skill involves doing something on the basis of the monitored bodily signal. Stop what you are doing. Do not keep on with how you are being. Or leave, exit, withdraw, get out. A patient may be talking with someone at a party.

Then the patient becomes aware of her heart beating hard and a tightening in her chest. She closes her eyes for a few seconds, confirms that these bodily sensations are indeed strong, and stops the conversation. She says, "Something is wrong. I must stop," and she withdraws from the situation. Or she says, "My heart is beating hard and there's a tightening in my chest. I have to stop for a while," and she exits. The general skill is that of stopping whatever one is doing and withdrawing. The specific skill is that of learning one's own particular bodily danger signals, learning how to stop whatever the particular patient is doing, and learning how to withdraw or exit in a way which fits the particular patient.

Another skill is that of using one's own particular bodily sensations as monitoring meters to rehearse a behavior, sample a behavior, or make a decision. The patient learns to be alone, either by physically being by oneself or by enveloping oneself in a zone of silence. Then the patient samples or rehearses by allowing a situation to occur in fantasy or imagery. Should I call my friend and tell her about the nasty remark our mutual acquaintance said about her? I close my eyes and allow the scene to take place. Then I receive the bodily sensations. My face feels flushed and full. These are unpleasant bodily sensations. I will decline to call my friend. Or, when I insert myself into the sampled situation, there is a pleasantly light tingling throughout my body, and I am therefore inclined to go ahead and carry out the action. Using bodily sensations to sample or rehearse or help decide upon some behavior is a general skill which many patients learn to use in the course of experiential therapy. It is a behavioral skill which is part and parcel of the therapy process itself, a class of "therapy skills" which all patients learn to some degree over the course of experiential therapy.

The clinical researcher predicts that the patient will move in the direction of using bodily sensations to monitor one's own behavior and of acting in accordance with the nature of these bodily sensations. As a footnote, each therapeutic approach has its own package of "therapy skills" which its patients learn in the course of becoming a patient in that therapeutic approach, and many of these qualify as predicted changes, outcomes, directions of potential change. This is one of ours.

There will be an increase in integrative behavioral reactions to oneself. As internal integration occurs, there is a change which typically involves the person himself or herself rather than necessarily involving other individuals. On the left in Figure 1, the person's relationships with herself are disintegrative, with little awareness of what she is doing, how she is being or behaving. The person's relationships are characterized by blinders, by defensive not knowing, by threat. The person is hidden from and blockaded from how she is being and what she is doing.

At the other extreme, disintegrative internal relationships may mean that the patient is supremely aware of one's own behavior and way of being. But the relationship is disintegrative. That is, the patient seems to be split so that while one part is being and behaving, another part is witnessing and observing, almost always in a negative way. Or the patient is in a perpetual stance of aggressively defending how one is being and doing or in a defensive posture of being attacked.

The clinical researcher predicts that the patient will move in the direction of integratively relating to oneself, behaving in ways which express a welcoming acceptance of one's own way of being and behaving, a welcoming acceptance which can be proud and pleased or critical and judgmental. The patient will be able to stand off and have a reaction to the way she is being and behaving, a reaction which is generally accurate, friendly, and open.

The core behavioral skill is that of being aware of how one is, how one is being and behaving. The patient notices that she is being surly and testy, or charming and delightful. She is able to have a reaction to what she just did and how she just behaved. If she is using an excessively loud voice in talking to her spouse, she is aware of using an excessively loud voice. In effect, she is aware of her own immediate reactions to what she is being and doing.

In addition, there is the behavioral skill of being able to react and respond to herself. The patient is in sufficiently integrative relationship with herself to be able to have integratively friendly, accepting, playful reactions. She can comment and react to the way she is being. Almost always, the reaction which her behavior or way of being invites others to assume she can assume to herself. If her way of being and behaving invites others to regard her as a tough leader, she can respond to herself that way: "I sound like a tough leader." If her way of being or behaving invites others to respond to her as childish and immature, she can have the very same response to herself: "Well, that's childish and immature!"

Many of these self-reactions are pleasant and happy. After singing a few bars, "That's a pretty good voice!" After eating her casserole, "Say, that's damned good cooking!" Looking at oneself in the mirror, "Not bad for an old broad." After explaining directions for how to reach the hardware store, "Good directions, eh! Clear! No frills! Simple." One can step aside, and have a reaction to oneself which is integratively positive and accepting.

But the integrative relationships between potentials also mean that the patient will be able to be concerned with and bothered about the way one is. Because of the integrative relationships with himself, he can stand aside and criticize, he can accept mistakes and errors and goofs. After telling an acquaintance about the new cottage he just purchased, he steps aside and says, "What a God damned show-off! There's something disgusting about that." After telling his five-year-old son to shut the door when he comes in, he is aware of the sharp brusqueness, and is on good enough terms with that to say, "What a nasty, brutal thing to do. I'm going to regret that for years." Integrative relationships mean that the patient can laugh at himself, criticize himself, see what a silly fool he is, identify what a petty bastard he is, tolerate his acts of petulant competitiveness.

The clinical researcher can make the general prediction that there will be an increase in these integrative behavioral reactions to oneself. That is a free prediction, applicable to all patients. The more the clinical researcher knows of the patient's own potentials, the more the clinical researcher can predict the patient will be able to react integratively to that particular way of being and behaving.

There will be an increase in integrative behavioral relationships with others. The clinical researcher predicts that the patient will show a new class of integrative behaviors in relationships with others in general, and specifically in relationships with those who had been externalized deeper potentials. If the patient had constructed and maintained the much older brother as the externalization of the patient's own deeper holier-than-thou superiority, then this eighth principle says that the direction of potential change is toward behaving in ways which build a new kind of integrative relationship with the older brother. There are at least four subclasses of such integrative behaviors.

One consists of integrative behaviors which allow other persons freedom to be however they are. The patient behaves so as to give the other person space, plenty of room to be whatever way the other person is ready to be. Instead of crowding the other person into being coldly superior, the patient behaves in integrative ways which simply let the other person be. This may consist of leaving the other person alone, having few if any relationships with him, no longer intruding into the other one, no longer forcing interactions designed to twist the other one into the externalized shape. It may consist of allowing the other person to be his own, real, authentic cold superiority, if that is what is there. Generally it means allowing the other person to be different, something other than the coldly superior one the patient had always forced the person into being. It is a behavioral means of letting others be whatever and however they may be, and it occurs both with the former externalized deeper potential and also with others in general.

A second subclass of behaviors consists of those which allow a measure of intimacy and closeness to occur. It is a matter of "allowing," rather than forcing or imposing or pressuring. If a measure of intimacy is here, it is allowed to occur. The patient can now build, with the other person, the same kind of intimate relationships which are present among the patient's own potentials. Accordingly, these behaviors are friendly, welcoming, gracious. Relationships with the other person can become close and intimate, but there is no having to be intimate, no force or pressure to impose intimacy.

A third subclass of integrative behaviors consists of allowing oneself to share whatever may be occurring in the other person right now. At times, the patient will feel something the other person is now feeling. The patient may share the older brother's sense of family loyalty and concern, or his pride in achievements, or his icy superiority. The patient's relationships are sufficiently integrative to allow some degree of this sharing of ongoing feeling. It is a matter of resonating or fusing with the feeling occurring in the other person.

The fourth subclass consists of behaviors which allow a measure of integrative encountering. This must be differentiated from aggressive confrontation or a tense having-it-out with the other one or a forced challenge. Instead, the patient can relate integratively enough to allow a playful staying with the other person, a friendly touching of where they are meeting. Instead of pulling back or avoiding, or even an implicit maintaining of safe distance, the patient is willing to move in a bit closer, to sample a playful integrative encounter. It is an encounter in that the patient is willing to take a step into the other, to approach the outer boundary of the private zone, to illuminate whatever is here even if it is somewhat risky or embarrassing or tense or bothersome or hidden. It is integrative in that it is friendly, gracious, respectful, easy, welcoming, and can end when it is perhaps no longer friendly, gracious, respectful, easy, and welcoming.

Principles 4–8 enable the clinical researcher to make specific predictions of the directions of potential change available to this patient as relationships between potentials move from disintegrative (as indicated on the left in Figure 1) to integrative (as indicated on the right in Figure 1). We now turn to the principles which refer to the change from deeper potentials to operating potentials.

DEEPER POTENTIALS BECOME
OPERATING POTENTIALS

The process of experiential psychotherapy brings deeper potentials into the operating domain. In Figure 1, the deeper potentials are indicated as DP5, DP6, and DP7. The direction of change is given on the right in Figure 1, wherein these become OP5, OP6, and OP7. This is a powerful direction of change. It means that potentials which were deeper, not directly experienced, not part of the way the patient is, not the basis of direct behaviors, convert into being a major component of the patient's operating domain. Principles 9 and 10 turn this general idea into researchable clinical predictions.

9) The Patient Will Have New
(Formerly Deeper) Experiencings

Where before the patient did not experience these potentials, now the patient can and does experience them. In the vocabulary of existential-humanistic thinking, this is referred to as actualization.

In order to predict the new experiencing, the clinical researcher must have a description of the nature of the person's deeper potential. The more the clinical researcher can describe of this particular person's deeper potential, the more the specifc clinical prediction can be made. Accomplishing this is work. It comes from a study of what happens in session after session. This is why notes for this prediction should be in pencil, for the process is one of continuous refinement. After one or two sessions, some gross prediction can be made, but as the data allow for a more accurately particularized description, a finer and more accurately individual prediction may be framed. After a session or two, the deeper potential may be described with words such as: hurt, alone, lost. However, after more sessions, the deeper potential is described as: forcefully excluded by them, actively rejected, always left behind, walled off from them, pushed away, kept at a distance, unwanted. These words provide a more specific picture of the content of the deeper experiencing. At this point, the clinical researcher can predict that the direction of change will consist of the potential for this particular kind of experiencing. The deeper potential will become actualized, realized, a part of the operating domain, a component of what the patient can experience.

But actualization is only half the story. The other half comes from what is called "integration." This means that the deeper potentials can convert to their good-feelinged form when they become part of the operating domain. A deeper potential is capable of converting from its bad disintegrative form to its good integrative form. That is the other half of the story of what constitutes the direction of potential change. In Figure 1, deeper potentials 5–7 are in their disintegrative form on the left. Relationships with other potentials are disintegrative, as indicated by the two negative signs in the channels of relationships between the deeper and the operating potentials. What can occur, the directions of possible change, are indicated on the right in Figure 1. Relationships between potentials 5–7 and all other potentials are positive, are integrated. This means that the very contents of the deeper experiencings convert from their bad form to their good form.

How does the clinical researcher figure out the good integrated form of the deeper potential? What are the data upon which this prediction can be made? There are at least three ways of answering these questions. One is to use moments in the session when the deeper experiencing actually appears in its new, good, integrated form. Therapeutic work will disclose such precious moments. Starting with the experiencing of being forcefully excluded by them, actively rejected, always left behind, walled off from them, pushed away, kept at a distance, unwanted, there are therapeutic moments in which this painful experiencing is revealed in a new integrated form. Now the patient is, for example, filled with the experiencing of being a person in his own right, being an intact and autonomous individual, letting go of the old relational ties, breathing free. Here is an experiential glimpse of the new, good, integrated form of the disintegrative deeper potential. The data consist of what actually occurs in the session itself. This is one way.

A second method is for the therapist or clinical researcher to "bracket" or set aside the painful disintegrative experiencing and to sample or taste or undergo the good integrative form. In effect, the therapist or clinical researcher actually undergoes the good, integrative form of the experiencing. While the patient is restricted and constrained to undergoing the disintegrative form of the experiencing, the therapist is free to undergo the same experiencng in its integrative form, and thereby grasp what this experiencing can be.

Suppose that the patient is experiencing the awful sense of being walled off from them in a scene in which he calls his parents from the apartment of a woman he just started living with. His mother is cold and withdrawn as she informs him that the family is getting ready to go to grandmother's house to celebrate her birthday, an event which he obviously is missing, and how could he do such a terrible thing. While the patient is groveling in the pool of being rejected by his family, the therapist is free to undergo the new, good, integrative experiencing of letting go of the old relational ties, of breathing a free sense of autonomy. The data consist of the actual experiencing of the integrative potential in the very scene in which the patient is experiencing the disintegrative potential.

A third method is to note commonalities in what actually occurs in patients whose disintegrative form of a specific kind of experiencing changes into the integrative form. Starting with a large number of patients whose deeper disintegrative potentials are strikingly similar, are there any commonalities in what happens as therapeutic work converts the disintegrative deeper potential to its integrative form? This is a problem of clinical research and study. In a sloppier form, this is what occurs over years of therapeutic work when therapists accumulate a body of experience. While I place only a limited degree of confidence in this third method, it is nevertheless another reservoir of guesses about the possible integrative good form of the disintegrative deeper potential.

The clinical researcher starts with the nature of the deeper potential and can predict that the patient will be able to have new experiencings. What is deeper can become a part of the operating domain. What is more, it can not only become "actualized" (i.e., move from the deeper to the operating domain), but also move from its disintegrative form to its integrative form.

The deeper disintegrative experiencing of lack of control, chaos, fragmentation, may transform into a sense of freedom and spontaneity. The deeper disintegrative experiencing of being hurt by the companion or partner may become the integrative risking of genuine intimacy. The deeper disintegrative experiencing of impotence, fecklessness, and incapability may become the delightful experiencing of passivity, trust, secure dependency. The bad-feelinged deeper experiencing of depression, heaviness, ending it all, may transform into the experiencing of leaving, having the capacity and choice of exiting, of declining, of freeing oneself, of having the choice of letting go. The disintegrative deeper experiencing of being a hated troublemaker, being bad, being the cause of problems may transform into a pleasant wickedness, devilishness, mischievousness, spontaneous spunkiness.

What had occurred as a fearful homosexuality may transform into a newfound sense of closeness and genuine intimacy with one's own sex. That hurtful inner sense of being abandoned and rejected may become the new experiencing of letting the other go, allowing freedom and space. When the deeper potential takes the form of the terror of death, dying, ending, that may convert to the integrative sense of peacefulness, inner harmony, and oneness. A lifelong inner sense of frightened awe may transform into a warm and loving respectfulness and pride in the other. That awful sense of being owned and defined by others, made into what they wish, may become an integrative sense of fitting into, of letting the role be, of trust in oneself.

All in all, there will be more to the operating patient. There will be new potentials for experiencing. This is a most significant direction of change which can be predicted by the clinical researcher.

10) There Will Be New Potential Ways of Being and Behaving for the New Operating Potentials

The clinical researcher starts with a picture of the patient's deeper potential. Whatever its described nature, the clinical researcher understands that the direction of change is that the deeper potential will become an operating potential. Principle 9 states that now the patient has the possibility of experiencing this new actualized and integrated, formerly deeper, potential. But there is more. The clinical researcher also knows that this new operating experiencing opens the possibility for new ways of being and behaving. This is one of the most significant payoffs of the therapeutic process, viz. movement of the deeper potential into the operating domain means the increased likelihood of new ways of being and behaving.

New operating potentials and new ways of being and behaving go together. Each provides for the other. New ways of being and behaving lock the deeper potential into the operating domain; symmetrically, the presence of a new potential for experiencing virtually calls for new ways of being and behaving.

The clinical research prediction is that the patient will be able to carry out new ways of being and behaving which provide for the experiencing of the new operating potential. That is about as specific as the prediction can be. In existential theory and in experiential psychotherapy, the choice resides with the patient. While the therapist and clinical researcher may firmly expect that the patient will indeed evidence these new ways of being and behaving, in fact all the theory allows is a prediction that the patient is now able to be this new way. Actually being this way is up to the patient.

What this means for clinical research prediction is that if the patient evidences the new ways of being and behaving, well and good. However, if the patient does not evidence such new ways of being and behaving, the clinical research prediction never promised that it will occur, only that the patient *will be able* to carry out the new ways of being and behaving.

Some of these new ways of being and behaving set the stage for experiencing by constructing appropriate situational contexts. Others more directly provide for the straightforward experiencing of the new potential. Each of these will be discussed in turn.

Potential new ways of being and behaving will construct new external situations. Given the new experiencing, the patient will be able to be and to behave in ways which construct the right kinds of external worlds, which fashion situations appropriate for the new experiencing. Here is a new person who behaves in ways which build new and fitting situations. By knowing the nature of the new experiencing, the clinical researcher predicts that the patient will be and behave in ways which construct new external worlds appropriate for this new experiencing.

If the new experiencing consists of freedom and spontaneity, open expressiveness, the having of plenty of space, the prediction is that the patient will be able to construct new situations appropriate for such experiencing. Some of these new situations may be slight revisions of her current life, fine-tuning within the context of already present situations. She already spends time with, enjoys playing with, her four-year-old daughter. The new way of being and behaving consists of granting her daughter the opportunity to do her own leading, to take a larger hand in choosing what to do and how to play. When they are together, the patient is now able to notice that the daughter is ready to explore their bodies, to touch and cuddle and physically play.

On the other hand, she may be able to be and to behave in ways which build altogether new situations, situations which are quite different from those filling her current world. She may seek out new persons with whom there is greater freedom and space. She may move from a constricting, lock-step government job to one which offers a far greater measure of freedom and space. She may dispense with evening and weekend commitments so that these times may be sculpted as she is spontaneously inclined to fashion them.

What kinds of new ways of being and behaving can build new situations for the newfound experiencing of intimacy? If his current world is designed for other experiencings, or if his current world is designed to minimize such experiencings, if there is little or no place for this newfound experiencing, then potentially new ways of being and behaving will begin to fashion new situations. He is now capable of living with another person instead of spending his life alone. Instead of legal sparring with his ex-wife, as he has for the past six years, he is capable of returning the intimacy of sexual relations with a woman who invites and shares intimacy. Instead of distance-insuring business relationships, he is able to bring into his life genuine friends. He is now capable of initiating contacts with his older brother and younger sister, to visit them in their cities, and spend a few days being with them after so many years.

The newfound experiencing consists of a sense of closeness and transparency, of warmth and oneness with one's own sex. New ways of being and behaving build situations which are appropriate for this kind of experiencing. Instead of living with a woman in endless arguments over his affairs with other women, he lives alone and surrounds himself with a small group of male friends who are receptive to close relationships of warmth and oneness. For the first time in his life he has long talks with his father, and joins his father in fishing trips where just the two of them are together. With men who are receptive, he can acknowledge all kinds of sexual leanings, including sexual relationships with other men. All of these are new ways of being and behaving which construct situational contexts for the newfound experiencing.

As she welcomed the new potential for experiencing trusting passivity and dependency, she was increasingly ready to be and to behave in ways which fashion new situational contexts appropriate for that experiencing. With her husband, she was able to request time alone with him, time in which she could put her head on his lap, be cuddled quietly, and even cry softly. She permitted herself to have occasional naps, and to fall asleep at night instead of staying up long after the whole family went to bed. She allowed herself to bring into her life women friends whom she could trust and upon whom she could depend. In conversation with others, she was able to acknowledge that she did not understand something, that she trusted their view on matters, that she counted upon their judgment. These new ways of being and behaving acted to build situations appropriate for new experiencing.

New ways of being and behaving will provide for direct experiencing of the new operating potentials. New ways of being and behaving will build situations which are appropriate for the new experiencing. While this may also offer a measure of actual experiencing, a fuller measure is given by a complementary set of new ways of being and behaving. In other words, building the situation is not enough; experiencing calls for direct new ways of being and behaving. Some of these are old ways of being and behaving, now reused, or now used in new ways and in new situations. Some are simply new ways of being and behaving.

Setting the situational stage consisted of bringing in new women friends whom she could trust and upon whom she could depend. But the actual direct experiencing of trusting passivity and dependency meant actively taking in and listening to what the other person says, seriously considering the other person's judgments on matters. Being able to be alone with her husband and to put her head on his lap set the stage, but then she was able to curl up like a little child, to feel and be a little child as she softly cried and told him of her bewilderments and uncertainties.

The experiencing of standing up to, of defying, of being a strong person in her own right may call for going to her sister's apartment and letting her know that there were things that her sister did that bothered the patient immensely. But the actual experiencing occurred as she held her sister's hands in hers, looked her sister straight in the eyes, and said, "You piss me off! I have the family over for every damned get-together, and now it's your turn, dammit!" It means raising her voice as she says, "Enough of dumping on Ellen! The days of my being the nice servant are over! It's the end of the era!" It means converting the sudden pressure in the chest into an outraged, "NO!!" It means standing up to her full five feet nine inches instead of hunching over. It means being able to say, "Not on your life, kiddo!" Direct experiencing calls for direct new ways of being and behaving.

Sexual experiencing can occur when the patient allows himself to be near attractive women. That helps. But the actual experiencing of sexuality also calls for new ways of being and behaving. At the open house and at the office, he allowed himself to be within reaching distance of women who aroused the right bodily sensations, but then he stepped into a whole new arena of sexual behaviors. He could now look directly at the other person. He could acknowledge bodily sensations. He could declare that he would like to be with a woman. He could allow himself to be sexually aroused when with some women. He could initiate and participate in being alone with a woman with whom he felt sexual attractions. He could share in physical touchings. He could welcome bodily intimacies and physical touchings.

The childlike experiencing of wonderment and open-eyed curiosity invites a load of new ways of being and behaving. There is a giving in to the spontaneous craving for a big ice cream cone. He gets down on the carpet, flat on his stomach, and looks deep into the eyes of the old brown dog. He looks intently at his right foot, as if seeing it for the first time, studying the shape of the nails and the way each toe pushes against its neighbor. He stares straight up into the sky, carefully following the slowly moving clouds. He rides a bicycle, for the first time in decades. He lies down in her lap and listens to her reading a story. He asks childlike questions that he wondered about as a child and still does not really know the answers to. He stares intently at the lovely caterpillar slowly inching its way across the sidewalk.

Being furiously outraged is the newfound experiencing which requires new ways of being and behaving. She learns how to raise her voice to the proper pitch and amplitude. She learns how to throw the appropriate things at the appropriate person in the appropriate situation and in the appropriate way. She learns how to rave and rant. She learns how to allow her arms, legs, torso, fists and face to share in the expression of wholesome fury. She learns how to make proper use of outrageously violent fantasies. She learns how to kick and scream and have full-blown temper tantrums.

All of these new ways of being and behaving are indicated as B5-B11 on the right in Figure 1. Some of these act to build the appropriate new situational contexts, and some provide for the simple direct experiencing of the newfound operating potentials. By knowing the nature and content of the new operating potentials, the clinical researcher can predict the classes of new ways of being and behaving which provide for the direct experiencing of these new operating potentials.

Principles 9 and 10 apply to the directions of potential change which take place as the deeper potentials move into the operating domain and become integrated and actualized operating potentials. The final category of change has to do with the fate of the former operating potentials.

THE OLD OPERATING DOMAIN
WILL EXTINGUISH

The old operating domain will no longer remain the way it was. It will change, perhaps radically. For the clinical researcher, this means that certain parts of the patient's world will no longer be present, and it means that certain ways of being and behaving will also extinguish.

The bases for such radical changes are contained in the previous ten principles. The first three principles related to the idea that therapy involved the bringing forth (actualization) of the good form of the operating domain. This means that the change is from the low or moderate degree of actualization to the high degree of actualization, and it means the change is from the disintegrative form of the operating potentials to the integrative form. These are radical changes. As the operating potentials undergo these changes, the former external world will tend to wash away, and so too will the related ways of being and behaving.

The next five principles involve therapeutic movement toward integrative relationships between the operating and deeper domains. As these relationships become integrative, operating potentials are deprived of their reason for existing. No longer having to block and avoid what is deeper, no longer denying and masking the deeper potentials, no longer having to establish disintegrative relations, these operating potentials tend to fade away, and this means the end of large parts of the patient's external world and ways of being and behaving.

Principles 9 and 10 speak to the change of deeper potentials into operating potentials. What is deeper moves into being a part of the operating domain. For many operating potentials, this means the end of their function, for they existed to serve the deeper potentials, to be the instrumental means for giving them a whiff of experiential air. As the deeper potentials move into the operating domain, the very heart of their justification is removed, and the consequence is that the external world and the ways of being and behaving tied to the old operating potentials tend to extinguish.

All in all, these components of the therapeutic process converge on sealing the fate of the operating domain. One way or another, it moves in the direction of extinguishing. In Figure 1, the risk of extinguishing is given by the dotted circles for operating potentials 1–4, on the right.

Consider the patient whose operating potential for experiencing a care-giving maternalness serves as a means of offering some whiff of experiencing to the deeper potential for manipulation and control. As the relationships become integrative, and as the deeper potential moves up into the operation domain, the basis for the operating potential is eroded away. Accordingly, it is quite likely that there will be an extinguishing of the patient's care-giving, controlling maternalness.

When she was a young girl, the deeper sense of distance and keeping away was achieved through the operating potential for experiencing explosive wildness. She would have sudden fits of screaming, she would spontaneously lash out at anyone, kicking them or spitting on them. Currently she operates on the basis of big sister protectiveness. Almost automatically, she ferrets out that which calls for big sister protection in others, and swings into action, thereby feeding the deeper sense of distance and separation. But then the changes occurred, the formerly disintegrative experiencing of distance and separation became a respectable part of the operating domain. There is then little or no basis for the experiencing of big sister protectiveness.

The deeper experiencing of being God-like, of having the magic of being the Special One, was fueled in childhood by the operating potential for being gifted and talented. He carved objects out of soap, composed melodies on the family piano, showed special promise in solving little architectural and design problems around the neighborhood. As an adult, there was the operating potential for experiencing the sense of assiduous dedication and unswerving devotion as a physician specializing in oncology. Yet the continuous deeper experiencing was that of being the God-like Special One. As therapy raised the deeper potential into the operating domain, changing its form from disintegrative to integrative, there occurred a washing away of the characteristic operating potential for the experiencing of assiduous dedication and unswerving devotion.

There may be a veneer of apparent good feelings attached to the operating potential for experiencing the sense of being competent, worthy, of substance. Yet it serves to fend off the deeper experiencing of nothingness, emptiness, vacuum. The direction of therapeutic processes is toward the unscrewing of the whole basis for having to be competent, worthy, of substance, and the result is the extinguishing of this operating potential. Having to be all sweetness and light will likewise tend to fade away, if the operating potential serves to hide and deny the deeper aggressive nastiness. No longer having to show the polar face, the whole basis for the operating experiencing of sweetness just undergoes extinction. A similar fate awaits painful operating potentials which hide the deeper potential by turning it around. It is hurtful and painful to experience the sense of being victimized, the one who is tortured and walked upon. While the deeper potential consists of the wholesale sense of being the powerful victimizer, the one who inflicts the torture, therapeutic change processes lead to the washing away of the operating sense of being victimized.

All of these changes mean that the former operating potential will no longer be present. In Figure 1, the change from a solid circle on the left to a dotted circle on the right means that there are changes in the external world and in the ways in which the patient behaves. These changes are concrete and identifiable, specific and measureable. In short, they lend themselves to clinical research prediction as principles 11 and 12.

11) The Operating Domain's External World Will Extinguish

Given any operating potential, there almost always is some external world which supports that experiencing. Particular parts of the external world provide for that experiencing, enabling it to occur. When the clinical researcher comes to grasp the particular situational context which enables the operating potential to be experienced, the prediction is that those parts of the external world will extinguish.

Here is an across-the-board risk. The operating domain's external world will extinguish no matter how the patient feels about the matter, regardless of whether the patient is attached to this part of the external world or is pleased about its eventual loss, regardless of whether the feelings accompanying the operating potential are happy or unhappy. Across the board, applying to everything in the external world linked to the operating potential, the risk is that it will fade away.

The extinguishing may take the form of the patient's turning her back and walking away from her job or lover or other situations wherein others pile garbage upon her. The extinguishing may mean that the former external world loses its meaning, its significance. Being the best basketball player in junior high school may gradually lose its charm. Surrounding oneself with fawning admirers may evaporate in its significance. A world of grasping and greedy clutching fingers may slowly fade out of meaningful existence. Whether actively or passively, the external world loses its former meaningfulness and significance.

The former external world may remain, in a sense, or it may no longer exist. While bosses may still be present, they no longer are powerfully authoritative. The patient may remain at the same job, but those problematic situations with the boss just no longer seem to occur. Something has changed. Mother may stay in the family, but there are few if any explosive crises threatening the breakup of the family. Again, something has changed. On the other hand, the patient may no longer be with that boss; the patient leaves, and her external world no longer includes powerfully authoritative bosses. Or the mother walks away from the family, and her external world no longer contains explosive crises threatening the breakup of the family. In both scenarios, the former external world may remain, in a sense, or may no longer exist.

There is the operating potential for experiencing being a victim, being assaulted, having no freedom, being the one who is done to. Pieces and bits of the external world have to be present in just the right ways to allow for this experiencing. For this patient, the experiencing occurs in situations in which her husband becomes enraged at her and beats her up, punctuated with yellings and screamings. It also occurs in situations in which her neighbor leaves trash on her yard. And it occurs regularly when her daughter takes on a supercilious air, looking down upon her ridiculed, low-class, unattractive, dumb mother.

The clinical prediction is that these situational contexts will no longer fill her external world. They will no longer be present. She may remain with her husband, but there are no further scenes in which he becomes enraged, beats her up, yelling and screaming at her. There may be conflicts and fightings, but without the beatings, the ragings, the same yellings and screamings. Or, she may no longer be with the husband, or any other person with whom the same situation exists. She may remain next door to her neighbor, but now there is no more trash on her yard. Or the trash recedes in significance and has no further experiential impact. Or she may move away and have no further trashy encounters with neighbors. With regard to her daughter, there may be no more situations in which her daughter ridicules her. Or these encounters may change to interchanges which provide for experiencings other than that of being victimized. Or the patient may extract herself from being with the daughter at all. In any case, the three situations no longer are present in her external world.

An operating potential may serve to deny and disprove the deeper experiencing of being a frightened, helpless little child, unsure of herself, confused and bewildered. In her current world, the operating potential consists of the experiencing of strength, of power and dominant control. What kind of external world can be constructed to accommodate this experiencing? What are the kinds of situations wherein she gains a measure of this sense of strength, power, and control? It occurs when her husband is on the phone, confidently reassuring the president of the massive conglomerate that he is of the opinion that they need not worry about the government investigation. Her husband is head of one of the most prominent law firms in the city. It also occurs when she chides one of her staff physicians for being late at the meeting. She is a physician and head of one of the departments in the general hospital of the city. There is an external world comprised of boards, staffs who are responsible to her and to her husband, an extremely large house, people who serve them as caterers, tailors, mechanics, landscape architects, a cook, a cleaning lady, all filling in an external world appropriate for the experiencing of power, strength, and control. It feels good.

Much of this external world may well fade out of existence as the operating domain extinguishes. That is the risk. The extreme is that the very external world which supports the experiencing of power, strength, and control will no longer be present in her life. There may no longer be a husband who is the powerful head of the powerful law firm. She may no longer be the powerful head of the department in the large general hospital. There may be no large house, no boards and committees, no caterers and no cleaning lady. If these are here to serve the operating potential alone, then these solid parts of her external world may well wash away.

How does the young woman arrange an external world designed to provide her with the experiencing of being out of place, not fitting in, being the sore thumb, the outsider? She dropped out of high school to have her baby and marry the first husband. Then she married the professor of fine arts at the university. She moved into a neighborhood of manicured lawns and picture book homes, flagging her lawn with tall grass and weeds. She befriended a slightly revolutionary political group without ever becoming a genuine member, and kept most of this hidden from her husband and friends. These were the kinds of situations which fuelled the operating sense of being out of place, not fitting in, being the sore thumb. The direction of change included the fading away of these situations. These parts of her external world lost their meaningfulness, their experiential bite, and dropped out of her world.

All of these are very real situations. They are parts of the external world which can be confirmed and verified by other persons. But the same direction of change holds for situations which are constructed in ways which are less open to confirmation and verification by others. Nevertheless, they are quite real to the patient. Consider the person whose operating potential consists in the experiencing of being taunted, found out, talked about. Certain people on the bus give him knowing looks; they know the evil thoughts he privately cultivates. The waiter places the dishes in the meaningful star pattern which indicates that he is aware of the essential wickedness of the patient. That man with the black dog allows the dog to approach him menacingly because he was assigned to taunt the patient in apparently innocent ways which the patient could never prove. In all of these situations there is a surging forth of the experiencing of being found out, taunted, talked about. As this operating potential undergoes its own alteration, the predicted direction of change is toward the fading away of these situations. They extinguish out of the patient's external world.

The clinical researcher knows the situational contexts, the parts of the patient's external world which support and provide for the present operating potential. Because therapeutic processes mean the extinguishing of the old operating domain, the clinical researcher predicts that these particular parts of the external world will also extinguish. But it is important to note that this refers rather specifically to those situational contexts and parts of the external world which are directly instrumental in providing for the operating experiencing. How defined and concrete the change is depends upon a careful knowing of the defined and specific situations and parts of the external world which provide for that experiencing. Those components of the external world extinguish; that is the prediction of the clinical researcher.

The special case of the compellingly axial external agency. There are some patients whose whole operating domain swings around some external agency. It is as if their whole being gets its meaning from the existence of some external figure who is the compelling axis around which their life revolves. The figure is powerful, fills the patient's whole world. Everything has significance only in relation to that figure.

This primitive figure lies behind spouses and bosses and enemies, behind movements and organizations and economic forces, behind bus drivers and neighbors and political forces. It may be God, the Devil, evil forces, menacing alien creatures. Yet there is always some agency around which the patient's whole existence has meaning. The patient rails against it and tries to overcome it, struggles to free himself of it and tries to please it, works to understand it and yearns to appease it, opposes it and defies it. The whole existence is that of a struggle at one end, with the compellingly axial agency at the dominant other end. It is as if the patient is the reactor, the one without an intact entity, whose very meaning and significance are defined by that other agency. The patient desperately needs that agency yet there is pain in relationship with it.

For such persons, the direction of change is a radical extinguishing of the whole operating domain, together with the compellingly axial external agency around which the operating domain swings. They go together. The whole operating domain exists predominantly in relationship to the primitively compelling external agency. As they exist together, so do they extinguish together.

Here is the woman who hates and fears the "man." She struggles to be dutiful to him, to please him, to defer to his wishes. She must be equal to him, be on a par with him, be acknowledged as a person by him. She hates him and must destroy him, yet he always reappears as the enemy against whom she must fight. She rails against his superior demands, his control and domination. She must be free of him, be a person on her own right, stand up to him and defy him. But all efforts are in vain, for her fruitless struggles always seem to be against the fresh reappearance of the hated and feared, loved and needed "man."

Here is the man whose life is filled with the struggles against "her." He tries to be her good little child and to be an adult who is strong against her. He strives to be free of her and to sense whatever she wants of him so that he can fulfill her wishes for him. He is terrified of being wholly swallowed up by her, and he longs to be one with her, to assimilate into her. He desperately hopes for a life forevermore with her, yet he anguishes for the peace of another life without her and with others. His whole life sings the theme of struggling against her as the central primitive anchor in his world.

Here is the patient whose whole world is dominated by menacing external agencies and forces. There are evil enemies, powerful forces, alien creatures. They chide him, torment him, poke at him. He is at their mercy, their whims and plots.

For these persons, their whole operating domain makes sense in relationship to the primitively compelling agencies. What these persons experience is reactively dependent upon the external agency. Everything the patient experiences is in relationship to the central figure. The clinical research prediction is that there is an extinguishing away of the centrality, the compellingness, the axial dominance of that external figure or agency. In Figure 1, the compellingly axial figure or agency is indicated as Externalized DP 5 or 6. It is missing from the right.

12) The Operating Domain's Behaviors Will Extinguish

Once the clinical researcher knows the specific nature of the operating potential, the risk is that this operating potential will extinguish, and that means the extinguishing of the patient's ways of being and behaving. Particular ways which are instrumental in constructing the appropriate situations and in enabling the direct experiencing will tend to wash away. Behaviors are a part of the operating potential's package. They go together so that when the operating potential is no more, so too are the behaviors ended. In Figure 1, these behaviors are indicated as B1–B4 on the left, and they are missing from the right.

The risk of extinguishing is universal across all kinds of behaviors. It includes behaviors which are prized by others, which are needed and highly valued by other people. It includes behaviors which feel good to the patient, which are accompanied with pleasant and happy feelings. It includes behaviors which are problematic, hurtful, painful, accompanied by all sorts of bad feelings and bodily sensations. It includes characteristic behaviors which have defined the person, and minor little assisting behaviors. It includes old ways of being which have been with the patient a long time, and behaviors which are the signatures of average, ordinary individuals.

The operating potential may consist of the experiencing of crowding gentleness and pressuring kindliness, serving as a means of providing a measure of experiencing for the deeper manipulation and control. She is thoughtful in remembering her friend's children, their birthdays and their food preferences and distastes. She is inclined to soft touches and gentle patting of others. Her smile is tempered and docile. Her voice is even and soothing. There is a slowness in her movements, radiating gentleness and kindliness. Few individuals are harsh with her, and a slight look from her tends to dampen the slightest offensiveness from others. Indeed, there is a gentle cushion of casual control and manipulation encompassing those with whom she interacts. As this operating potential extinguishes, there is a receding away of these ways of being and behaving. They just fade out of existence.

As a means of providing for the deeper experiencing of distance and separation, the older woman operated on the basis of big sisterly concern and protection. She was the confidante of her younger siblings, as well as their spouses and children. She protected the nurses under her supervision. With nearly everyone, she was skilled in swinging the conversation around to their own personal concerns, and her home was filled with a parade of acquaintances who basked in her big sisterliness. Few came very close to her, and even fewer were bothered by the absence of genuine intimacy. Yet all of these ways of being and behaving tended to slide away as the operating potential itself extinguished. These concrete behaviors were no more.

The physician gained a sense of assiduous dedication and devotion by being instantly available to his patients, by living within walking distance of both the hospital and his office, by spending extra hours with his residents, by reading virtually everything available in the field of his specialty, and by maintaining regular contact with patients who had improved. His ways of being and behaving were truly dedicated and devoted. This operating potential served the deeper potential for experiencing a sense of being God-like, the Special One. As the therapeutic process brought changes in the deeper potential, there was no further basis for the operating potential, and the ways of being and behaving which instrumented this operating potential tended to wash away.

Given the deeper potential of experiencing abject worthlessness, having no impact, being overlooked and unwanted, he operated on the basis of a patrician lordliness, ever competitive, ever seeking office after office. His voice oozed. He slithered his way into the intimate gatherings of important people. He cultivated underlings and helpful superiors. His posturings and facial expressions were noble and high-born. As significant changes occurred in and in relation to the deeper potential, the operating potential faded away, and with this came the extinguishing of these ways of being and behaving. With no further basis for the operating potential, it fades away and takes along its ways of being and behaving.

He operated on the basis of the experiencing of driving others wild, of frustrating others covertly, always presenting a face of bumbling innocence. If his companion was in a hurry to get back to the office, he would manage somehow to delay, by having to spend a half hour in the restaurant restroom or by leaving his wallet at the hardware store or by twisting his ankle and being unable to walk at a reasonable pace. When he sensed someone was trying to pin him down, obtain a direct answer, nail down a commitment, he became cloudy and vague, confused and indirect, bewilderingly noncommittal. As this operating potential itself extinguished, so too did all the various ways of being and behaving which were devastatingly effective in providing for this experiencing.

While the deeper potential consisted of the awful sense of being unwanted, uncared for, an extra piece of baggage, her operating potential was the experiencing of doing for her self, prizing her self, showering her self with loving attentiveness. She would spend hours selecting the right kind of panties, carefully considering every nuance of their effect on her precious skin, the proper texture and color, how they compared and contrasted with the panties she already had. Her days were filled with writing and rewriting the lovingly typed memoirs of each thought she had about her self, when she had the thought and how it related to other thoughts. Each brief contact which she had with any other individual was the agenda for hours of sifting and thoughtful analysis as she sat in her apartment in the evenings, quietly going over the events in preparation for insertion into her memoirs. Yet all of these ways of being and behaving extinguished as the operating potential itself finally faded away.

In general, the clinical research prediction is that the extinguishing of the operating potential will be accompanied with the extinguishing of the linked ways of being and behaving. Whether pleasant or unpleasant, subtle or gross, these will undergo the inevitable risk of fading away.

The special case of bodily phenomena. Some bodily phenomena serve the operating domain by taking their place alongside the ordinary ways of being and behaving. Accordingly, these bodily phenomena share the same fate as the regular behaviors of the operating domain, i.e., they tend to extinguish. Unlike regular behaviors, however, these bodily phenomena are generally not missed, for they typically are bothersome problems.

There are several actual behaviors which enable the experiencing of being engulfed, taken over, invaded, deprived of mandate and intactness. Among these is a bodily tendency to become dizzy and to pass out. As the operating potential fades away, so too may the bodily phenomenon of becoming dizzy and passing out.

Aggressively tinged avoidance of sexual intercourse may be experienced in a number of ways which involve the body. The person has sudden and powerful headaches or low back pains or overwhelming fatigue. While these may be singled out as problems, they are also instrumental means of providing for the operating experiencing of aggressively avoiding sexual intercourse. As this operating experiencing extinguishes, so too do the headaches, the low back pains, and the bouts of evening bodily fatigue.

The patient's body is obese. This obesity is a bodily means of contributing to the operating potential. For example, the patient experiences a sense of being a force to be reckoned with, grossly substantial, exceedingly present. Or the experiencing is that of being surrounded with a moat of protective fat, maintaining the needed distance from all the outside intruders. Whatever the nature of the experiencing, as it fades out of existence, so too will the obesity.

Consider the operating experiencing of avoiding punishment. There are many behaviors which may provide for this experiencing, but bodily phenomena can also play an effective role. The sense of "It's not my fault . . . I'm not responsible for that" may be gained by means of so-called epileptoid fits and seizures, fugue states, all kinds of powerfully incapacitating "physical illnesses." At the height, the experiencing is that of avoiding punishment. It is the sense of escaping responsibility. When the operating potential extinguishes, these bodily phenomena likewise fade away.

The clinical researcher grasps the bodily phenomena which are instrumental in providing for the experiencing of the operating potential. Then the reasoning is that these bodily phenomena will themselves extinguish as the operating potential washes away. This is the clinical research prediction of the direction of potential change.

CONCLUSIONS

In traditional psychotherapy research, there are some standard meanings of psychotherapeutic change. One has to do with a change in psychopathological condition. A second consists of a change in the patient's "problems." A third involves a change along some personality dimension. An existential-humanistic theory of human beings and its experiential theory of psychotherapeutic practice propose an alternative meaning of psychotherapeutic change. It consists of the framing of specific and concrete directions of potential change, particularized to the individual patient. This is proposed as a new and different meaning of psychotherapeutic change, one which evolves from an alternative conception of personality, of what psychotherapy is and what it does, and of the meaning of psychotherapeutic change.

This meaning of psychotherapeutic change makes sense to therapists and clinical researchers who understand experiential psychotherapy's own meanings of change. One is the actualization of the good form of the operating domain. A second is the promotion of integrative relationships with deeper potentials. A third is that deeper potentials become operating potentials, and a fourth is that the old operating domain will tend to extinguish. These are not research predictions of change. They are four meanings of change which must make sense to the therapist and clinical researcher in order for specific predictions to be framed.

From these alternative meanings of psychotherapeutic change, the chapter proposes 12 principles for predicting the directions of potential change for the individual patient. By knowing and understanding these 12 principles, the therapist and clinical researcher can formulate rather specific changes which are available to this patient, directions of potential change particularized to this individual patient.

How does the therapist or clinical researcher use these 12 principles? After each session, the clinician adds to or modifies a schema of the individual patient's potentials for experiencing, meaningful behaviors, and external world. These are the data for a cumulatively refined picture of what this person is like. Given these data, after each session, the clinician uses the 12 principles to generate another picture, another schema. This second picture is of what this individual person can be or become, i.e., the directions of potential change for this patient (see Figure 1).

The existential-humanistic theory of human beings and the experiential theory of psychotherapeutic practice cannot use the traditional meanings of psychotherapeutic change. They simply do not fit. Using these 12 principles to generate a picture of the directions of potential change for the individual patient—that fits. But there are some real difficulties in using this in research. One is that the clinical researcher must be familiar with the 12 principles, with our theory of human beings, and with our theory of practice. A second is that the data are gathered progressively and cumulatively, session by session. A third is that the gathering of data requires the help of an experiential psychotherapist. The fourth is that all of the predictions are highly particularized to the individual patient. In short, this meaning of psychotherapeutic change is fitting for a careful, sensitive, meaningful study of the directions of potential change in a given patient. If the researcher is prepared for this kind of investigation, then this meaning of psychotherapeutic change is exciting and useful. If not, then the difficulties will be too much to overcome.

Indices of Psychotherapeutic Movement
3

On the basis of an alternative conceptualization of human beings, personality, and psychotherapy, chapter 2 proposed one alternative meaning and measurement of psychotherapeutic change. The general purpose of the present chapter is to propose a second alternative meaning and measurement of psychotherapeutic change. It is based on the idea that virtually every approach to psychotherapy can identify when something good is occurring in its sessions. Each approach may have its own set of indices, but each approach can recognize when something therapeutically good is occurring. We may refer to this as significant moments, moments of progress, improvement, change, or indices of psychotherapeutic movement.

The purpose of this chapter is to review the field of psychotherapy and to propose a general list of these "indices of psychotherapeutic movement" which would be of use to the clinical researcher. In so doing, the complementary purpose is to define the "indices of psychotherapeutic movement" expressly from the perspective of experiential psychotherapy. It is surprising that there is no such list. If we ask the field of psychotherapy for a simple list of indicators that something good is occurring in the session, we will be disappointed. There ought to be such a list. One would think that there are indications of movement, change, progress, even if these vary with different approaches.

I wish to acknowledge the assistance of members of my psychotherapy research team, especially Wayne Nadler, in the preparation for this chapter.

Background and Scope

The meaning of "indices of psychotherapeutic movement." Psychotherapists depend upon the idea of in-therapy events which indicate movement. It is exceedingly common for therapists to point to moments in the session when something good occurred. Here is a moment when the therapy process moves along well. Here is an indication that some change is happening. This shows that progress is occurring. Something valuable is going on right here. In virtually every session, most therapists can point to moments when something occurred which the therapist regards as welcomed, desirable, good. The reasons why that moment is good may vary from therapist to therapist, patient to patient, and approach to approach. But most psychotherapy rests on the idea of some moments of movement, some indices of change, some significant in-therapy events.

By "index of psychotherapeutic movement" is meant some event, occurrence, or epoch in the therapy session. It generally occurs over a space of a few seconds to perhaps 10 to 20 seconds or so. It refers to some kind of valued, welcomed, desired indication that something significant is occurring. Its significance may be that the therapeutic process is moving along well, or that some welcomed change is taking place. It is not important why the event is considered significant. It is not important what kind of movement is occurring, as long as there is movement, as long as the event is considered welcomed and desired, a good one.

Some meanings of "psychotherapeutic movement" or "significant events" may happen very seldom in a session. If there are two or three such moments in a session, that is about all that one may expect. For example, a genuinely good insight may only occur once or twice every session or so, or maybe even less. On the other hand, some moments of movement may occur frequently over most sessions. If psychotherapeutic movement is occurring when the patient is engaging in genuine self-exploration, then there may be sessions where this occurs 10 or 20 or 30 times or more over a session. Moments of movement can occur seldom or frequently, depending upon the meaning of the significant moment, on the therapist, and on the patient.

However, psychotherapeutic movement does not refer to moments when the patient is fulfilling the basic requirements of being a patient. It is not regarded as a significant moment of movement when the patient talks about some problem, gives the requested background information, brings a dream, remembers childhood events, or is relatively punctual about appointments. In some psychoanalytic schools, patients are expected to lie on a couch and to talk about whatever comes to mind, and to do so with little or no censorship or selection. Doing this is not considered a significant moment, an index of psychotherapeutic change.

Most meanings of psychotherapeutic movement highlight the patient rather than the therapist. If good therapeutic process is occurring or if good therapeutic change is occurring, the major referent is the patient. It may refer to the patient alone or to the patient in interaction with the therapist, but the movement, process, or change is generally with reference to the patient predominantly. But this is not always the case. Some researchers focus upon the therapist at the center of good therapeutic moments. Therapeutic movement is occurring when the therapist is being or behaving in certain ways, rather than the patient. For example, Auerbach and Luborsky (1968) considered good therapeutic process as occurring when the therapist is judged as responding effectively to whatever seems to be troubling the patient:

> A good hour could be defined in many ways. For the present paper we define it in terms of one of our variables, Therapist Responds Effectively to Patient's Main Communications. . . . What is meant by a therapist's reasonable and effective response? . . . If he says anything reasonable concerning the patient's communications, we are apt to consider this at least a moderately effective response. He is hitting close to what is troubling the patient, and this is likely to be helpful eventually. (p. 162)

Nevertheless, the present meaning of indices of psychotherapeutic movement refers to events which center upon the patient rather than upon the therapist.

Accordingly, indices of psychotherapeutic movement refer to relatively short epochs, moments or events (e.g., up to 10–20 seconds or so) which are regarded as welcomed, desirable, valuable, and good because they signify the occurrence of psychotherapeutic movement in the patient in terms of therapeutic process, progress, or change.

Paucity of reviews of indices of psychotherapeutic movement. There are only two reviews of the indices of psychotherapeutic movement. In 1949, Raskin compiled a list of five indices used by psychotherapy researchers to gauge in-therapy progress or movement. These were: positive expression of attitudes toward the self, acceptance of and respect for the self, understanding and insight, maturity of behavior reported by the patient, and reduced instances of exhibited or reported defensiveness. In 1978, Orlinsky and Howard reviewed in-therapy process events which were found to be related to outcome criteria of successful treatment. On the basis of this single strategy for identifying outcome-related indices of psychotherapeutic movement, they concluded that three components seemed to emerge: (a) patients communicated in a manner which was expressive, i.e., their speech was concrete, responsive, and not too "rational"; (b) patients talked about themselves in a personal manner; and (c) patients related to their therapists in a likeable, accepting, and support-seeking manner.

In this chapter, I will argue that there are at least five strategies that psychotherapy researchers have used to identify indices of psychotherapeutic movement. Orlinsky and Howard (1978) reviewed research using only one strategy. If we accept all the strategies used to identify such moments, then the current status seems to be that there is indeed a paucity of reviews and, accordingly, a need for a comprehensive integrative review of the indices of psychotherapeutic movement.

Why the clinical literature is excluded. By "clinical literature" is meant the body of writings characterized by vignettes of what occurs in therapy, case reports and discussions, speculations about the therapeutic process, commentaries about what therapy is, how it works and why it works. This entire, rich, complex literature is excluded from the present review.

The reason the clinical literature is excluded is that it contains far too much of what is maddeningly irrelevant for our purposes. Suppose that we go to the clinical literature with the following question: What are indices that something good is occurring in a session, something that is therapeutically welcomed and desirable, something which indicates that there is therapeutic movement? One problem is that the clinical literature has thousands of little incidents whose subjectively idiosyncratic therapeutic significance defies research utility. In describing a particular session, the writer indicates that at this point the patient reached out and touched the therapist's hand. Or the meaningful moment is when the patient once again recounted the story about going fishing with his father. Or the moment of movement is the session was when the patient presented a particular dream. If the clinical researcher compiled a list of these moments, it would not only go on for perhaps a few hundred pages or so, but also touch upon nearly everything which nearly all patients do nearly all the time, without ever really capturing the essence of the indices of therapeutic movement.

A second problem is that answers to the question are so general, vague, abstruse and abstract, so couched in the lingo of particular vocabularies, that they are once again essentially useless. For example, at this segment of the session there was a resolution of the deep-seated ambivalence, or there was a restoration of self-defenses, or there was an emergence of the anti-libidinal ego, or there was a lifting of the blind cognitive paralysis, or the patient is appreciating the choice between autistic withdrawal and ethical socialization, or there is an easing of the transference neurosis, or there is a resolution of the patient's "child" and the patient's "parent," or the inner self responds to the therapist's empathic understanding, or there is a reduction of inhibitions to appropriate behavior yielding social rewards, or an excellent working relationship is now established, or the patient is gaining a "success identity," or the patient now is understanding and accepting himself. All of these are descriptions which may perhaps point in the general direction of useable indices, but they defy actual use by clinical researchers. While the phrases may have some meaning to the initiated, it would be well-nigh impossible to listen to a tape of a session and to come to some reasonable agreement that *right here* what is occurring is *this particular moment of movement.*

The problem is that clinicians write about indices of psychotherapeutic movement in ways which are seductive but essentially useless to the clinical researcher. It would be wonderful if someone would frame a useful list of indices of psychotherapeutic movement on the basis of sensitively tough study of this rich clinical literature. That task remains to be done.

On the other hand, a few rare clinicians have tried to study sessions and to identify moments of movement. To my understanding, the pioneer was Carl Rogers. I have deep respect for his simple pursuit of the task of identifying what he called "moments of movement" and of learning from them. He deserves a lot of credit for introducing the idea of indices of psychotherapeutic movement, and for showing how a sensitive clinical psychotherapist can also be a sensitive clinical researcher in studying these moments of movement:

> . . . during this past year I have spent many hours listening to recorded interviews—trying to listen as naively as possible. I have endeavored to soak up all the cues I could capture as to the process, as to what elements are significant in change. Then I have tried to abstract from that sensing the simplest abstractions which would describe them. . . . I came . . . to appreciate what I think of as "moments of movement"—moments when it appears that change actually occurs. (1970, pp. 128, 130)

Rogers was one of those exceedingly rare clinicians who could also examine psychotherapy from the perspective of a clinical researcher. That is, he and his coworkers could also look at psychotherapy in a way which was careful, rigorous, and could yield new ideas by means of sensitively systematic study. Rogers' work bridges the gap between the exclusively clinical literature and the clinical research perspective. Our review, however, excludes the straightforward clinical literature and concentrates upon the psychotherapy research literature.

How the research literature is included. The research literature will be asked: What indices of psychotherapeutic movement do you consider worthy of investigation or use? It does not matter whether the significant moment has been confirmed, tested, or found to be a good one. It does not matter what psychotherapeutic approach the researcher uses or works within, or what clinical psychotherapeutic literature the researcher takes the indices from. As long as psychotherapy researchers use it, study it, investigate it, the index will be included in our list. Accordingly, the list of indices reflects whatever the research literature deems worthy of study and use, and includes, without being restricted to, those which have been shown to be tested or proven or confirmed by the research.

It does not matter what strategy the researcher uses to arrive at the indices of psychotherapeutic movement. For example, here are five strategies which seem to be used by psychotherapy researchers to arrive at indices of psychotherapeutic movement, and all of these strategies will be included in the review:

1) Psychotherapeutic movement can be identified by looking at those in-therapy events which are expected to be related to successful outcome. Whether or not the in-therapy event is really linked to measures of successful outcome is irrelevant. The key is that the researcher has reason to expect that the in-therapy event could or should be related to successful outcome.

2) Psychotherapeutic movement can be identified by starting with a picture of what successfully treated patients should be like, or what patients would be like if their behavior were mature, adjusted, normal, or optimal. If patients show (evidence, demonstrate) those characteristics in therapy, the events are those indicating psychotherapeutic movement.

3) Psychotherapeutic movement events can be identified by asking theories of psychotherapeutic practice what in-therapy events would indicate therapeutic movement, change, progress, good process. Essentially, the researcher does the work of getting the authoritative statement from the clinical therapeutic literature.

4) Psychotherapeutic movement can be identified by first targeting defined complaints, behaviors, or problems, and then noting instances in the session where there are welcomed changes in the targeted complaints, behaviors, or problems.

5) Psychotherapeutic movement can be identified by means of post-session evaluations, judgments, and ratings by therapists, patients, and other observers.

Whatever strategy is used, as long as the research literature identifies or uses the index of psychotherapeutic movement, it will be included in the list.

Some speculations on why there is so little research attention to indices of psychotherapeutic movement. In the psychotherapy research literature, the issue of indices of psychotherapeutic movement is a mere footnote. Yet, for practicing therapists what constitutes good moments in the session is a dominant theme. It is surprising that researchers generally disregard this issue: "There has been surprisingly little research regarding what constitutes or correlates with the occasional experience of therapists and patients that something particularly 'good' (or 'poor') has transpired during a therapy session" (Hoyt, 1980, p. 159). Auerbach and Luborsky (1968, p. 162) approach this through the medium of the "good hour": "In discussions among psychotherapists, one often hears the term 'a good hour.' Most of us are not sure exactly what this is, but we know that we like it. Clearly more needs to be known about it." Elliott (1983c) is explicit about the disregard by researchers of significant moments of movement: "There are significant or critical events which are central to the personal change process in psychotherapy. Since these events are infrequent, they should be studied in detail with the aim of making psychotherapy process research more relevant to practicing therapists. . . . Unfortunately, previous psychotherapy process and outcome research has entirely ignored significant change events" (pp. 113–114). We know virtually nothing about such significant change events or moments of movement. There is something embarrassing in our avoidance of this topic which is so central to genuine practitioners. How may we account for this state of affairs?

Perhaps this topic does not lend itself well to research because such moments are too subtle, too "clinical." These good moments may be so tied to the particular patient in this particular part of this particular session that researchers are entitled to throw up their hands in frustration. A meaningful pause, a special look, a particular phrase, a quiet word or two, mention of a given topic, a slight shift in voice quality—all of these are subtle indicators used by a therapist with this given patient, and they are simply too subtle for research use.

The clinical literature is full of good moments whose very subtlety and delicate distinctiveness render them impervious to the research net.

Perhaps there is little reason to pay attention to these moments because they are drowned out by the more molar process of psychotherapy itself. If psychotherapy is a process, then why bother to look at one or two little moments in the session? Because there is a larger encompassing process of therapy going on, these little moments are mere indicators of a richly complicated process which may extend back to the whole session and to previous sessions, and which may include all sorts of complicated and evanescent determinants in and out of the therapy sessions. All in all, these little moments make little difference in the overall process of psychotherapy. They are tiny blips in the big unfolding picture.

Perhaps moments of movement are overlooked when their private, personal, subjective nature means that researchers cannot get a grasp on them. For example, suppose that significant moments are those in which the patient "works through" something, realizes something, feels an inner change in something, makes an inner connection, has a sense of easing, comes to accept that part of herself, undergoes a meaningful silence. When this is the meaning of a moment of movement, it will tend not to be identifiable by anyone except perhaps the patient herself, who might note that moment in reviewing an audiotape or videotape of the session (cf. Elliott, 1983a). Moments of movement will ordinarily be beyond most researchers' means of study when they consist of quiet, inner times of working-through, special realizations, and feelinged awarenesses of an inner shift or change.

Perhaps moments of movement are overlooked because what is "good" does not occur in moments. There are no discrete events. Movement and indications that something good is occurring refer instead to patient characteristics and traits and processes which gradually emerge over time. For example, the patient is showing more motivation for therapy, or the patient is now "learning to learn," or the patient is starting to relate to the therapist as a parental figure, or the patient is now starting to function more as an adult than a child, or the patient is demonstrating a capacity and willingness to engage in therapeutic interaction, or the patient is now showing fewer pre-schizophrenic signs. These are dimensions of personality, emerging ways of being, changes in psychopathological state, characteristics of a good patient. As such, they do not lend themselves to occurrence as discrete moments or events. Rather, they are "process dimensions" or "therapeutic conditions." For example, in psychoanalytic therapy the process may be regarded as going along well when there is a gradual increase in transference behavior and a gradual decrease in resistance behavior (Graff & Luborsky, 1977), or a gradual decrease in the amount of tension in the patient's speech (Dollard & Mowrer, 1947; Raimy, 1948). But these are dimensions which can be gauged as increasing or decreasing over time, rather than discrete moments, events, or epochs.

In all of this, the focus is the patient. But perhaps the important focus is the therapist, not the patient. If psychotherapy is a process which is mediated and brought about by the therapist, then therapy is rolling along well when the therapist is doing a good job (cf. Auerbach & Luborsky, 1968). If, for example, the therapist is doing a good job in providing the right facilitating conditions within a client-centered framework, then good moments occur when the therapist is providing these conditions. If the therapist is supposed to provide appropriate interpretations, then we should look to the therapist and identify as good moments those in which the therapist is doing a good job of providing appropriate interpretations. Looked at in this way, good moments refer to the therapist's doing a good job doing whatever the therapist is supposed to be doing. There would then be little payoff in studying events involving the patient.

Perhaps in-therapy moments are overlooked because the truly good moments occur outside of therapy. If therapy is working, then significant changes should occur in the extra-therapy world. What occurs in therapy is helpful and instrumental in getting the process of change started. But the payoff changes, the genuine outcome of the therapy process, occur in the everyday world outside of therapy. Accordingly, it would be less profitable to study moments of movement in the session and more profitable to study moments of movement outside of the therapy sessions.

These are some speculations as to why there is so little research on moments of movement in therapy. It is a pity, but perhaps it is understandable.

A Review of the Research Literature

Although there is very little research on significant in-therapy events or moments of movement, there are lots of studies which back into using such indices in investigating other questions. It is as if the idea of moments of movement is quietly implied in studying such questions as what events in therapy are related to good outcome, how successful patients differ from less successful patients, what the in-therapy consequences are of favorite therapist methods, comparisons among various schools of therapy on a number of dimensions, in-depth examination of the psychodynamics of symptom formation, studies of the efficacy of specific treatment programs on behavioral target complaints. The research literature does not seem to feature or acknowledge significant in-therapy events as an object of study. Yet the research literature uses or presumes the idea of significant moments of movement in studying other issues.

Accordingly, there is a fair number of research studies which can provide an answer to the central question of this chapter, i.e.: What are the various indices of psychotherapeutic movement? The long and formal question may be phrased as follows: What has the research literature identified or used as indices of psychotherapeutic movement, from any and all approaches to psychotherapy, using any reasonable strategy whatsoever, and accepting indices as relatively short epochs, moments, or events which are regarded as welcomed, desirable, valuable or significant because they indicate psychotherapeutic movement, progress, improvement, change, or good process?

Following this review of the research literature, the same question will be put to the experiential theory of psychotherapy. Then the important task will be to present a comprehensive summary list of the indices of psychotherapeutic movement, based on both the research literature and the experiential theory of psychotherapy.

The present section is organized under five strategies used by researchers for identifying or arriving at whatever they regard as moments of movement or change. It is important to understand that these studies do not merely show that some moment is significant. Rather, these studies dignify certain events as moments of movement merely by using them in their work. Each of these five strategies will be discussed in turn.

Good events as bearing expected relationship with outcome criteria. The reasoning begins with a special valuing of measures of outcome. If some in-therapy events are expected or found to be associated with criteria of successful outcome, then the in-therapy events are justified in being called indices of psychotherapeutic movement. They are good events because successful outcome should follow. There are two ways of arriving at this expected relationship. One is to start with some in-therapy events which the researcher has reason to believe might be or should be related to good outcome measures. A second way is to start with indications of good outcome and see what kinds of in-therapy events seem to be related to these outcome criteria.

It is important to keep in mind the target question of this chapter. We are looking for whatever in-therapy events researchers use, the ones researchers consider sufficient to investigate. Whether or not the findings validate or confirm the in-therapy event is irrelevant here. If studies validate or confirm an in-therapy event, it shall be included in our taxonomy. But we shall also include those in-therapy events the research uses in the first place, regardless of the findings. At the end of this chapter, in the section on discussion and commentary, it will be argued that the process-outcome strategy is generally ineffective in either discovering or testing in-therapy psychotherapeutic movement events. For our present purposes, however, the question is what in-therapy events are revealed by a strategy which expects they will be or are related to outcome criteria.

Let us start with the more restrictive question, viz., what in-therapy events were found to be related to outcome criteria? Using various outcome criteria that the therapy was successful, that there was improvement, what are the in-therapy, process events which seem to be related to these outcome indices? In a comprehensive review of these studies, Orlinsky and Howard (1978) concluded that at least three in-therapy process events seem to be confirmed by this research strategy: (a) Patients communicate in a manner which is expressive, i.e., their speech is concrete, responsive, and not too "rational." (b) Patients talk about themselves in a personal manner. (c) Patients relate to their therapists in a likeable, accepting, and support-seeking manner.

Where do the researchers get their in-therapy possibilities in the first place? How do they know what in-therapy events to throw into the research pot? Generally they turn to predominant theories of practice, and ask these theories which in-therapy events should be expected to be related to measures of good and successful outcome.

One of these is the loose amalgam of psychodynamic/psychoanalytic theories of practice. Reasoning from this body of thought, Gomes-Schwartz (1978) suggested that good outcome should be related to in-therapy evidence of patient involvement and active engagement in the therapy interaction. This would be evidenced by the patient's willingness to communicate, commitment to change, trust in the therapist, recognition of the patient's own responsibility for effecting change, willingness to ally oneself with the therapist and to work at changing.

Representing both the psychoanalytic and client-centered approaches, Schauble and Pierce (1974) suggest that successful outcome should be linked back to in-therapy events in which patients clearly take responsibility for and accept their own behaviors and feelings.

The client-centered approach has provided researchers with a number of in-therapy events which are expected to be associated with successful outcome criteria. For example, effective in-therapy events should include client self-exploration. The client is to be actively and spontaneously engaging in an inward probing into the self, getting in touch with and discovering meanings, feelings, and experiencings. Client-centered researchers have devised measures to assess the degree to which clients engage in this self-exploration (e.g., Carkhuff, 1969; Carkhuff & Berenson, 1967; Truax & Carkhuff, 1967).

Probing further into the components of this self-exploration process, Rice and her coworkers have suggested that important and useful indices of this self-exploration process include the activity and energy shown in the client's voice, good "expressive stance," and vividness and richness of the client's words (Butler, 1974; Butler, Rice, & Wagstaff, 1962; Rice, 1973, 1974; Rice, Koke, Greenberg, & Wagstaff, 1979; Rice & Wagstaff, 1967; Wexler, 1975).

The activity and energy shown in the client's voice include animation, high energy, spontaneity, freshness and involvement in what is being spoken. The energy may be emotional (energy overflow rather than control), focused (energy turned inward in an exploring fashion), or externalizing (energy turned outward with a "talking at" quality). The "expressive stance" includes two components: subjective reaction (client focuses on the subjectivity of his own reactions to things impinging on him, an immediate subjective response to a specific stimulus), or differentiated exploration (probing an inner experience in an immediate and differentiated fashion without subjecting it to cognitive operations). Vividness and richness of language include figures of speech, colorful use of imagery and metaphor, a strong sensual quality that draws upon visual, auditory, and/or kinesthetic modalities.

Good events as in-therapy expressions of optimal functioning. The strategy begins with a picture of what persons are like who are functioning optimally, i.e., who are mature, adjusted, mentally healthy, normal, and representative of good outcome, effective treatment, successful therapy. From this picture, the reasoning is that good moments are those in which the patient evidences such characteristics. In effect, these are moments which bring the good outcome right into the therapy session. They are in-therapy good outcomes, a kind of foretasting or sampling of what optimal persons or successful therapy can be like.

Perhaps the most direct application of this strategy is given in a study by Hoffman, reported in Raskin's (1949) review. Using judges who rated the degree of maturity of behaviors reported by the patient, psychotherapeutic movement or progress consisted of moments when these mature behaviors were expressed or reported. Similarly, if successfully treated patients have a characteristic of "focusing on experience," then significant epochs in therapy are those in which the patient is evidencing a high degree of focusing on experience (Gendlin, Beebe, Cassens, Klein, & Oberlander, 1968). Further, if optimal functioning is held as consisting of very little evidence of defensive behavior, then significant therapeutic moments are those in which there is a decrease in defensive behavior, either as exhibited or as reported by the patient (Haigh, 1949).

Some studies begin with general classes of what successfully treated patients should be like, and then refine these general classes to fit the individual patient. For example, Horowitz, Sampson, Siegelman,

Weiss, and Goodfriend (1978) started with the idea that successfully treated patients should be characterized by two classes of behaviors. One consisted of being directly cooperative, concurring, and complying; the second consisted of being directly defying, disagreeing, disapproving. In their examination of a single case, they particularized these two general classes on the basis of a careful study of the therapist's process notes over the first 10 sessions, and emerged with a list of specific behaviors which, when exhibited or reported in the session, would evidence moments of psychotherapeutic movement for that particular patient.

Raimy (1948) and Braaten (1961) are representative of those who see successful outcome in terms of the patient's relation to the self, in accord with the concepts of self psychology. For Raimy, both successful outcome and in-therapy progress were indicated in a shift from self-disapproving statements to positive, self-approving statements. Braaten regarded both successful outcome and in-therapy progress in terms of movement from non-self to a feelinged awareness of both the inner and interpersonal self. Statements signifying a feelinged awareness of the inner self included inner self-exploration, awareness of being and functioning as a separate entity, internal communication, dialogues with the self. Statements signifying a feelinged awareness of the interpersonal self involved the self in relationship to significant others, awareness of the feelinged interaction and reactive relationship.

In a similar vein, Dollard and Mowrer (1947) gauged the self-concept change in terms of one component, tension reduction. Accordingly, in-therapy progress could be gauged by assessing the reduction in tension or, more carefully, the relationship between patient statements indicating discomfort and those indicating relief. This discomfort-relief quotient, then, served as an in-therapy index of verbal tension, and significant changes would identify progress as reduced tension. A number of studies aimed at refining this measure and using it to study in-therapy progress (Assum & Levy, 1948; Cofer & Chance, 1950; Hunt, 1947, 1949; Hunt & Kogan, 1950; Kauffman & Raimy, 1949; Mowrer, Hunt, & Kogan, 1953; Mowrer, Light, Luria, & Zeleny, 1953; Murray, 1954; Murray, Auld, & White, 1954). While the net result of this series of studies casts doubt on the use of this measure, it is important to note that efforts to examine the measure called for the development of other measures of in-therapy movement, and these are included in the present review.

Good events as given by theories of practice. In this strategy, the researcher turns to the clinical literature and asks selected theories of practice to identify what they would regard as moments of move-ment or change, progress, improvement, good process. The burden of responsibility lies with the researcher for organizing the material offered by the selected theories of practice. Indeed, for our purpose of assembling a list of significant events, the researcher's contribu-tion consists essentially in framing whatever the theories of practice would regard as moments of movement or good events.

It should be understood that while each strategy is different, there ought to be a fair measure of overlap and complementarity in what is found. For example, a similar set of indices should emerge whether the clinical researcher concentrates on asking theories what events signify movement and change, whether the researcher looks for what-ever would characterize successfully treated patients, or whether the researcher uses in-therapy events which are expected to bear strong relationship with outcome criteria. Accordingly, this and subsequent sections will begin to confirm prior indices of psychotherapeutic movement.

By studying the writings of Fenichel, Sullivan, and Rogers, Ditt-man (1952) identified what should be indices of therapeutic move-ment in the classic psychoanalytic school, Sullivan's interpersonal school of psychoanalysis, and client-centered therapy respectively. For Fenichel, the moments should consist of free and realistic expres-sion of basic impulses. For Sullivan, significant moments should con-sist of increases in awareness of the interpersonal consequences of behavior. For Rogers, therapeutic movement was held as consisting of moments when the patient evidenced increases in positive attitudes toward self or others. The marker for "improvement" consisted of the patient's immediate response in the light of the immediate and penultimate response-statements.

As given in his early review of significant moments of movement, Raskin (1949) highlighted client-centered theory's upholding of the client's positive self-attitudes, a concept which was later formalized into a researchable scale (Rogers, 1958), and further refined by

Walker, Rablen, and Rogers (1960) into a scale for assessing the client's owning, communicating, and exploring inner experiencing, feeling, and personal meaning.

Given client-centered theory's identifying client self-exploration as a significant moment of therapeutic movement, researchers could then study this event as a welcomed and desirable in-therapy event. For example, it was now possible to study whether reflective statements would be followed by client self-exploration (Adams & Frye, 1964; Auerswald, 1974; Barnabei, Cormier, & Nye, 1974; Bergman, 1951; Frank & Sweetland, 1962; Hekmat, 1971; Highlen & Baccus, 1977; Hill & Gormally, 1977; Hoffnung, 1969; Kennedy & Zimmer, 1968; Kurz & Grummon, 1972; Mahrer, Brown, Gervaize & Fellers, 1983; Merbaum, 1963; Merbaum & Southwell, 1965; Powell, 1968; Waskow, 1962).

Another researchable index of therapeutic process, also derived from client-centered theory, is the extent to which " . . . the individual's words and actions refer to, or freshly phrase his ongoing felt experiencing, and to what extent are they rather 'mere' words, not involving and carrying his felt experiencing any further" (Gendlin, Beebe, Cassens, Klein, & Oberlander, 1968, p. 220); good process is when the patient is " . . . focusing on his not yet conceptually clear, but directly felt, experiencing" (p. 218), or when the patient is describing feelings in some detail, showing a fair measure of awareness of feelings, and is searching for personal meaning and understanding of feelings (Kiesler, 1971b). As occurring in the session, this can be assessed by means of the patient experiencing scale (Klein, Mathieu, Gendlin, and Kiesler, 1970).

Moving from internal, focused self-exploration and experiencing to external feeling expression, Isaacs and Haggard (1966) designated significant moments as those in which patients verbalize affect by using words expressing subjective feelings. Here is a shifting from the client-centered school to the feeling-expressive, abreaction, and catharsis approach to psychotherapy (cf. Nichols & Zax, 1977; Scheff, 1979). Moments of psychotherapeutic movement become those in which the patient is undergoing straightforward abreaction or catharsis (e.g., Lifshitz & Blair, 1960).

When the affect is expressed toward the therapist, we are approaching good moments associated with the psychoanalytic concept of transference. As assessed by Lower, Escoll, Little, and Ottenberg (1973) on a five-point rating scale, the moment consisted of either negative affect (e.g., anxiety, guilt, anger, rebellion, irritation) or positive affect (e.g., warmth, closeness, dependent longings) expressed directly toward the therapist. Also valuing the importance of transference events, Luborsky, Graff, Pulver, and Curtis (1973) used the following definition for research purposes: " . . . transference could be conceptualized as the revival in a current object relationship, especially to the analyst, of thought, feeling, and behavior derived from repressed fantasies originating in significant conflictual childhood relationships" (p. 70). They used this in asking clinical judges to rate the degree of transference behavior in 30 five-minute excerpts from tape-recorded sessions of a psychoanalytic treatment of a single case.

Also reasoning from psychoanalytic theory, Strupp, Chasson, and Ewing (1973) interpreted patterns of intercorrelations among ratings of therapy sessions by psychoanalytic therapists as indicating that therapists valued moments in which patients were showing a cooperative attitude toward the therapist, especially within the context of a positive transference, were working hard on their problems, and were achieving emotional insight, all indices central to psychoanalytic theory.

Of these, one seems almost too slippery for research use. "Working hard on their problems" appears to defy use in research. For example, Cook (1964) regarded some periods of silence as indicating that the patient is working hard on problems, attending to and working through something important. Accordingly, " . . . it seems not unlikely that silence might well be a necessary condition, or at least an index of a necessary condition, for movement in psychotherapy" (p. 42).

On the other hand, insight is a standard psychoanalytic index of therapeutic movement (e.g., Elliott, 1983a; Raskin, 1949; Strupp, 1980a). In a careful examination of the complete process recordings of two cases seen in time-limited psychoanalytic therapy, Strupp (1980a) confirmed what he termed rare moments of mutative change in which the patient is in a state of emotional arousal and is ready to apprehend a new way of seeing oneself that " . . . results in or is a function of cognitive reorganization or, if you will, insight . . . the patient somehow realizes on a deep level that it is a more satisfying, gratifying, and rewarding way of seeing himself and the world" (p. 601). Insight is a respectable index of psychoanalytic movement.

Others reason from psychodynamic/psychoanalytic theory that significant moments are those in which there is an occurrence of material which has been previously warded off and pushed away. Such contents would include cognitions, feelings, and impulses which were relatively unavailable to the patient early in treatment, produced discomfort when they first emerged early in treatment, were accompanied by some kind of defensive process, and come to emerge later in treatment relatively free of discomfort and defensive processes (Gassner, Sampson, Weiss & Brumer, 1982; Horowitz, Sampson, Siegelman, Wolfson, & Weiss, 1975).

Good events as reduction in target problems and complaints. This strategy begins with identifying some target problem, complaint, difficulty, or symptom. As common sense indicates, good moments are those where there is a reduction. By its very nature, such a strategy tends to be tailored especially for the particular patient (chapter 2).

An early example of this strategy was the case study reported by Murray (1954) in which it was determined that the particular patient's problem was targeted as low hostility and high defensiveness. Hostility was defined in terms of quite specific figures in the patient's world, and defensiveness was tied specifically to intellectualization and physical complaints around hostility. Significant moments of movement were then identified as including expression of hostility toward the designated figures, and especially decreases in both defensive intellectualization and physical complaints.

While Luborsky and his colleagues were more interested in the psychodynamics of symptom formation than in therapeutic change, they noted the in-therapy significance of changes in such targeted symptoms and problems as stomach pains (Luborsky & Auerbach, 1969) and momentary forgetting (Luborsky & Mintz, 1975). Good moments are those where the target problems seem to reduce appreciably.

This strategy is the keystone of the behavior therapies, where defined programs are aimed at reducing targeted problems, complaints, difficulties, and symptoms. Clinical research studies document how some targeted problem behavior was reduced, and the research index of improvement or change is the reported or exhibited in-therapy behavior. Behavior therapies differ on the favorite treatment methods, on the principles used to explain how and why the methods work, and on the breadth and depth of what is to be included in the pot of targeted problems and complaints. But they generally agree on the strategy of regarding reported or exhibited reductions as welcomed and desirable therapeutic moments. Here is where experimental research and common sense come together. For example, if the patient complains about becoming anxious and vomiting after eating, if a behavioral program is directed at that complaint, and if the patient then eats in the session and self-reports reduced anxiety and reduced urge to vomit, it is sensible to flag these as good moments in the session (e.g., Leitenberg, Gross, Peterson, & Rosen, 1984). This is the essence of the behavioral therapies' use of this strategy.

While the targets are typically behavioral, some wings of the behavior therapy family work upon cognitions, attitudes, beliefs, and ideas which may be regarded as maladaptive, psychopathological, self-defeating, self-constricting, or irrational. Often it is a little more difficult to gauge the reduction of these targets. Nevertheless, they use the same strategy of regarding moments of movement and change as those in which the targeted cognitions are reduced, as indicated by reported or exhibited in-therapy behavior or by use of such measures as semantic differentials before and after sessions (Hoehn-Saric, Frank, & Gurland, 1968; Hoehn-Saric, Liberman, Imber, Stone, Frank, & Ribich, 1974; Hoehn-Saric, Liberman, Imber, Stone, Pande, & Frank, 1972).

Good events as identified by post-session evaluations. This final strategy invites participants or third party observers to provide post-session evaluations which point toward selected in-therapy events as significant. The evaluation may be done by the therapist (Duncan, Rice, & Butler, 1968), by both therapist and patient (Orlinsky & Howard, 1967; Stiles, 1980), by patients (Elliott, 1983a, 1983b, 1983c, 1984b; Elliott, Cline, & Shulman, 1983; Kagan, 1975), or by third party judges (Hoyt, 1980; Hoyt, Marmar, Horowitz, & Alvarez, 1981).

Duncan, Rice, and Butler (1968) asked therapists to provide selections of their good or poor sessions. Then the researchers examined parameters of the therapists' speech, including intensity and pitch level. Although the present review concentrates upon patient events rather than therapist events, the strategy may be used also for identifying significant moments of patient movement.

Orlinsky and Howard (1967) asked therapists and patients to fill out a questionnaire after each session. One item dealt with the rating of the session as good or poor, and other items dealt with supposed characteristics of good sessions. By correlating these characteristics with therapists' and patients' global evaluations of the session, the following descriptors emerged: "(a) . . . we found the good therapy hour to focus on experiences of the most intimate personal relationships, past and present; early family relationships, erotic attachments, and explorations of fantasy and self-experience" (p 631). (b) The patient acquired insight and understanding. (c) The patient's behavior and feelings were those of being likeable, trusting, optimistic, secure, relaxed, confident, and, expecially in relationship with the therapist, warm, friendly, accepted and supported.

Elliott concentrated on patients' reviewing videotapes or audiotapes immediately following the sessions, and identifying explicit moments of "helpful impacts" (Elliott, 1983b, 1983c, 1984a, 1984b; Elliott, Cline, & Shulman, 1983; Kagan, 1975). These identified descriptors were sorted, categorized, and placed into clusters. One cluster consisted of personal insight, awareness, problem clarification and solution. A second cluster consisted of an interpersonal relationship with the therapist, a relationship characterized by understanding, reassurance, involvement, and personal contact.

Instead of using post-session evaluations of therapists or patients, Hoyt, Marmar, Horowitz, and Alvarez (1981) used third party judges. The researchers compiled a list of specific activities which define what patients do in psychodynamic therapy, a list taken from descriptions of psychodynamic therapy, from the researchers' own impressions, and from process-outcome studies. This list was then correlated with judges' ratings of sessions as good ones. On this basis, for example, Hoyt (1980) concludes that " . . . sessions were rated as being more 'good' when patients' actions emphasized the expression of thoughts and feelings and the discussion of their meanings" (p. 161).

By following these five strategies, researchers have flagged a number of indices of psychotherapeutic movement. It is possible to organize these into a list of good moments in psychotherapy. But this will be delayed a bit while we turn to the experiential theory of practice and give that theory a chance to throw its moments of movement into the pot. Indeed, the experiential theory of practice will add four moments of movement to those already cited in the present section.

Indices of Psychotherapeutic Movement:
The Perspective of an Experiential Theory
of Practice

This theory of practice (Mahrer, 1983) is constructed around four kinds of significant moments of psychotherapeutic change. As shown in Figure 2, the method carries the patient through four kinds of experiencing, and they proceed along a particular sequence. For purposes of research, the question is how to identify and assess these four moments of psychotherapeutic movement.

Psychotherapeutic research already has some measures of general experiencing. There is the experiencing scale of Klein, Mathieu, Gendlin, and Kiesler (1970), and there is the Truax and Carkhuff depth of experiencing scale (1967). Although in the same general family, these do not capture the distinctive characteristics of the four kinds of experiencings which comprise this theory of practice. Accordingly, each of the four will be described in turn.

It is to be noted that these four kinds of experiencing, occurring in the sequence given in Figure 2, are the explicit aims and goals of this theory of practice (Mahrer, 1978c, 1979, 1980, 1983). All of the methods and operations are designed to implement each of these four kinds of experiencings. In other words, the purpose and aim of each method or operation are to bring about the subsequent kind of experiencing, and the purpose and aim of achieving that experiencing are to open the way toward the subsequent experiencing. Accordingly, each session opens by using methods and operations which are designed to enable the patient to experience the carrying forward of potentials or to enable the patient to experience the relationship with the deeper potentials (Figure 2). Once in the proper beginning state of readiness, the therapist and patient use methods which explicitly bring about one or both of these two kinds of experiencings. When this is achieved, the therapist and patient then use methods and operations which bring the patient to the experiencing of being the deeper potentials, and finally, methods and operations which provide the

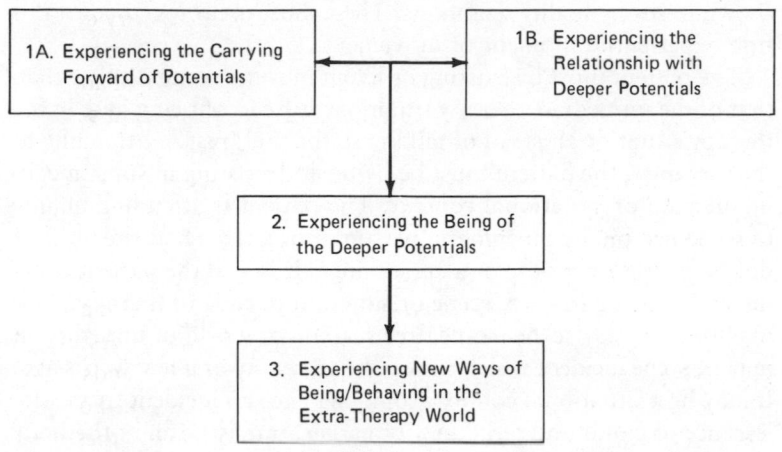

Figure 2. The Sequence of Experiencings (Moments of Movement) in a Session of Experiential Psychotherapy

patient with the experiencing of new ways of being and behaving in the extra-therapy world. Here are four explicit moments of movement around which this therapy is constructed, the attainment of which is the functional goal of its methods and operations.

The data consist of an audiotape or videotape of the session, and the task of the clinical researcher is to listen to or observe the session in order to identify each of these good moments of experiencing, these moments of psychotherapeutic movement. The clinical researcher should picture the patient and therapist in reclining chairs, with feet on hassocks. The patient's eyes are closed throughout the session, and the therapist's eyes are likewise closed during most of the session. With this picture in mind, we now turn to a description of the four kinds of therapeutic experiencings, the four kinds of significant moments of psychotherapeutic movement and change in experiential psychotherapy.

1A) Experiencing the carrying forward of potentials. There are two indications that this kind of experiencing is occurring. One has to do with the situational context in which the patient is existing, and the second has to do with the strength of the experiencing as shown in strong bodily sensations. These must occur together for this first experiential moment of movement.

The patient must be existing or living in some context other than that of the immediate therapy situation. Instead of being here in the therapy situation, instead of talking to the therapist or attending to the therapist, the patient must be living and existing in some meaningful state or situational context. The patient is attending mainly to some personally meaningful person or object such as the ulcer or dog or parent or spouse or acquaintance. It is as if the patient is living and existing in some scene or situation outside of therapy. This may be a fantasy scene, some dream scene or world of unreality. It may be some incident which took place yesterday or a few weeks ago. It may be a situational context from long ago, an incident from adolescence or childhood or infancy or earlier. It may be an in-the-body context or an out-of-body context. What the patient is attending to and existing in may be real or fanciful, mundane or dramatic, alone or with others.

The key feature is that the patient is predominantly living and being in this context or state, rather than with the therapist. As long as the patient is mainly in this other meaningful context or state, the first requirement is met. The patient may be somewhat aware of the therapist, somewhat talking to the therapist, but most of the patient's attention and existence are in this other context or state.

The yoked second requirement is that experiencing is to be strong. As far as the therapist is concerned, the requirement is that experiencing is carrying forward with a good measure of strength, whether at the operating level or at the deeper level. The experiencing may consist of passivity, toughness, vulnerability, looseness, intimacy, controlling, blending into, or whatever is occurring in this particular context or state.

The clinical researcher uses several indications that strong experiencing is occurring. One is that what is coming from the patient is strong. Whatever the patient is doing, there is amplitude, volume, loudness, force. Even if it reaches this plateau for just a half second, it is strong. It is noisy, intense, resounding, clamorous, powerful. It is not a light titter; it is hard laughter. It is not soft tears, but loud wailing.

Another indication of strong experiencing is bodily movement. Verbally this includes exclaimings, shoutings, yellings, screechings, gruntings, groanings, swearings, bellowings, laughings, cryings, shriekings, yelpings. Nonverbally, it includes slappings, twistings, shakings, poundings, contortings, paroxysms, liftings, catchings, fallings, hittings, flailings, kickings.

A third indication of strong experiencing is bodily sensations. Strong events are occurring in and to the body. They may be on the surface or inside the body. They may be ordinary or extraordinary. They may feel pleasant or unpleasant. They may be located in one part of the body or include the whole body. But they are strong. There may be chills down the back, pounding headaches, dizziness and swirling, nausea, butterflies in the stomach, pronounced heaviness in the legs, shakings in the head or arms, seizures all over the body, tight muscle crampings and lockings-up of muscles, loss of body integrity, floating sensations, a sensation of viscera spilling out, leatheriness over the skin, arms like clubs, oozing softness of the whole body, blood pouring out of the eyes and ears, sensations of heat or cold, prickly sensations, a hot heavy ball in the chest, internal churnings and turnings, sensations of the whole body swelling to incredible proportions, hard sweating, pressures from inside or outside, sensations of dropping or falling, sensations of rushing forward or rising straight up, sexual sensations in the breast or groin or pelvis or whole body, pulsating and gyrating sensations, enlarging and ballooning, drifting and gliding, eyes popping, pains and hurts and aches.

It is relatively easy for the clinical researcher to judge that the patient is predominantly existing in some meaningful context or state other than being predominantly in the therapy situation. Patients are mainly attending and talking to someone other than the therapist. For example, the patient is predominantly in a non-therapy situation in the following:

Pt: The cancer is slimy. It is greenish, and full of force! My God, you're going to destroy me. I can't get rid of you! You don't care!!!

Pt: I liked Stockton. I have friends there! Why are they taking me away? Please . . . (crying.) I don't wanta move away. I love my room and my toys . . . (crying). . . . Please don't make me move . . .

It is also relatively easy for the clinical researcher to judge that what is coming from the patient is strong, and that there are strong bodily movements. Sheer volume and loudness are indications. Even if the data consist of an audiotape rather than a videotape, the clinical researcher can detect strong yellings and groanings, beatings and poundings.

What may be more difficult is for the clinical researcher to detect the presence of strong bodily sensations. In order to identify when there are strong bodily sensations, the method used by the experiential researcher is to say and do what the patient is saying and doing, and in the very same manner as the patient (Mahrer, 1983). Mimic the patient. Do it just the same way as the patient. As the clinical researcher does this, she becomes aware of bodily sensations. If they are strong, then this criterion is met. There are strong bodily sensations when they occur in the clinical researcher who says and does it right along with the patient.

1B) Experiencing the relationship with deeper potentials. Here is where the clinical researcher must be knowledgeable and skilled in experiential psychotherapy. The clinical researcher must be familiar with the experiential theory of practice and have sufficient competence to detect when the patient is experiencing the relationship with deeper potentials. Psychotherapeutic movement is occurring when the patient is undergoing strong experiencing in direct encountering relationship with the therapist who is speaking with the voice of the patient's deeper potential, and who is likewise engaged in a strongly experienced, direct, encountering relationship with the patient.

The patient must again be undergoing strong experiencing. There is loudness and volume, amplitude and strength, intensity and force. There are bodily movements, verbal or nonverbal, and again these are of strong proportions. There are also bodily sensations. Some are pleasant and some are unpleasant, but they are of strong proportions. These indications are similar to those which are tied to the experiencing of the carrying forward of potentials. What is distinctive is that the patient is engaged in a relationship with the therapist. Most of the patient's attention is targeted upon the therapist, and the experiencing occurs in this interactive relationship. What the patient says is directed to and at the therapist.

So far there is little that might not be assessed by the ordinary researcher. So far, this index of psychotherapeutic movement is no different from many aspects of the psychoanalytic transference or the encountering relationship between patient and external therapist. Here is where the researcher must be familiar with experiential theory and practice. In the psychoanalytic transference, the patient projects or transfers deeper personality processes onto the external therapist. In the ordinary meaning of encounter, deeper personality processes of patient and of external therapist clash with each other. In this second index, the experiential therapist takes on the identity of the patient's deeper personality process, exists and lives as the deeper process, speaks with its voice, gives it life and form and identity.

The patient experiences the relationship with the deeper potential when the strong experiencing occurs in the relationship or interaction with the therapist as the deeper potential. Rather than being an intact, external individual, the therapist is the interacting identity of the deeper potential. For most researchers, it would be difficult to discern that the therapist is interacting from within the identity of the deeper potential. For clinical researchers familiar with experiential psychotherapy, this would be a relatively easy judgment.

For the non-experiential researcher, then, the moment of psychotherapeutic movement seems to be when the patient is undergoing strong experiencing in relationship to and with the therapist. For the experiential researcher, the moment of strong experiencing is when the patient is undergoing strong experiencing in relationship with and to the therapist as the voice, being, and identity of the patient's deeper potentials. The former is sloppy and misses a lot; the latter is the method of the experiential researcher.

2) *Experiencing the being of the deeper potentials.* As indicated in Figure 2, this moment of psychotherapeutic movement tends to occur only following one or both of the others. When the patient undergoes the carrying forward of potentials and/or when the patient undergoes the experiencing of relationships with the deeper potentials, then the stage is set for this third moment of psychotherapeutic movement.

As far as the researcher is concerned, the distinguishing feature of this moment is that the patient undergoes a shift in personality.

It is as if the patient is no longer the person he was, but is now a qualitatively new and different person — not just more of the same person, not just the same person in higher gear or in some heightened state, but actually a different person. The patient sounds qualitatively different and acts and behaves as a qualitatively different person. To the observer, this has an exciting, exhilarating, or a chilling, eerie quality to it.

Patients often shift from one operating potential to another. The patient who is experiencing a sense of gloominess and depression may later experience sharp anger and defiance. The sweet and kindly experiencing may later give way to rollicking silliness. These are significant shifts, but not the kind we are referring to. Here again is where the researcher must be a clinical researcher, with some knowledge in the theory and practice of experiential psychotherapy. The shift is to be from the operating domain to a deeper potential. That is, the patient is to undergo the radical change into being a potential which is deeper, out of the ordinary operating domain.

For the clinical researcher with some knowledge in experiential psychotherapy, the presence of the deeper potential can usually be determined somewhat before the shift. The determination does not require data from a previous session, or even data from much earlier in the session. A moderate number of therapist and patient statements before the shift should be sufficient to identify the shift as one into a deeper potential.

Even more pointedly, this moment of psychotherapeutic movement has some in-therapy cues. It almost always occurs following steps 1A and/or 1B (Figure 2). It almost always occurs as a consequence of specific methods designed to enable the patient to disengage from the ordinary person that he is and enter fully into a different being or personhood or identity. Finally, there is a palpable sense of a qualitatively new and different person.

3) Experiencing new ways of being/behaving in the extra-therapy world. The final index of psychotherapeutic movement can be used by researchers not necessarily familiar with experiential psychotherapy. It occurs as the final step in each session, and it may be described as a tasting or sampling of new ways of being and behaving within the context of the extra-therapy world. The moment occurs when the patient is experiencing what it is like to carry out some new behavior in the world outside the therapy situation.

The new behavior is specific and concrete, a defined action. It is saying "no" to your father, renting a car and driving to the restaurant, telling your neighbor to pay back the money, taking a nap in the afternoon, painting a picture, caressing her face, shining his shoes, calling your mother on the phone, telling the kid to stop interrupting.

The patient must actually experience the new behavior, visualize doing it, practice carrying it out, imagine it happening, sense and feel what it is like initiating and carrying it through.

The context must be the world outside therapy. It may take place this evening, or tomorrow, or in a few days or weeks, or possibly later. But in this moment the patient must be living and existing preponderantly in that extra-therapy context rather than in the immediate therapy context or the context of recent or remote scenes. It is in the world of the available, imminent future.

The accompanying feelings are good and pleasant. They may be exciting, fun, exuberant, silly, delightful; they may have a tone of wickedness or riskiness, devilishness or audaciousness. But the feelings are not tight, fractionated, anxiety-ridden, fearful, gloomy, awful, bad ones.

Generally it is the experiential therapist who takes the lead in framing the new way of being and behaving within the extra-therapy world. The therapist sees it or undergoes it, defines or concretizes it. More than suggesting or advising, mentioning or talking about, the therapist enters into the actual being and doing of the new behavior within the extra-therapy world. But the patient must also partake and undergo. The patient tastes or samples or feels what it is like to be and behave in new ways within the available future world outside the therapy context.

These are the four kinds of experiencings around which experiential psychotherapy is built. They are the four indices of psychotherapeutic movement from this perspective. Furthermore, the theory of practice dictates that these are to occur more or less in sequence, and are to occur each session. There may only be three or four such good moments in a session. The moments may be short. Or the moments may occur over and over again, and each may be somewhat lengthy. In any case, these are the four additional indices of psychotherapeutic movement which experiential psychotherapy offers to the clinical researcher.

A Provisional Taxonomy of the
Indices of Psychotherapeutic Movement

If we put together the indices of psychotherapeutic movement proposed by experiential psychotherapy and those used by psychotherapy researchers, it is possible to develop a provisional taxonomy of indices of psychotherapeutic movement, change, improvement, progress, and good process. If there are good moments which occur in psychotherapy, what are they? More carefully worded, what are the indices of psychotherapeutic movement (change, improvement, progress, process) which occur in a session and which are (a) taken as indicating that something good, significant, worthwhile, and meaningful is occurring; (b) relatively short epochs of perhaps a few seconds to upwards of a minute; (c) referring to audiotaped or videotaped or verbatim events of a session; (d) taken from the experiential theory of psychotherapeutic practice and from the research literature, including indices used by researchers without being restricted to those confirmed by research findings; (e) focused upon the patient rather than predominantly upon the therapist; (f) representative of a wide variety of approaches to psychotherapy; (g) framed in a vocabulary that is essentially free of the technical jargon of any given approach to psychotherapy?

The spirit in which this taxonomy is offered is one of a somewhat hesitant initial probe. It is a genuinely provisional proposal on the firm expectation that it begs revision, reorganization, extension, and refinement. While it is perhaps understandable that no such taxonomy is available, it is nevertheless surprising and disconcerting. Given these disclaimers, the provisional taxonomy follows:

1) Providing meaningful material about personal self and/or relationships. The patient is providing (giving, reporting, telling about, exhibiting, describing) material which is meaningful (useful, important, revealing, significant) and which involves (a) the patient's private inner self, personal problems, inner fantasy life, current or historical material relevant to the patient's personal self, and/or (b) the patient's present or past interpersonal relationships such as erotic relations, aggressive interactions, or problem-related involvements.

Pt: There's this thing, voice, sometimes too much for me. A voice, mad and angry and it is inside my head, here, in here. A voice. Sounds mad all the time.

Pt: My sister, couple of years older than me. When we were kids she'd play with me. In bed. She'd, uh, well, she'd play with it. Touch my penis. Touched it. Put it against her, her . . . We never talked about it. I always felt, you know, real bad!

2) *Describing/exploring the personal nature and meaning of feelings*. The patient is engaging in a meaningful personal description and/or inner exploration of significant feelings, including what it is like to have the feeling, the nature and content of the feeling, the personal meaning of the feeling. The description and/or exploration is meaningful and personal rather than removed, distant, casual, uninvolved, or intellectual.

Pt: It's like I get weak, suddenly, can't breathe. Just even in the street, there are some women. I can't stop. It's like my whole body gets weak. Like I feel like something too much for me, something scary is going to take me over. I feel like . . . passing out . . . that's the way.

Pt: All I have to do is look at her, a miracle, my own baby, and I start to cry. She's so wonderful. It feels warm and tender, and unbelievable. My very own. I feel soft and like everything is OK when I hold her and look at her. Tender and like a real nice melting, loving, just so being with her . . .

3) *Emerging of previously warded-off material*. The patient is now remembering (dealing with, showing, exploring) material which is significant and therapeutically meaningful, but which had been warded-off earlier in therapy. The material may include cognitions

and ideas, impulses, feelings, interpersonal relations, memories and early incidents. Its emergence is accompanied with strong feelings such as pain, hurt, discomfort, distress, or it is accompanied with much reduced feelings of pain, hurt, discomfort, distress.

Pt: He was sick, my Dad, and he came back from the hospital. I was eight, I think. That was a bad time for me. But I remember I used to pray at night and . . . Jesus, I can't believe this! I used to pray that he'd die! I remember praying and asking God to take him out of the house! I never thought of that, but I remember just as clear! Please, God, take him to heaven. I can't believe this!

Pt: Lately I have been starting to remember stuff about my aunt. I always thought she was peculiar. Went to the hospital. But I think I used to do things with her. She gave me a little bottle with something in it. I kept it, magic. Had it in my room. And she'd bury little birds. I'd help her bury them along the garage. We'd do it together. So many little birds! I don't know where these memories are coming from. They seem like dreams! I'm getting scared, feeling funny!

   4) *Showing insight/understanding.* The patient is showing (having, expressing) insight/understanding which is meaningful, significant, and therapeutically important, in that (a) its occurrence is accompanied by feelings of emotional arousal, (b) it indicates a substantial change in the way the patient sees himself and his world, and (c) it has significant implications for the patient's well-being and personal and interpersonal behavior. The content may refer to the patient's current and past behavior, connections within and between areas of the patient's life, connections between past life and current functioning, inner processes and the patient's current cognitions, behaviors, and interpersonal relationships.

Pt: Sure! I'm smiling, and I know I come across as nice, but my stomach is churning and tight! It's like an act, you know? If I were honest, well, I don't know how I'd be, but I'm beginning to see that I'm not all that sweet and nice. No way! I've been a good actress, that's all!

Pt: I've always thought I was so different from my Dad. He's a wimp, and I always felt tough. But maybe I'm not so damned different, huh? I never realized how passive I am. Like him. Oh no! What a damned waste, all those years. We really are a lot alike. Shit!

5) Communicating expressively. There are two yoked defining characteristics of significant, meaningful, important expressive communication. One consists of a voice quality which is active, energetic, fresh, spontaneous, alive, vibrant. This may include the energy turned outward in an expressive manner, or it may occur with the energy turned inward in an exploring manner. The other consists of vividness and richness in the spoken words: figures of speech, colorful use of imagery and metaphor, a strong sensual quality that draws upon visual, auditory, and/or kinesthetic modalities.

Pt: The last time I went to Calgary the plane slid on the runway and I got so thrown around I felt like I went one way, my body went another, and I suddenly became mixed up between peeing, shitting, and vomiting. I think my body forgot how to be terrified, and I wasn't around to remember what to do when I panic! I hope the pilot doesn't really mind if I sit on his lap, with a priest on one side and you on the other, while I fondle my parachute and wonder what you were trying to tell me about masochism . . .

Pt: They'll be reading the list at graduation, everything deadly quiet, Davidson, closer, Derrick, then here it comes, Doberman, and my Dad will scream out, "That's my boy!" The chancellor's eyeballs will glare at me in the front row, I'll pull the hood down over my head, and my blood pressure will explode. Trying to put a lid on my Dad at graduation is like asking an elephant to do Swan Lake with Pavlova. You can dress him up, but you can't get him to behave!

6) Manifesting a meaningfully significant working relationship with the therapist. The patient is actively involved and engaged in a meaningfully significant working relationship with the therapist. This exceeds mild or moderate cooperation, e.g., answering the therapist's questions, talking about requested material, being friendly and receptive toward the therapist. The meaningfully significant level of a working relationship may be manifested in a high level of trust in the therapist, highly active cooperation, strong allegiance with the therapist, acceptance of a strong measure of genuine responsibility for effecting personal change.

Pt: So my wife invited her sister and she'll be here Thursday, staying till Sunday, sleeping in the bed in my den. (Pause.) I know, I'm being silent, and I should be saying what I'm thinking. Well I'm ashamed. I know, that avoids what I'm thinking. Ooooh, all right, I picture that gorgeous body, those long lovely legs, sleeping in that bed. Ooooh! I got sexy thoughts. I got to tell the sexy thoughts. Maybe I should talk about the erection I'm getting?

Pt: I'm still thinking about what you said a minute ago, that I don't really show how deeply I feel to him. Your words are still ringing. I think that's true. You said that last time too, and I kept hearing your words even at work, and yeah. It's really up to me to show him. If I want to it's my choice, I have to be the one to change, not him. Yeah. That really makes sense.

7) *Expressing strong feelings toward the therapist.* The patient is expressing feelings which are strong, may be either positive or negative, and are expressed directly toward the therapist. The therapist is the direct, immediate target of the feelings. Positive feelings may include warmth, love, acceptance, closeness, trust, confidence in and toward the therapist, and feelings of being loved, accepted, understood, protected, cared for, prized by the therapist. Negative feelings may include defiance, disagreement, disapproval, mistrust, hatred, guilt, anger, rebellion, irritation, annoyance. The strength of the feelings is indicated by loudness and volume, by yellings, bellowings, shriekings, gruntings, groanings, hearty laughings, racking cryings, and by strong bodily sensations such as shakings and tremblings, pains and hurts and aches, tinglings, stingings, pricklings, crampings, clutchings, dizziness, kickings and flailings, turnings and twistings.

The expression of strong feelings directly toward the therapist may be described as "transference" when the feelings are understood as derived from repressed fantasies originating in significant conflictual childhood relationships, and revived in the current relationship with the therapist. The expression of strong feelings directly toward the therapist may be described as "external encountering" or "internal encountering" when the patient is engaging with, respectively, the personal processes of the external therapist or the therapist as the internal voice of the patient's own deeper processes.

Pt: I couldn't wait for today's session 'cause I wanted to tell you 'cause I knew you'd be so pleased! It's so good to know you're there. Just knowing you're here and you really care, I count on that so much. You really understand! It's like a wonderful gift, just being able to be with you!

Pt: I don't think I want to do that; it sounds like another of your gimmicks. I don't know why you end each session by trying to rattle me like this. Maybe you have some personality quirk where if I leave here all shook up I'll come back for another six months. What's your reason for wanting me to do that? Do you have a reason? Do you have the brains to understand what I'm trying to tell you? Should I spell it out for you?

8) Expressing strong feelings in personally meaningful life contexts. The patient is expressing strong feelings within the context of personally meaningful life situations other than that of the therapy situation. It is as if the patient is mainly existing in some recent or remote scene, real or fantasied context, or in an emotional or experiential state other than being present with the therapist, talking to and interacting with the therapist. The predominance of the patient's attention is within that personally meaningful context, directed toward some figure or object other than the therapist. The patient is in effect existing more in the other context or state than here with the therapist in the therapy situation.

The patient is expressing strong feelings. These may be either positive or negative. Positive feelings may include warmth, love, acceptance, closeness, trust; negative feelings may include defiance, disagreement, disapproval, mistrust, hatred, guilt, anger, rebellion, irritation, annoyance. The strength of the feelings is indicated by loudness and volume, by yellings, bellowings, shriekings, gruntings, groanings, hearty laughings, racking cryings, and by strong bodily sensations such as shakings and tremblings, pains and hurts and aches, tinglings, stingings, pricklings, crampings, clutchings, dizziness, kickings and flailings, turnings and twistings.

Pt: OK, so here I am driving in a lot of traffic on the freeway, and it's OK with cars I can see. But the cars from the side, they're the buggers. I always think one'll mush me from the side, slam into me!! Dammit, my hands are shaking already! I can't hack this! I don't have eyes all over! I know I'm gonna get hit and I hate this!

Pt: Momma, Momma! You have to let me go! I can't spend the rest of my life being your good little girl! I gotta get away! But you don't understand, and you are so helpless all by yourself, and I sometimes feel so selfish when I get like this. I don't know. Please help me Momma! Help me. I don't know what to do, and I'm so mixed up. (Cries softly.)

9) Radical shifting into deeper personality states. The patient undergoes a radical shift in personality, and no longer is the former, continuing, substantive personality. Instead, the patient undergoes a transformation or radical personality change, and becomes a qualitatively new and different person who is the expression of a deeper personality state. This deeper personality state was latent, potential, available within the patient, and the patient is now being and expressing this deeper personality state. This radical shift in who and what the patient is may be accompanied with feelings which are good and pleasant or bad and unpleasant. In either case, the patient has shifted into being a genuinely new and different person.

Pt: (The little wimp has spent his life being dominated and victimized by a series of powerful persons, and now slides into being the incredibly powerful state which had been latent and available.) It really feels strange, new. I feel like the whole world turns to me and waits for instructions. When people talk, they say what I want them to say. I determine their conversation, control their movements. Waitresses bring me the food I want and I just think it. I got power! I can determine fates and destinies! It's more than, uh, mental telepathy. It's mental control! Control! Over everything!

Pt: (The patient succumbs into being a deeper personality state involving a free-wheeling, impulsive spontaneity.) There's energy in me! Like I got a charge in me! I want to dance, and sing and kiss everyone. I want to tell Hilda that she's divine, and throw my arms around Harry! You're a great guy! And I want to make love like I never. I can't stop! I feel like I got shot up with something wonderful. (Laughs hard.) Help everyone, come on out for volleyball! And a lot of friendly screwing! Wow! I can't stop!

10) Risking new ways of being and behaving within the real world of the imminent future. The patient is risking new ways of being and behaving within the real world of the imminent future. Risking new ways of being and behaving means (a) intending to undertake the new ways of being and behaving, being cordially welcoming and receptive to these new ways of being and behaving, and (b) actually undertaking them, trying them out, tasting and sampling them, expressing and doing them. These new ways of being and behaving may be slight changes or gross new ways of being and behaving. They may occur within the patient's current and imminently future world, and they may invoke slight or gross changes in the patient's current and imminently future world.

Pt: I don't think I ever just touched her face, uh, lovingly, just even, or looked at her and caressed her hand or anything. It's not so hard! I feel like I want to be with her and touch her. What's happening? I like this! I feel like I want to go be with her and touch her—and Mamma! Hold her hand! Holy shit, I'm becoming a damned touchie-feelie! And I like it!

Pt: It always seemed like nothing's going to change, but I think I'm going to lose about 40 pounds. I can see what it would be like to be around 130, and I want to lose it and be healthy. I can feel little sexual perks in my body, and I want to help them.

Losing weight, and getting back to good old-fashioned sex. I used to love it. I miss it! I want to ride a bike again and take long baths and get outside and walk. Ha! I don't know what to do first. It all seems so, uh, easy! Now!

11) Expressing/reporting positive target behaviors. Positive target behaviors are those which have been flagged as the behaviors which therapy is to bring about. These generally fall into two classes. One includes behaviors which have been flagged as positive targets for this particular patient. For example, this particular patient is to be able to drive a car, have orgasms, eat eggs, walk without crutches, go on vacations, touch furry animals, speak fluently, be assertive, use elevators. The second class is broader. It includes positive behaviors which are held as characteristics of adjusted, adapted, normal, mature, optimal, successfully treated patients in general. Depending on one's version, this class may include having a job, having friends, crossing streets, leaving the house, having heterosexual relations, being relaxed, accepting responsibility for one's own feelings and behaviors, standing up for oneself, being aware of and in touch with feelings.

The patient may express the positive target behavior in the therapy session or by reporting its occurrence in the extra-therapy world.

Pt: My skin feels fine. No prickly anywhere, not even on my arms, and I'm stroking the cat and even rubbing the back of my arm over her fur. This is something! First time ever! Yes, my shoulder's still relaxed, and there's only the slightest tension in my stomach, normal, that's normal for the past minutes. I think I'm doing it! This is great!

Pt: Yesterday I finally did it OK. I was in line again, at the market, and this old big guy got in line two people ahead. He just put his cart in front. No one said anything, but I said, "This is a line, and we are in our place. Please go to the back of the line." It worked! (Laughs.) I don't know what he said, but he got in the rear, and the lady in front of me said, "Thank you," and I felt like the training worked. I didn't even feel mad, just like I was saying what's what.

12) Expressing/reporting reduced negative target behaviors and ideas. The patient expresses or reports a reduction in negative target behaviors or ideas. These are behaviors and ideas which are to be reduced, extinguished, occur less frequently, or no longer occur under defined conditions and circumstances. The negative target behaviors and ideas include specific complaints, behavioral problems, symptoms, attitudes, beliefs, cognitions and ideas which are regarded as problematical, sick, neurotic, distressing, abnormal, psychopathological, self-defeating, maladaptive, maladjustive, psychotic, hurtful, painful, bothersome. These may include nail-biting, vomiting, forgetfulness, compulsive masturbation, hand washing, facial tics, stuttering, being too scared to use elevators, the idea that one must be loved to be of any worth, the belief that others are plotting against the patient or that one's child is the devil.

The patient may manifest reduced negative target behaviors and ideas in the session, or the patient may report reduced presence and occurrence from the extra-therapy world.

Pt: It's been two weeks now, and I haven't stolen anything. Nothing. The best part is that I hardly get the urge anymore. What a helluva difference that makes. Joe and I shopped yesterday in the market and we spent the whole afternoon, like a test? Nothing. Didn't rip off a thing. We even bought some stuff. I'm getting all better!

Pt: Just like now, I can say, "That's enough!" and it goes away. I can control the thought and I don't have the idea of going crazy. I can say, "I'm normal!" and the thought goes away. Even when I'm at work alone, you know, after hours. It comes and I can say, "Stop . . . I'm normal" and it just goes away. I think I'm on top of it, and it was easier than I thought.

13) Expressing/reporting a state of well-being. The patient expresses or reports a state of well-being, a general state of good feelings and positive attitudes. This may include an expressed or reported state of happiness, relaxation, security, confidence, competence, psychological soundness, comfort, satisfaction, pleasure. This state of well-being may be a generalized condition; it may be in relationship with oneself (e.g., self-satisfaction, self-respect, self-confidence, self-acceptance, self-regard); it may be in relationship with others (e.g., loving the spouse, feeling good with one's family, accepting one's group).

Pt: Oh, I just feel so good! I never felt so at peace, and just, good! Every day seems . . . well, I feel happy. I just feel good all over!

Pt: I got nothing to complain about anymore! Life is great. I feel alive. Business is fine. We love each other. Sex is better than ever. My body is terrific. I feel like a pig in shit! I feel like I just woke up and became a different person. I'm happy! Is it OK to say it? I am damned happy and I never felt so good!

These 13 indices of psychotherapeutic movement constitute the provisional taxonomy, and are the answer to the central question of this chapter. The theory of experiential psychotherapy is represented in indices 7-10.

Discussion and Commentary

The actual framing of a list of moments of psychotherapeutic movement invites discussion and commentary on the actual research use of the taxonomy, on the lines of investigation which may be opened by such a list, and on the place of traditional outcome procedures in regard to examining or modifying the list.

Some considerations in using the taxonomy in research. There are several considerations which have emerged from actual experience with a research team's efforts to use the above taxonomy. Members of the research team independently listened to tape-recorded individual psychotherapy sessions, following the dialogue with a verbatim typescript. At weekly meetings, the problems were discussed. On the basis of these discussions, the following considerations were highlighted:

(a) It is quite difficult for an individual researcher to use all the indices simultaneously. It is much easier to select a few (e.g., one to four or so), particularly those which make psychotherapeutic sense for the individual researcher. An experiential researcher will be inclined toward experiential indices, and these proclivities should be respected.

(b) Especially if the researcher is a clinician, problems will come into bold relief if the selected indices clash with the researcher's own implicit or explicit indices of psychotherapeutic movement, change, progress, improvement, or good process. Even if the researcher only uses the few which seem to make psychotherapeutic sense, actual use of the indices will disclose differences between those indices and those which are implicitly held by the researcher and are not included in the list. These differences may be "bracketed" so that the researcher can use the indices reasonably well. These differences may also be respected and used as a basis for a careful modification of the taxonomy.

(c) Most of the indices lend themselves to scaling along a dimension. At one end, there seems to be some movement, some change, some mild or moderate progress, improvement, or process. In terms of that index, the moment seems to be a fairly good one, indicating a low degree of significance with regard to that index. For example, the patient is showing some degree of insight and understanding, and the moment may be regarded as moderately significant, valuable, important in terms of insight and understanding. At the other end, there is great, wonderful movement, change, progress, improvement, process in terms of that index. This is a stellar moment, a real high point, a significant turning point, a most impressive moment, a highly valuable and therapeutically important moment, an outstanding instance of that index.

The definition and description of each index talk about a meaningful degree, a significant amount of it, a therapeutically important measure of whatever the index is. For each index, it has to occur in a way and to a degree that impresses the researcher as meaningful, important, valuable, as indicating that something good is happening right here, a moment when the therapeutic process is moving along quite well, some significant change is occurring, as indicating meaningful progress, process, improvement—and all in regard to the particular index.

Our provisional taxonomy does not specify a criterion level for any of the indices. Until there are ways of defining that criterion level well, together with good examples, the researcher must rely on a measure of best judgment. The researcher must ask, "Given this particular index of psychotherapeutic movement, does it seem to be present to a genuinely significant degree, is it a meaningful instance of this kind of movement, is it an important and valuable moment with regard to this index?"

(d) Some of the indices seem to be continuing conditions which may be present continually throughout a session. For example, throughout a session the patient may frequently manifest a good working relationship with the therapist (index 6) or communicate expressively (index 5). Each time the patient meets the criterion, it is to be noted, even if this means the patient is showing this index of psychotherapeutic movement throughout the session.

An alternative approach is to regard a given level as a characteristic of the patient. "He is an expressive communicator." "She just has a good working relationship with the therapist." Then the researcher flags instances which seem to be above this baseline level characteristic of the patient. Although this alternative approach is possible, it has many drawbacks and it distorts the meaning of indices of good process, important and valuable conditions in psychotherapeutic movement.

(e) A few of the indices call for some contrast between the way the patient is now as compared with the way the patient was earlier in this or maybe even previous sessions. In index 3 (emerging of previously warded-off material), the researcher must know that the material had been warded-off. This may be shown by contrast with what occurred earlier in the session, by what is contained in the nearby statements of the therapist, or in the actual patient statements in which the material emerges. Again, this calls for some judgment.

The same considerations apply to index 12 (expressing/reporting reduced negative target behaviors and ideas) and index 11 (expressing/reporting positive target behaviors). The researcher must have some idea of what the targeted behaviors were. Again, a fair measure of judgment is called for so that expressed or reported behaviors can be identified as the targeted ones.

Sequences. It would seem that the indices may well fall into sequences or steps or phases in a session or over a series of sessions. In experiential psychotherapy, the four indices are explicitly organized into a sequence of steps in a single session (Figure 2). This issue of sequences was raised by Horowitz, Sampson, Siegelman, Weiss, and Goodfriend (1978) in their examination of what they term cohesive and dispersal behaviors, i.e., classes of behaviors in which patients show or report more direct engagement and involvement with others. Are there sequences of psychotherapeutic movement? Which indices seem to organize themselves into sequences? Are there sequences within single sessions? Are there sequences over series of sessions? Are there sequences of indices characteristic of given approaches to psychotherapy? By using the taxonomy, psychotherapy researchers are invited to address these questions. Indeed, the use of a taxonomy of indices of psychotherapeutic movement would seem to lend itself to the careful addressing of such questions.

Process indices and outcome indices. It seems that some of the indices are "process indices" and some are "outcome indices." It also seems that whether the index is considered process or outcome depends upon the psychotherapeutic approach. And it seems that each of three major families or approaches to psychotherapy has its own distinctive set of indices, with the psychoanalytic/psychodynamic approaches using mainly process indices and the experiential/humanistic and behavioral approaches using mainly outcome indices.

Some of the indices seem to say that psychotherapeutic movement is occurring because the "therapeutic process" is moving along. What is meant by psychotherapeutic movement has little to do with outcome, i.e., how the patient is to be following therapy or when therapy brings about successful outcome or change. For example, when the patient is manifesting a good working relationship with the therapist (see Figure 3), "psychotherapeutic movement" means that the therapeutic process is proceeding along well, even though a successful "outcome" would probably not include the patient's manifesting a good relationship with the therapist.

On the other hand, some indices refer to actual changes in the patient's behavioral way of being, changes which are coterminal with the way the patient is hoped to be later in treatment or following treatment. In effect, these are "in-therapy outcomes" of the same form and shape as many of the traditional meanings of therapeutic outcome. For example, when the patient actually shows a positive change in the target behavior, that is an index of psychotherapeutic movement and also qualifies in many approaches as an outcome of successful or effective psychotherapy.

In addition, whether the index of psychotherapeutic movement is regarded as process or outcome varies with the therapeutic approach (see Figure 3). For example, in some experiential/humanistic approaches, it is regarded as a mark of successful therapy that the patient becomes a person who describes and explores the personal nature and meaning of feelings (outcome). In many psychoanalytic/psychodynamic therapies, on the other hand, this way of being is looked upon more as a part of the therapeutic process and less as a characteristic of the successfully treated patient.

Finally, each approach to psychotherapy seems to have its own distinctive package of indices. It is always a real judgment call to organize a group of psychotherapeutic approaches. There are lots of groupings. Figure 3 offers one among many. I have organized therapies into psychodynamic/psychoanalytic, experiential/humanistic, and behavioral families. Using this loose three-fold organization, it seems that there is considerable distinctiveness over the first nine indices, i.e., each of the three families seems to have its own package from the first nine indices. On the other hand, each of the three families seems to accept indices 10-13. All in all, dividing therapies into these three families, there seems to be some commonality and considerable variation in the choice of indices of psychotherapeutic movement.

The clustering of indices. Do different indices seem to point toward similar patient behaviors? When one index seems to announce that here is a moment of psychotherapeutic movement, do other indices also target the same moment? Do indices seem to cluster on particular kinds of patient behaviors?

If the answer is yes, this could have several explanations. One is that the clustering indices are really only a single package, described in differing vocabularies. A second explanation is that the clustering indices differ mainly in level of analysis, so that perhaps one is a more concrete version of another which is a more general category.

Process or Outcome

	Psychodynamic/ Psychoanalytic	Experiential/ Humanistic	Behavioral
1. Providing meaningful material about personal self and/or relationships.	P		
2. Describing/exploring the personal nature and meaning of feelings.	P	O	
3. Emerging of previously warded-off material.	P		
4. Showing insight/understanding.	O		
5. Communicating expressively.		O	
6. Manifesting a meaningfully significant working relationship with T.	P	P	
7. Expressing strong feelings toward T.	P	O	
8. Expressing strong feelings in personally meaningful contexts.		O	
9. Radical shifting into deeper personality states.		O	
10. Risking new ways of being-behaving within the real world of the imminent future.	O	O	O
11. Expressing/reporting positive target behavior.	O	O	O
12. Expressing/reporting reduced target behaviors and ideas.	O	O	O
13. Expressing/reporting a state of well-being.	O	O	O

Figure 3. Indices of Psychotherapeutic Movement as Process or Outcome Over Three Families of Psychotherapy

A third explanation is that the clustering categories bear some kind of underlying commonality or basis for intercorrelation. If this third explanation seems feasible, it would mean that we might learn more about very particular kinds of psychotherapeutic movement. For example, if "showing insight/understanding" and "communicating expressively" go together regularly, it may have something to teach us about the kinds of insightful statements which qualify as moments of psychotherapeutic movement.

This is a worthwhile research question. Indeed, it is the central research question in studies by Raskin (1949) and Kauffman and Raimy (1949). Raskin examined the coterminality and intercorrelations among five indices of psychotherapeutic movement applied to ten therapy cases. Kauffman and Raimy compared the DRQ (Discomfort-Relief Quotient) tension index with an index of self-evaluation. Both studies found extensive and interesting similarity and overlap in the indices they studied, and both discussed the implications with regard to theories of psychotherapeutic change. Yet they just opened the door to the study of such questions. Much more study is to come.

Therapist methods instrumental to bringing about the moments of psychotherapeutic movement. If we can locate given moments of psychotherapeutic movement, then it is possible to take a look at the antecedent therapist methods. What did the therapist (or therapist and patient) do to help bring about this moment of psychotherapeutic movement? What about this other moment of psychotherapeutic movement? Are there different kinds of antecedent therapist methods for each kind of moment of therapeutic movement? These are the kinds of questions which can be answered once we have located particular moments of movement.

An example of such a study started with the identifying of strong hearty laughter as moments of psychotherapeutic movement (Gervaize, Mahrer, & Markow, in press). They then studied antecedent therapist statements and named five kinds of therapist statements which occurred just before the strong hearty laughter as compared with instances of no laughter and instances of mild or moderate laughter. This may well prove to be a powerful strategy in seeing what kinds of therapist methods are instrumental in bringing about each of the moments of psychotherapeutic movement.

A critique of the traditional outcome strategy in discovering or confirming moments of psychotherapeutic movement. If we wish to discover or to confirm "good moments in therapy" or "moments of psychotherapeutic movement," can this be done by the traditional outcome strategy in which pre- and post-therapy measures are used? Is it useful to examine which patients improved or were successful or scored better on outcome measures? Is it a useful strategy to relate what occurs in therapy to extra-therapy or post-therapy outcome? Will the traditional outcome strategy help us to learn more about good moments, significant in-therapy changes, meaningful epochs in therapy? My conclusion is that the answer is no (Mahrer, 1983) to all these questions, a conclusion reached by Murray in 1954:

> It is not clear why only some patients improve. Current research using measures before and after therapy, or comparing therapy with no-therapy, yields little useful information; such an approach establishes no relationship between what actually occurs during therapy and the outcome. Thus, there is no rationale for gradually improving tactics or understanding the changes in various kinds of patients. (p. 305)

It is the same conclusion reached by Rice and Wagstaff (1967):

> Particular therapist behaviors or other experimental variations are so remote in time from the actual assessment of therapy outcome, with so much intervening interaction, that their effects are problematic without some more immediate index such as changes in client process. (p. 557)

It is the same conclusion more recently offered by Stiles (1980):

> These questions are fundamental, yet they cannot be answered directly because outcome cannot be assessed until long after any particular intervention and may then reflect the cumulative effect of many diverse psychotherapeutic encounters. (pp. 176–177)

The commonality among Murray, Rice and Wagstaff, and Stiles lies in the difficulty of relating in-therapy events with remote outcome assessments which take place so much later and after so many confounding intermediate events. But there are other considerations which lead toward the conclusion that traditional outcome strategies, however sophisticated, are not the way either to discover, identify, confirm or disconfirm significant moments of movement.

In rough outline, the logic of the outcome strategy goes like this: If we have a fair number of cases, administer pre-therapy and post-therapy evaluations, and compare those with successful outcomes against those with less successful outcomes, then we should be able to discover, identify, confirm or disconfirm significant moments of movement in therapy by looking at the presence and distribution of these significant events in the successful cases as compared with the less successful cases. Although there are all sorts of sophisticated refinements of this general strategy, these are the overall contours of the standard outcome model. Let us now look at two considerations a little closer.

This research strategy will work when the significance of the in-therapy event lies preponderantly in its having a more or less direct instrumental connection with outcome. The moment of psychotherapeutic movement must be the "means" and the outcome must be the "end," and therein must lie the major worth of the in-therapy event. The rigorous implication is that if the research findings are not "positive," the in-therapy event should be dropped. That is, if the results of a fair number of well-done studies fail to confirm that the hypothesized significant moment of movement occurs more in successful outcomes than unsuccessful outcomes, then the logic dictates that the significant moment should be abandoned.

Furthermore, it must be noted that such a research methodology is virtually ineffective in discovering any new moments of movement. It is limited to confirming or failing to confirm the significant moments of movement already entertained by therapists.

It is essential that the significance of the moments of movement lies mainly in their direct, instrumental connection with outcome. If the significance does not lie there, if the meaning and worth of the moment of movement lie in what is occurring in the session itself, then this research strategy loses most of its power and rigor.

Suppose that some therapists hold that in significant moments of movement the patient is manifesting good insight and understanding. The interpretive efforts of the therapist have paid off and now there is significant evidence of insight and understanding. If the research indicates that insight and understanding are related to successful outcome rather than unsuccessful outcome, what can be concluded? We can probably conclude that there is some added faith that insight and understanding are related to that particular criterion of successful outcome. However, suppose that the results of a fair number of well-done studies are that there is no significant difference between successful and unsuccessful cases. The research logic would then dictate that such therapists abandon efforts at achieving insight and understanding. Right? Not quite. Very few therapists hold that the primary value of achieving insight and understanding lies in their direct instrumental connection with criteria of successful outcome. Instead of abandoning insight and understanding, therapists who hold these as valuable would find reasons to question the research in a justifiable effort to retain their faith in insight and understanding. Why is their faith justified? It is justified because they never accepted the essential logic of the research strategy, namely that the preponderant significance of insight and understanding lies in a straightforward, direct, instrumental connection with successful outcome. Indeed, virtually all therapists who value insight and understanding would reject such a proposition, and instead hold that the value of insight and understanding lies elsewhere. It lies in the immediate therapeutic process. It lies in notions of what is occurring intrapsychically in the patient. It lies in all sorts of therapeutic considerations which are more important than the proposition essential to the standard outcome research strategy. So the very foundation of this research strategy was never there in the first place.

Of all the significant moments in therapy, of all the indices that something therapeutically good and effective is occurring, how many of these would conform to the proposition that (a) the preponderance of the significance lies in direct, straightforward, instrumental connection with outcome, and (b) if the results of a well-executed body of studies fail to show that the hypothesized moments occur significantly more in successful than unsuccessful cases, the hypothesized moments of movement should be abandoned? There may be one or two throwaway exceptions, but I believe that there would be precious few which would conform to such a proposition. I certainly would not accept such a proposition for the significant moments of movement offered by experiential psychotherapy.

Consider a representative study such as that by Schauble and Pierce (1974). They examined three in-therapy process dimensions, each of which constitutes an index of good process, a moment of therapeutic movement: (a) active engagement in inward probing and self-exploration, (b) "owning" and accepting one's own feelings and behaviors, and (c) commitment, desire, willingness to change, and cooperation with the therapist. Their therapists were generally client-centered and psychoanalytic. The hypothesis was that successful cases would demonstrate higher levels of these three in-therapy process dimensions than would less successful cases, and they used MMPI scores as the outcome measure. If a respectable number of studies used this design, and if they all failed to support the hypothesis, would client-centered and psychoanalytic therapists be persuaded to abandon trying to effect their patients' active engagement in inward probing and self-exploration, or efforts to have their patients own and accept their own feelings and behaviors, or attempts to promote patients' commitment, desire to change, willingness to change, and cooperation with their therapists? I doubt this, and the reason for doubting this is that the value, worth and meaningfulness of these three in-therapy process dimensions do not lie predominantly in their direct, straightforward, instrumental connection with changes in MMPI scores. The study of direct connections between indices of psychotherapeutic movement and indices of successful outcome has little to do with why the indices of psychotherapeutic movement were regarded as significant in the first place.

The standard outcome strategy is rather inert in discovering new in-therapy significant moments of movement. It may have some worth in confirming or disconfirming significant moments of movement only for those whose therapeutic significance lies in their having direct, straightforward, instrumental connections with measures of successful outcome — and researchers would have a hard time identifying more than possibly one or two of these. So this first consideration suggests that the traditional outcome strategy is feeble both for discovering or "testing" moments of movement.

The second consideration has to do with overlap or coterminality between the indices of psychotherapeutic movement and the measures of successful outcome. If the index of psychotherapeutic movement is similar to the measure that successful outcome has occurred, then the research conclusion is embarrassingly circular.

Suppose that the research started with 100 cases of severe stutterers, and the index of in-therapy movement is a reduction of the stuttering and the occurrence of fluent speech. If the indication of successful treatment is that the patients no longer stuttered, then what may be concluded? The conclusion is restricted to one of generalization, i.e., that stutterers who showed evidence of no longer stuttering in therapy may show evidence of no longer stuttering in the outcome measures.

To the extent that the in-therapy index of psychotherapeutic movement is similar to, overlaps with, or is coterminal with outcome measures of successful treatment, the research is limited to showing that the change in therapy also occurs on the outcome measure. That is hardly a powerful conclusion if one is seeking to confirm or disconfirm the in-therapy indices of psychotherapeutic movement. Nor is the example of stuttering a distorted one. Many outcome measures bear remarkable similarity to the in-therapy significant events. Accordingly, to acquire power, it must first be demonstrated that there is clear separation and distinctiveness between outcome measures and in-therapy indices.

Furthermore, it is again notable that such a strategy — i.e., one in which there is a fair measure of overlap between the outcome measure and the in-therapy indices — is not equipped to discover much that is new, and that deprives the strategy of a great deal of what research could and should accomplish.

Is this consideration a manufactured one? I doubt it. This problem of overlap has plagued such research from the very beginning. In 1955, Auld and Murray cited this problem in reviewing studies which examined (a) in-therapy instances of patients' discussing their problems with some significant indication of insight, and (b) in-therapy instances of patients' demonstrating their intention to formulate plans for new ways of responding. In all of the studies reviewed, the outcome measure consisted of judgments of the case as successful or nonsuccessful. However, as noted by the reviewers, judgments of whether the case was successful or unsuccessful included an assessment of whether the treated patients (a) discussed their problems with some significant indication of insight, and (b) demonstrated an intention to formulate plans for new ways of responding!

> This result is hardly an independent confirmation that the cases judged to be successful *were* successful, since the judges undoubtedly reacted to just such changes in the client's verbalizations when deciding whether cases were successful. (Auld & Murray, 1955, p. 382)

It is more common than we would want to admit that whatever is regarded as evidence of good in-therapy movement and whatever is regarded as successful outcome are confounded with one another. Indeed, it would seem to be a stout task to demonstrate rigorous separation between the two. But this must be done to preserve the power, if any, in the standard outcome strategy.

All in all, solid prospects for the traditional outcome strategy are grim. It seems that a research strategy which ties indices of psychotherapeutic movement to outcome measures is not designed to provide us with new knowledge about these moments. If the clinical researcher wishes to discover new moments of psychotherapeutic movement, the standard outcome strategy is just not a very powerful choice. This is a pity. It would be nice to discover the events or epochs in a session where something good is happening, when there is progress or therapeutic change. But it seems that we will not be helped much by the time-worn, pre-post, outcome-measured, compare-successful-and-less-successful-cases research strategy.

If we are hard put to discover any new moments of movement by using that research strategy, can it be used to test the ones we already believe we have? Can it be used to confirm or disconfirm our present set of clinically accepted moments of movement? I suggest that such a research strategy can be used for those purposes only under three conditions, each of which the researcher must demonstrate:

(a) The researcher must demonstrate that the presence (or absence) of significant differences between successful (improved) and less successful (less improved) cases is connected to the hypothesized moments of movement. As pointed out by Murray (1954), Rice and Wagstaff (1967), and Stiles (1980), this is very difficult to do. If there are no significant differences between successful and unsuccessful cases, if there is no pre-post improvement, the researcher must take into account the length of time between the in-therapy moments of movement and the post-therapy outcome assessment, and the researcher must take into account the possibility of all sorts of other factors which may affect outcome scores.

(b) The researcher must demonstrate clear separation between the indices of psychotherapeutic movement and the measures of successful outcome. Indices of psychotherapeutic movement and outcome indices cannot overlap, be coterminal, have common components, or be merely different aspects of a single category.

(c) The researcher must demonstrate that the preponderant significance of the moment of movement must reside in a close, direct, straightforward, intimate connection with the outcome which is used. There must also be a demonstrated logic whereby the moment of movement is to be abandoned if an adequate body of research fails to yield positive findings.

On balance, it appears that the traditional outcome strategy has little to offer those who are inclined either to discover new moments of psychotherapeutic movement or to confirm or disconfirm indices already entertained by therapists. For these purposes, the traditional outcome strategy should be replaced by others such as those proposed in this book.

Conclusions

One way of studying psychotherapeutic change is to gather your own pertinent data of the patient, organize these within a topographical map of the patient's personality, and to use principles which enable you to predict the directions of potential change available to the individualized patient. This meaning and measurement of psychotherapeutic change are discussed in chapter 2. Chapter 3 introduces another meaning and measurement of psychotherapeutic change. As with the first, it is fitting and appropriate for experiential psycho-therapy, and it also can be used by other approaches to psychother-apy and research. It starts with the notion that there are moments or epochs which can be described as psychotherapeutic movement or progress or process or change, i.e., moments in which something therapeutically good or valuable is occurring. By reviewing the re-search literature and the theory of experiential psychotherapy, the aim was to develop a list of indices phrased in a vocabulary which may be used by the clinical researcher. On this basis, a list of 13 in-dices of psychotherapeutic movement was proposed on the presump-tion that such a list lends itself to further refinement and use for clinical research purposes. Finally, some ways of using this list were discussed, including a suggestion that the standard outcome research strategy is rather inert both for discovering or for confirming/dis-proving these or other indices of psychotherapeutic movement.

4
Therapist Statements as Prescriptions-for-Change

The purpose of the present chapter is to introduce a third meaning and way of measuring psychotherapeutic change. While it evolves from an experiential theory of psychotherapy, it is a method which lends itself to virtually all kinds of therapies and therapists.

Briefly, therapist statements are regarded as containing prescriptions-for-change. That is, each therapist statement is examined in terms of its implicit or explicit laying out of how the patient is to be or become, what the patient is to do or be like, the kind of person the patient is to be. From these data, dimensions of change are generated for that therapist with that patient in that session or series of sessions. Changes are measured by assessing the degree to which the patient moves along those dimensions, becomes that kind of person, evidences those ways of being and behaving (Mahrer, Clark, Comeau & Brunette, in press).

Background

What psychotherapists do when they are talking is generally taken as carrying out some kind of therapeutic technique or method. We say that the therapist is reflecting feelings, pointing out inconsistencies, avoiding patient traps, getting background information, establishing rapport, getting around defenses, self-disclosing, and so on. We may get close to the data and describe these techniques or methods at the concrete molecular level, or we can get kind of loose and general and describe these techniques and methods at a more molar

I wish to acknowledge the assistance of the members of my psychotherapy research team, especially Irit Sterner, in the preparation for this chapter.

level. But it is easy to confine ourselves to seeing what the therapist is doing in terms of therapeutic techniques and methods. Let us leave all that aside. Let us consider the other perspectives for making sense of the statements that therapists make. For our purposes, four backgrounds converge in the proposed way of understanding therapist statements as prescriptions-for-change rather than as techniques and methods of therapeutic praxis.

Therapist statements as means of instrumenting therapist-patient role relationships. One background for this way of understanding therapist statements resides in Laing's (1970) surgical analysis of parents' statements to their children. The actual statements could be understood chillingly as the imposing of crazy roles which the children are defined as fulfilling, together with quite explicitly defined relationships they are supposed to carry out in relationship with the parents. It is an eye-opening tiny step to understanding many statements by therapists similarly—not as therapeutic techniques and methods to move the therapy process along, but as attempts to define the role the therapist is to fulfill, define the role the patient is to fulfill, and define the relationship between the therapist and patient (Bugental, 1964; Laing, 1982; Lawton, 1958; Mahrer, 1978a, 1978b, 1980, 1983; Mahrer & Gervaize, 1983). Statements by the therapist are thereby understood as saying, "I shall fulfill this role, you are to fulfill that role, and we shall have this relationship with one another." While the traditional perspective looks at therapist statements as, for example, reflecting the patient's inner uncertainty or interpreting the patient's ambivalence, this other perspective looks at the same words and describes something different, e.g., the therapist is defining a role of being the knowledgeable authority, defining the patient as a mixed up and confused little child, and defining their relationship as one in which the patient is to trust and depend upon the knowledgeable authority. Therapist statements lend themselves nicely to understanding as means of instrumenting therapist-patient role relationships.

Therapist statements as linguistic-communication acts. A second convergent background looks at therapist statements from the perspective of psycholinguistics. What the therapist says is seen as an instance of communication, a linguistic act, as a mere "speech act" (Shapiro, 1979).

Looked at from this perspective, many of the classes of linguistic speech acts emitted by the therapist lead rather directly to what I mean by therapist statements as prescriptions-for-change. For example, Labov (1972) and Labov and Fanshel (1977) define one class of (therapist) statements as "requests for action." The therapist's words request or direct that the patient is to do this or that, behave in this or that way, carry out this or that behavior. The requested action may include providing information, giving confirmation, offering attention, and so on (cf. Mahrer, Edwards, Durak, & Sterner, in press). This class of therapist statements can exert a significant impact upon the patient; " . . . our examination of requests for action and information in actual discourse shows that their interactive significance goes far beyond the communicative functions we have discussed so far. We find that most of these requests are employed to accomplish other purposes which strongly affect the social and emotional relations of the person" (Labov & Fanshel, 1977, p. 93).

In the same family as "requests for action" is what Searle calls "directives": "The illocutionary point of these consists in the fact that they are attempts . . . by the speaker to get the hearer to do something. They may be very modest 'attempts' as when I invite you to do it or suggest that you do it, or they may be very fierce attempts as when I insist that you do it" (1976, p. 11). Similarly, Claiborn (1982) sees therapeutic communications as the means whereby one person forces the other into particular kinds of interactive relationships: "Each person's communications are his or her attempts to control the actions of the other. . . . Each person strives to entice the other to act in ways that will render the interaction to the person's purposes" (p.167). Whether called requests for action, directives, or, as Watzlawick (1978) terms them, "injunctive language forms" or "behavioral prescriptions," the commonality lies in communications as means of prescribing what the other person is to do.

Lennard and Bernstein (1960) studied the dyadic communication between therapists and patients, and were impressed with the extent to which therapist statements determine the actual content of what the patient says: "Clearly what the therapist says or does not say will have an influence upon what the patient is likely to say or not to say. So long as the patient is responsive, verbal stimuli from the therapist are among the factors that determine what he will talk about" (p. 133). For example, Lennard and Bernstein noted the degree to which therapist statements directed patients' attention to feelings and emotions, and constituted invitations or directives for patients to respond by talking about feelings and emotions. It is as if therapist statements constituted a progressively accumulating prescription for patients to talk about their feelings and emotions:

> . . . as therapy proceeded, the therapists increased the frequency with which their propositions inquired into and solicited patient verbalization about feelings, and also . . . our patients began to verbalize more voluminously about feelings . . . a therapist explicitly teaches his patient to put his feelings into words while implicitly moving his patient in this direction by making emotion the target of his own references. As the therapist increases his interest and inquiry into feelings, thus documenting their validity for the patient, the patient increases his own discussion on them. (Lennard & Bernstein, 1960, pp. 70, 71)

This implicit drawing of patients' attention to particular topics is also found in what Pentony (1981) refers to as "meta-communications," viz., higher order communications which comment upon lower order communications and serve, as Lennard and Bernstein also observed, to focus the patient's attention and verbal behavior.

From a linguistic-communicative perspective, other therapist statements fall into a class characterized by the putting forward of the truth of a belief or observation; it may assert the truth of that to which it refers, it may put it forward as an hypothesis, or it may gently point in the general direction of a discoverable truth. Searle (1976) names this class "representatives," and we may borrow from this class in providing an alternate way of making sense of some therapist statements which are generally termed "interpretations" and related kinds of therapist statements (Mahrer, Durak, Lawson & Nifakis, in press).

When we look at therapist statements from this perspective, when we allow these statements to disclose themselves as, for example, requests for how the patient is to behave and act, or invitations for the patient to accept the truth in the therapist's statement, then a new picture emerges of the therapist's statements. It begins to look as if the therapist is expressing a distinct way that the patient is to be, to become, to behave. "When the technique of the therapist is exposed in detail, the analysis produces the illusion that the therapist is manipulating the patient in a crude and obvious way. This is an inevitable product of the analytical study of spontaneous interaction" (Labov & Fanshel, 1977, p. 347). This "illusion" is at least as sound as other "illusions" of how therapist statements may be described.

In keeping with the linguistic-communicative perspective on therapist statements, it is sensible to consider the kinds of tasks which are assigned by the words of the therapist. Very close to "how the patient is to be and become" is "what task the patient is to carry out." The researcher sees what the tasks are by studying the therapist's statements, a method termed "task analysis" and described by Greenberg (1975, 1979, 1984) and by Rice and Greenberg (1974, 1984). Our method grows directly out of Greenberg and Rice's task analysis method.

Therapist statements as acts of intention. We are looking at therapist statements to see if they contain prescriptions or pictures or demands for how the patient is to be or become. A related recent development in psychotherapy process research is to look at therapist statements to see what the therapist is intending to accomplish. This tells us little about how the patient is to be or become, so it is not a direct root for our method. It is, instead, an indirect root in several ways. For one, it is a departure from seeing therapist statements as methods, techniques and praxis. Instead of considering what the therapist is doing and saying in terms of reflection, interpretation, observing splits, and so on, it provides a new way of getting meaning from therapist statements in terms of something that the therapist intends, wants to accomplish, an explanation and rationale for why the therapist did that particular thing. Instead of considering what the therapist is doing and saying in terms of larger aims and goals such as providing support, offering facilitating conditions, building a relationship, it isolates very particular statements and inquires into the goals, intentions, and hoped-for aims linked to that particular statement. Accordingly, it demonstrates that therapist statements can be understood as something more than or different from mere methods, techniques or praxis.

It also is an indirect root in a second way. It looks at therapist statements in terms of hoped-for, intended, reasonably expected consequences. The difference from our method is that we look for the consequences in regard to how the patient is to be or become, while the researchers who look at therapist statements as acts of intention focus their attention on what the therapist is intending to do.

For example, Elliott and Feinstein (1978) proposed the following set of intentions intrinsic in therapist statements: to gather information, to communicate understanding, to explain, advise, guide, reassure, disagree, share the therapist's "self," and "other." Building on this beginning, Hill and O'Grady (in press) developed and used a list comprised of the following therapist intentions: set limits, get information, give information, provide support, focus discussion, clarify, provide hope, promote catharsis, identify cognitions, identify behaviors, promote self-control, identify-intensify-accept feelings, promote insight, promote change, reinforce change, overcome resistance, challenge, enhance working relationship, protect-relieve-defend therapist needs.

It is not a great step from therapist statements as intentions to reassure or promote self-control to therapist intentions for the patient to be, behave, or become some particular way. As such this background also converges upon framing therapist statements as prescriptions for patient change.

Training the patient to fulfill the role of patient. A fourth converging background consists of explicit training programs and research on showing patients how to fulfill the role of (good) patients. The idea is that if patients are explicitly trained to be good patients, therapy would be more efficient and more successful. These training programs have been carried out prior to therapy and in the early phases of therapy, in everything from short orientations to explicit skill-training programs. In examining the communication aspects of therapist statements, Lennard and Bernstein (1960) were struck with how much of the early phases of therapy were devoted to prescribing the kind of role the patient is to fulfill; " . . . we became aware of psychotherapy as a prototypic role learning situation. It is a situation in which the patient learns the 'learning of roles'" (p. 196).

Modalities include films, interviews, demonstrations, and other methods of showing/training patients how to be and behave as patients. Such training programs have been called role preparation, role induction, vicarious pre-therapy training, productive client behavior training, and other appropriate terms. Among the prominent methods and research are those of Hoehn-Saric, Frank, Imber, Nash, Stone, and Battle (1964), Jacobs, Charles, Jacobs, Weinstein, and Mann (1972), Sloane, Cristol, Pepernik, and Staples (1970), Strupp and Bloxom (1973), Schonfield, Stone, Hoehn-Saric, Imber, and Pande (1969), Truax and Carkhuff (1965), Truax and Wargo (1969), and Warren and Rice (1972).

Such training programs carry a significant component of prescribing how the patient is to be, to behave, to become. They are explicit role prescriptions which define the kind of person the patient is to be and become.

These background themes may be taken as converging on a way of understanding therapist statements as prescriptions-for-change. If therapist statements are reasonably rich in providing such data, then perhaps it is possible for clinical researchers to use these prescriptions-for-change as a useful meaning of psychotherapeutic change, and to study psychotherapeutic change by examining patient changes in the light of an organized picture of how the patient is to be, to behave, and to become.

*Researchability of Conceptualizing Therapist
Statements as Prescriptions-for-Change*

The idea of measuring the individualized patient's potential directions for change (chapter 2) is not new. Nor is the idea of looking for indices of psychotherapeutic movement in the session itself (chapter 3). But some discussion is called for in regard to the researchability of this present method, for it is relatively novel.

Some appealing features of this method. There are some singular features of this method. Whether they are appealing or not depends upon the researcher.

1) The data are objective, concretely present, plentiful. Virtually every therapist statement is loaded with prescriptions of what the patient is to do, how the patient is to be, the kind of person the patient is to become. The data stand right here in front of us. Persons who are not psychotherapy researchers can look at a therapist statement and see what the patient is to do and how the patient is to be and become. There is no mysterious process of clinical intuition. One need not be a psychodiagnostician or an expert in psychotherapy. The way the patient is to be is not extracted from a battery of tests. Even someone who knows little or nothing about psychotherapy research can look at a given therapist statement and conclude that the patient is to do this or that, to be this way or that way. There is something appealing in having the data right here in front of you.

2) The data are a faithful manifestation of how the therapist wants the patient to be and to become. Psychotherapy has taught us that there is often quite a difference between a person's actual manifest behavior as compared to what the person says about his behavior, his wishes and wants. In the same way, we can go directly to the therapist's statements and notice that the therapist is directing-forcing-guiding-wanting-telling the patient to get a job, show his jealousy more openly, be aware of his clenching fist, be the kind of person who can express caring consideration. By looking at the therapist's actual statements, we can get a faithful picture of how the therapist wants the patient to become. We see it directly. Aside from the therapist's theories and clinical intentionalities, notions of how the patient is to be are manifested faithfully in the actual statements themselves.

I believe that this is a more faithful portrayal of how the therapist wants the patient to be and to become than the typical methods of asking the therapist to describe how the patient is to be and become. In many research methods, the therapist is to give some impressions or write a report about or answer a questionnaire about the way the patient is to become. Or, the researcher must get some indication about the theoretical approach espoused by the therapist, and then find some way of reasoning from that theoretical approach to some ways the patient is to be. All of this is given directly in the therapist's actual statements.

I contend that there may be considerable differences between the ways the therapist wants the patient to be and to become as manifestly indicated in the therapist's actual statements and, in contrast, what the therapist may say are the welcomed or desirable directions of change. Indeed, the proof or disproof of what the therapist may say that she wants or intends is contained in the actual statements she makes in the session itself. All in all, the data of the actual therapist statements are a faithful manifestation of how the therapist really wants the patient to be.

3) The therapist's statements alone provide a good picture of what this therapist sees this particular patient as becoming, the directions of change, how this particular patient is to be. The first proposed way of measuring psychotherapeutic change (directions of potential change for the individualized patient) called for the clinician-researcher to know something about the patient's personality structure, and then to use a set of principles to predict what this particular patient can become. This is different from the present method. In the present method, we can get a picture of how this very particular person is to be, the directions of change, by studying the therapist's statements themselves. Here is another means of arriving at a highly specific picture of what this particular patient is to become.

4) How the patient is to be and become are neatly measureable. These are not vague predictions softly wafted in the air. Each statement gives rise to a picture which is reasonably objective and measureable. Most clinical researchers can look at the behavior of a patient and determine whether or not the patient is looking at her grandmother or not, and whether the patient is or is not saying, "I love you, Gramma," or words to that effect. Compare this with the ordinary attempts to frame some sort of picture of how the patient is to be. How do we measure with any real assurance whether the patient has a stronger ego, has a good support system, has better sexual relations? One of the appealing features of this method is that the clinical researcher has something specific, objective, and measureable to look for in seeing whether there have been any changes in the patient.

5) This method can identify modifications in the picture of how the patient is to be and become, modifications which occur over the sessions. In the first few sessions, the therapist may operate on the basis of one picture of how the patient is to be. Soon, some of this picture may be let go, and a somewhat modified picture emerges of how the patient is to be and become. Our method is sensitive to the changing picture of how the patient is to become as this picture grows and modifies over the course of the sessions.

In contrast, most clinical researchers use a paradigm where the important picture of how the patient is to be and to become is the pre-treatment one; then the treatment is applied, and the researcher sees if the pre-treatment problem is resolved (Campbell & Stanley, 1963; Dahlstrom, 1975; Fiske et al., 1970). Research designs, plain and fancy, and statistical procedures, simple and complex, begin with ways of comparing pre-and post-treatment measures. This standard paradigm holds whether the design is factorial (Paul, 1969) or quasi-experimental (Campbell, 1963; Campbell & Stanley, 1963). It holds whether we rely on analysis of covariance (Lord, 1963) or correlational methods (Bereiter, 1963; DuBois & Manning, 1961; Tucker, Damarin & Messick, 1966). This standard paradigm is essentially unable to accept changes in the picture of how the patient is to be and to become, changes of greater specificity in precisely how the patient is to be some way, changes in the very directions of how the patient is to be and to become, changes which occur in phases so that the accomplishing of one opens the way for a subsequent new way of being and becoming. All of these fall outside the clunky pre-post treatment paradigm of standard research.

All in all, I regard these as appealing features, especially in the light of the ordinary alternatives. I commend this method as eminently researchable.

Why psychotherapy researchers may have ignored looking at therapist statements in this way. There are two main reasons. One is that psychotherapy researchers have plenty of places to look for how patients are to be and to become, and plenty of measures of psychotherapeutic change. Why bother with a whole new place to look? Virtually every therapeutic approach tells us how patients are to be and to become. If we want to know about the meaning of psychotherapeutic change, just ask psychoanalytic theory or the theory of rational-emotive therapy or client-centered theory or the theory of any other approach. Virtually every psychotherapy measure is filled with notions of what patients are to be and to become. They are built into our tests and assessment devices, our psychometry and our scales. There is essentially no need to look at therapist statements.

The second reason is that psychotherapy researchers almost exclusively operate out of a perspective in which therapist statements are the process which leads to the outcome. Therapist statements are things that therapists do to bring about change; they are interventions, they are instrumental means for effecting change, they are factors and variables which constitute the therapy. The category systems for therapist verbal behaviors cast therapist statements into such classes as reflections, interpretations, confrontations, self-disclosures, restatements, and similar classes. These are the process things therapists do, the interventions, the therapist variables. There is little room for another perspective in which therapist statements may also be regarded as containing and expressing prescriptions-for-change. Accordingly, it seems understandable that psychotherapy researchers have largely overlooked therapist statements as a resource for arriving at a picture of how patients are to be and to become.

The Method

There are two steps in the method.

Generating the dimensions along which the patient is to change. The data consist of a verbatim transcript of each session. Consider that a therapist statement may be understood as all the words spoken by the therapist, preceded and followed by the words of the patient. Looking at each therapist statement independently, the clinical researcher answers the following question: On the basis of this statement, what is the patient to do now, how is the patient to be, what sort of person is the patient to be, how is the patient to change? All the researcher studies is that particular therapist statement, nothing more. So the contents of that therapist statement define the boundaries of how the researcher answers the question.

If the therapist says, "Say it louder, with more feeling in your voice," then what is the patient to do now, how is the patient to be, what sort of person is the patient to be, how is the patient to change? One answer is that the patient is to say particular words louder, with more feeling in his voice; the patient is to be the sort of person who is able to speak with feeling. While this raises all sorts of questions about what theoretical perspective the judges are to use, how specific and how general should the answers be, and so on, the method allows the judges to arrive at some answers to the above questions when looking at a given therapist statement.

Most therapist statements will enable answers to these questions. In other words, most therapist statements will contain some picture of how the patient is to be, become, change. While some therapist statements will be inert, will not give rise to answers to these questions, the judges are to go through each therapist statement, and to frame out an answer to these questions for each therapist statement which enables the judges to do so.

A few examples illustrate therapist statements as prescriptions for change, as exerting a demand for the patient to be and behave in explicit ways.

T: So look at him, your brother, just look right at him, and say, "You piss me off!" — and say it like you mean it!

The patient is to be the kind of person who can look directly at his brother and say, with genuine meaning, "You piss me off!" At a slightly more general level, the patient is to be the kind of person who can express anger and annoyance directly to significant figures.

T: What do you think you do to provoke her into these rages?

The patient is to be the kind of person who is aware of and who can identify his own behaviors which provoke others, specifically his wife, into rages.

T: How do you feel now? What's it like for you when you get silent like this?

The patient is to be the kind of person who can identify and describe feelings, e.g., the feelings which are present when the patient is silent, and to talk about feelings rather than remain silent.

T: Your hand is clenched, like a fist. Every time you talk about the way your son talks back to you. I wonder what that means.

The patient is to be the kind of person who is aware of the meaning of clenching her fist, and who can connect her clenched fist with her feelings about her son talking back to her.

T: You're saying sentences to yourself that keep you from making sexual contact with women. Now, what sentences are you saying to yourself?

The patient is to be the kind of person who can verbalize the sentences he is saying to himself to keep from making sexual contact with women, and to be the kind of person who can verbalize more generally the sentences he says to himself.

T: I wonder whether we could get into the feeling a bit more. As if you were with him now, the sort of feeling you might have.

The patient is to be the sort of person who can describe the personal feelings she has in regard to significant others.

At first, only a selected few therapist statements seem to give rise to prescriptions for change. Once the researcher settles into this perspective, however, it is as if a whole new facet is disclosed of therapist statements. It appears that most therapist statements exert respectable demands for patients to do defined things, be particular ways, become identified sorts of persons, change along explicit dimensions. It then becomes a matter of seeing how specific or general the prescribed changes are to be framed, and to locate filler statements, i.e., therapist statements which have little or no yield as prescriptions for change.

After going through a session or a number of sessions, the researcher will have a whole list of prescriptions for change. The problem is how to organize all of these prescriptions for change into sets or classes or a manageable number of clusters. A method has yet to be worked out, one which balances rigor with clinical good sense. Experience seems to indicate that a manageable work unit is a session, rather than a whole series of sessions, and that the task is not all that difficult when a clinician-researcher works with a single session. My own experience suggests that in a single session, prescriptions for change seem to fall into two to five clusters. Nevertheless, careful rules and guidelines remain to be worked out for a task which seems to be eminently do-able.

As an illustration, here is a method I have used to organize prescriptions-for-change into clusters. I was one of six judges who studied a session of 80 therapist statements. Of these, we emerged with 50 prescriptions-for-change. How could we organize these into clusters? Each judge was asked to organize the 50 prescriptions-for-change into anywhere from two to five clusters, whatever number seemed to make best sense. Four of the six judges emerged with four clusters, and there was remarkable agreement on the specific therapist statements comprising each cluster. Two of the judges had five clusters. An inspection of our differences revealed that these two judges had divided one more general cluster into two somewhat more specific clusters. As a group, we agreed that either the four or five clusters made both clinical and research sense, and that it was a matter of group decision whether we would choose four or five. What was impressive was the agreement in clusterings, including the therapist statements which comprised each of the clusters. Whatever method is followed, it seems to be a reasonably rigorous task to organize the prescriptions into a small number of clusters.

Once the clinician-researcher organizes the prescriptions for change into clusters, the net result is a small number of dimensions for change. It provides an answer to the question: On the basis of the therapist's own statements, how is this patient to be, to behave, to become? Along what dimensions is the patient to change? For example, one dimension may be framed as follows: The patient is to be and to become the sort of person who can openly and directly express aggressive feelings toward significant persons in his world. Mainly, this includes being able to tell significant figures such as his brother, a coworker, and his neighbor that he is angry, that he's had enough, that he's not going to take any more abuse from that other person. Another dimension may be framed as follows: The patient is to be and to become the sort of person who is aware of and in touch with certain bodily-felt sensations. These include a "clutching-up" sensation of tension in the stomach, a sensation of tightness across the upper chest, and a sense of muscular constriction in the throat.

Some dimensions of change may be broader and some narrower. Some may be more behavioral and some more descriptive of personality. Yet the method yields a set of dimensions of how this particular patient is to be or become. This is the first step in the method. It culminates in a set of dimensions of change, together with the therapist statements from which the particular dimensions were generated.

Assessing the degree to which the patient changes along the prescribed dimensions. The second step is the assessment of the degree to which the patient changes along the prescribed dimensions. For example, how does the researcher assess the degree to which the patient shows evidence of being a person who can openly and directly express aggressive feelings toward significant persons in his world? One option is for the researcher to look outside therapy for indications that the patient is more openly and directly expressing aggressive feelings toward significant persons in his world. This is an option, and some researchers may of course elect to follow this option, but it is not the option I would favor. Reasons for declining this option are discussed in chapter 5.

My preference is to use the data of the actual therapy session. Where the therapist statements contain the prescriptions-for-change, the patient statements contain the data for assessing the degree to which the patient changes along the prescribed dimensions. Given the prescribed dimensions for change, the patient statements are apt data for measurement.

For example, suppose that one dimension of prescribed change consisted of open and direct expression of aggressive feelings. From the therapist statements which comprised this prescription, a fuller description may be framed, e.g., telling significant others to go to hell, saying "you sonovabitch!" to key figures, bawling out critical figures with toughness, raising his voice in anger, responding to aggressive provocations by loud and angry growling. Suppose another dimension of prescribed change involved self-reflectiveness. Again, from the therapist statements comprising this prescription, the fuller description may be as follows: The patient is to be able to comment on himself, react and respond to what he just said and did, applaud how he just was, be critical of what he just said and did, be pleased and bothered with his behavior. He is to step aside from himself and have responses and reactions to himself and his behavior.

Given these two dimensions of change, the researcher may assess the patient's statements and behaviors in the session(s) and scale the degree to which they represent or manifest these dimensions. On this basis, judges are able to assess the degree to which the patient changes along each of the prescribed dimensions (cf. Mahrer, Clark, Comeau, & Brunette, in press). Once the dimensions of prescribed change are organized and described, patient statements and behaviors enable the researcher to assess these changes as they occur throughout the session(s).

As an illustration, consider a design in which a group of judges are given a paragraph or so of description of a given dimension of change, together with a series of patient statements. These patient statements may either be immediately consequent to the relevant therapist statement, or they may be taken from all of the patient statements in the session(s), regardless of the antecedent therapist statement. Consider also that the patient statements are randomized so that the judges have little or no idea where they came from in the session(s). In any case, a decision has to be made as to whether or not the judges are also to be given the antecedent therapist statement for, in many instances, the antecedent therapist statement is helpful in order to make sense of the patient statement.

Given the description of the dimension for change, judges are to assess the degree to which the patient statement exemplifies, manifests, and expresses that dimension of change. For example, judges may be asked to assess whether the patient statement indicates that the patient is being the prescribed kind of person (a) to a strong degree, (b) to a moderate degree, or (c) not at all, e.g., the patient may be described as disregarding, avoiding, refusing, disagreeing, questioning, or objecting to the prescribed change.

Consider the therapist statement: "So look at him, your brother, just look right at him, and say, 'You piss me off!' — and say it like you mean it!" Suppose the dimension of change is that of being the kind of person who can express aggression, anger, frustration, and annoyance easily and directly to key other figures. The immediately consequent patient statements represent increasing degrees of being, expressing, manifesting this dimension of change:

Pt: (In a dull, flat tone of voice) My mother called me last night. She wants me to come home this weekend.

Pt: (After a pause) I don't see what good that would do.

Pt: (With mild feeling) I really don't like a lot of things he does. He's always making trouble for me.

Pt: (Animatedly) You bastard!! You piss me off! I'd like to knock your damned head off!! LOOK AT ME, YOU BASTARD!!

By unscrambling the patient statements, and by placing them in sequence across the session(s), it is thereby possible to assess the degree to which the patient changes along the prescribed dimensions. Here then is a method for generating and assessing dimensions of change, derived from actual therapist statements and using actual patient statements in the actual therapeutic sessions.

An illustration. The present illustration is taken from a series of three sessions conducted by Dr. Joen Fagan and published verbatim (Fagan, 1974). In the initial session, the patient explains that she is bothered by feelings of loneliness and depression. Dr. Fagan quickly moves to the patient's feelings as a child, feelings in relationship to her grandfather who died during the patient's childhood. This session was selected because it was used in a study (Mahrer, Clark, Comeau & Brunette, in press) of therapist statements as prescriptions for change, and because a set of judges had found considerable agreement in framing the prescriptions for change in the therapist's statements. While the prescription for change will be given for each therapist statement, the reader may also judge the degree to which the subsequent patient statement indicates that the patient is carrying out the prescription, i.e., doing what the therapist requests, fulfilling the prescription, being the way the statement is inviting the patient to be or become. The excerpt begins with the therapist's 29th statement:

T: Would you be willing to talk to him now? OK. Would you put him over there and describe him. (*The patient is to be a person who can describe significant figures in her life.*)

P: Hm. He's got on an old dingy sort of turned-up overalls. Lee overalls. And a blue work shirt. And his shoes are old and muddy. One of them is a little torn and he can pick it up with his toe and stick his toe out and tease us with it. And he's pretty much bald-headed except for a little thing of hair around here. And he wears wire rims and, uh, he's got a square chin, something like mine, only square. He's an old man. When he works he's always in the field. He's got on a safari hat when he works, and when he don't work he's sitting on the sofa, like he's doing now. And either watching TV or just sitting on the sofa, like he's doing now. And either watching TV or just sitting there, not saying much. Um, sometimes, he has a little can of beer, not very often, just once or twice. And he just sits here, and rests.

T: As you see him, how are you feeling towards him? (*The patient is to be a person who can identify and describe her feelings toward significant figures in her life.*)

P: I miss him, actually.

T: Would you say that to him now? (*The patient is to be a person who expresses her feelings directly to the significant other figure.*)

P: I miss you.

T: Go ahead and say some more about missing him and about what he meant to you. (*The patient is to be a person who communicates openly and directly to the significant other figure deeply felt and personal feelings for that figure, for example, feelings of missing the other, and how much the other figure meant to the patient.*)

P: I miss sitting on your lap. (P. begins crying heavily.) And sitting out on the well with you, and you used to talk to Minnie Pearl, that was one of the chickens, she was crippled. Um, I don't know . . . just sitting in the rocking chair, just, just following you around really, that's really about all I ever did, but I miss that.

T: So, there was a lot of warmth, ah, you're appreciating him as you watch him—what you got from him. Would you say to him what watching him and feeling that way meant to you? Tell him that. (*The patient is to be a person who communicates deeply felt personal feelings and meanings for the other figure directly to that other figure, for example, feelings of warmth and heartfelt appreciation.*)

P: Well, I felt like I had me a buddy. Somebody that wanted me around, really, which he did. He did. I was his favorite grandchild.

T: Somebody that really likes you. (*This statement has a low yield of prescription-for-change. It is a soft invitation for the patient to respond to it as a statement to be agreed with.*)

P: Yeah. And I always preferred men to women, somehow. I don't know. Now I feel more comfortable around women as such, but I still try to be around men.

T: I hear you, almost as if you're trying to back off from your feeling right now? (*The patient is to be a person who values the therapist as someone who knows her well, who knows how she is really being and behaving.*)

P: Yeah, I guess I am.

T: I think what you had going was mighty important and I'd like to see you get to it a little bit more. . . . Are you saying to him, "I don't want to say good-bye to you?" (*The patient is to be a person who agrees that the therapist has accurate understanding about what the patient is "really" feeling and meaning.*)

P: Yeah, I reckon.

T: Would you say that and see what happens? (*The patient is to be a person who says the words the therapist tells the patient to say, e.g., words signifying deeply personal feelings about a significant figure.*)

P: I don't want to say good-bye to you.

T: Would you tell him what you would like to do, what you got from him? (*The patient is to be a person who verbalizes what the therapist tells the patient to say, specifically to tell a significant figure what the patient would like to do and what the patient got from the significant figure.*)

P: I'm trying to figure, well, I've got the memory, I guess that's not good enough, though, or I wouldn't be doing this.

Here is an illustration of how the therapist's statements may be taken as prescriptions for what the patient is to do, how the patient is to be and become. It also is an illustration of one way to assess the degree to which the patient fulfills the prescriptions-for-change. In the actual procedure, judges would use the pool of prescriptions-for-change to organize a small set of dimensions along which the patient is to change. With this set of dimensions, judges would then assess either subsequent patient statements or the larger body of patient statements to assess the degree to which the patient carries out or fulfills or manifests the dimensions of prescribed changes. We now turn to some of the limitations and problems in the method.

Some Limitations and Problems in the Method

In the actual use of the method, a number of limitations and problems are underscored. Here are a few of the major ones.

Staying close to the therapist's statement versus expanding into generalizations. Given a particular therapist statement, the judge may stay rather close to the data in describing how the patient is to be or become. On the other hand, the judge may expand into increasingly more general levels of description. For example, if the therapist says, "Listen to your tone of voice as you say that. How does it sound to you?", the judge may stay rather close to the data. Accordingly, the description of how the patient is to be may be framed along the following lines: "The patient is to be aware of and to describe the meaning of his tone of voice." On the other hand, the judge may expand into larger and larger generalizations, ending up with a statement along lines such as the following: "The patient is to be aware of his behavior." On this issue, I lean toward staying reasonably close to the data of the therapist's statement.

Simple description versus theoretical language. Each judge may be expected to approach the task from his or her own theoretical perspective. Looking at the same therapist statement, and attempting to frame a description of how the patient is to be and to become may be expected to lead to quite different answers from an experiential perspective, a rational-emotive perspective, a Jungian perspective, a classical Freudian perspective, and so on. What is more, the temptation is to use jargon and vocabulary from whatever theoretical languages are used. One solution is to cluster judges using similar theoretical approaches and languages. I prefer a solution in which the emphasis is upon simple description, staying rather close to the actual data of the therapist statement, and emphasizing the use of language that is relatively jargon-free. Nevertheless, this is a problem.

Identifying high-yield versus low-yield therapist statements. Many therapist statements may be understood as containing prescriptions for change, ways the patient is to be and to become. These are high-yield therapist statements. However, other therapist statements may be identified as containing little or no prescriptions for change. Here are some examples:

T: Uh-huh.
T: Your brother? You mean your older brother?
T: Yeah, I could be wrong about that.
T: I think I would like to see you twice a week.

The problem is that if one is sufficiently single-minded, practically every therapist statement can be used to squeeze out some hint as to how the patient is to be and to become. The judge can always figure out some reason why the therapist might have said that statement, some reason which has a whisper of a hint as to how the patient might perhaps become. Or the judge can easily frame a delicate inference about how the patient is to be even when the therapist is silent or gives the simplest of acknowledgments. Every statement by the therapist can be a delicate message from which hints may be extracted about how the patient might become. The identifying of high-yield and low-yield therapist statements is a problem which calls for reasonable judgment. I favor a rather strict division between high-yield and low-yield therapist statements.

Interpretive statements as prescriptions-for-change. If we look upon therapist statements as prescriptions-for-change, there is a large group of therapist statements which constitutes a special problem. In general, this is the large group of interpretive statements. It includes the backbone of many therapies, i.e., interpretations. This refers to statements in which the therapist tells or points toward or explains or describes to the patient what the patient is like. The therapist indicates themes, connections, observations, patterns, causality, personality descriptions. Cutting across many therapeutic vocabularies, these interpretive statements include everything from direct telling of the patient what he is like to reflections which dip somewhat below the patient's conscious awareness. The statement may be gently guiding or authoritatively directive, introducing new material or providing selective summaries of what the patient has already indicated.

The problem is that such therapist statements offer at least three options when they are looked at in terms of providing prescriptions-for-change. One option is that the patient is to be or become the way which is implied in the contents of the interpretive statement. If the therapist says, "I wonder why you must control your daughter so carefully," one prescription-for-change may be that the patient is to move in the direction of being less controlling of her daughter. If the therapist says, "Every time you feel angry but don't say anything, you seem to have a headache," an implied way the patient is to become is that of saying something when she is angry, and no longer having headaches. The actual words and contents of many interpretive statements can be used to build a picture of how the patient is to become. This is one option.

A second option is that the patient should be or become a person who adopts the therapist's frame of reference or way of making sense of the patient and the patient's world. Essentially, the patient is to take on the therapist's mode of insight or understanding or way of interpreting oneself and one's world. Accordingly, the patient is to become a person who can have insight into or demonstrate understanding of why she must control her daughter or why she has headaches or understanding what happens when she feels anger but does not express it.

I would like to introduce a third option which emerges when the therapist offers interpretive statements in the light of prescribed ways the patient is to be. Interpretive statements may be seen as invitations for the patient to value the worth of the therapist and the therapist's statements. That is, the patient is invited to give serious consideration to the authoritative significance of the therapist and the therapist's statements, to weigh and respect and reflect upon the meaningfulness, wisdom, and truth in what the therapist says. The patient is to regard the therapist as an authority, as someone with special knowledge and understanding, whose statements bear the stamp of significance and worth. The patient is to validate the worth of the therapist and the therapist's statements.

Such a conceptualization of therapists' interpretive activity grows out of a framing of psychotherapy as the mutual construction of role relationships between therapist and patient (Mahrer, 1978a, 1978b, 1983; Mahrer & Gervaize, 1983). With regard to interpretation, this kind of statement is understood as explicitly instrumental in building a role relationship in which patients validate and enhance the therapists' own sense of self-esteem and self-worth, their sense of being persons whose statements are meaningful and significant, especially with patients for whom talking about themselves is a highly valued enterprise, and who are ready to relate to therapists in that manner. This conceptualization of therapists' interpretive activity was supported in research which examined patients' statements antecedent to and following therapists' interpretations (Mahrer, Clark, Comeau, & Brunette, in press; Mahrer, Durak, Lawson & Nifakis, in press.)

If the therapist says, "I wonder why you must control your daughter so carefully," or "Every time you feel angry but don't say anything, you seem to have a headache," there are at least three different perspectives on the prescriptions-for-change. One is that the patient is to be less controlling of her daughter, or the patient is to be more expressive of angry feelings, and to have fewer headaches. The second is that the patient is to become a person who has insight and understanding of why she must control her daughter, or why she has headaches, or what happens when she feels anger but does not express it. The preferred third option is that the patient is to value the worth of the therapist whose statements are meaningful, significant, helpfully authoritative, wise. The patient is to show that she respects the therapist and takes those statements seriously. These are three different meanings of interpretive statements in the light of prescriptions-for-change. Which one or ones to use is a problem. I favor the third option.

Conclusions

There is a background, both from theory and research, for looking at therapist statements as prescriptions for how the patient is to be, behave, and become. There are also eminently researchable features of this method, both in terms of generating the dimensions along which the patient is to change, and also in terms of assessing the degree to which the patient changes along these prescribed dimensions. While there are some limitations and problems, this method is proposed as a third meaning and method of measuring psychotherapeutic change for virtually all patients in virtually all therapies.

5

The In-therapy
Change Paradigm

Chapters 2–4 proposed three relatively new meanings of psychotherapeutic change. The next question is this: What are the considerations in deciding whether to measure these three kinds of psychotherapeutic change within the context of psychotherapy itself or within the context of the patient's extra-therapy world? The extra-therapy world generally refers to tests, interviews, assessments, measurements taken outside the actual therapy sessions, typically after therapy is over. The thesis of this chapter is that the three proposed meanings of psychotherapeutic change call for the measurement of in-therapy change. Another way of framing this thesis is that our alternative three meanings of psychotherapeutic change introduce the "in-therapy change paradigm" as an alternative to the traditional "process-outcome paradigm."

What Is the Real Payoff in Psychotherapy? The
Process-Outcome Paradigm

Most psychotherapy research comes from the perspective that what occurs in psychotherapy is the process which leads to the extra-therapy outcome. What happens in the session is the means which lead to the outcome-end, the instrument which results in the extra-therapy outcome, the treatment which hopefully results in the post-treatment change, the process which leads to the outcome.

If this chapter had been completed a few months later, or if *Patterns of Change* by Laura N. Rice and Leslie S. Greenberg had been available a little sooner, this chapter would have linked its central thesis to much of that book. I commend their 1984 book to readers interested in what I term the "in-therapy change paradigm."

In this paradigm, the real payoff occurs outside of the therapy session. Genuine changes, the goals of therapy, refer to how the patient is in the real life outside therapy. This is where to look for the payoff of psychotherapy, so that one would not expect to look for these kinds of changes in therapy itself. It would be rare indeed if such changes were to occur in the session. Besides, even if it happened to occur in the session, the only significant place for outcomes to occur is in the patient's extra-therapy world. What good would a therapy be if the patient showed changes only in the session itself and not where it really pays off, i.e., in the patient's actual extra-therapy world?

In-therapy patient changes as process. If the patient evidences a change in therapy, the change is a *process* event. It is not the outcome, for outcomes are really extra-therapy events. In-therapy patient changes may be considered welcomed and desirable because they indicate that therapy is moving along, that the process of therapy is occurring. For example, if the patient shows insight, that is good. It indicates progress, movement, process. But insight is not the real payoff; extra-therapy outcomes are the payoff.

In some psychotherapies, the therapist is to help the patient resolve inner conflicts, and the therapist is to accomplish this mainly through interpretations. If this is done well, there should occur, in the session, a resolution of unconscious conflicts. "Resolution of unconscious conflicts" is a significant in-therapy patient change, but it is not an outcome. Instead, the outcome of "resolution of unconscious conflicts" is a payoff change in the patient's extra-therapy life style, symptoms, and character traits: " . . . to the extent that a resolution of unconscious conflicts occurs via the expressive-interpretive aspects of therapy, there is at least proportional change in symptoms, character traits, and life style" (Wallerstein, 1968, p. 595). Changes which occur in therapy are process changes. They are of a different order than the genuine outcomes which occur outside of therapy.

For researchers who follow the process-outcome paradigm, in-therapy patient change is not the real payoff. It cannot make sense that in-therapy patient changes are sufficient. They must be linked to the real payoff, and that can be nothing other than demonstrated extra-therapy life changes:

Even interview measures that seem to have face validity as indicators of progress may not be related to extra-therapy outcome measures. Thus, a client may communicate more openly, describe himself more positively, and report fewer symptoms during therapy sessions and still not improve in his everyday life. For instance, the client may be able to communicate with a benevolent therapist in the protected situation of the consulting room but may find all other human relationships too threatening for comparable openness. (Murray, 1975, pp. 110–111)

The process-outcome paradigm must grant the real payoff to consist of extra-therapy patient changes. It simply cannot accommodate itself to regard in-therapy patient changes as more than process changes which have to be linked to extra-therapy changes to have genuine worth.

Research questions appropriate for the process-outcome paradigm. If therapy is conceptualized as the process, and if the real payoff consists of what occurs in the patient's actual extra-therapy world, then a straightforward research question has to do with the relationships between these two. Will assertion training (process) help the patient to stand up against his controlling wife (outcome)? Will meditation cure the cancer? Will desensitization therapy enable the lathe operator to stay on the job? Will this brand of therapy make the patient happy in her daily world, stop her from vomiting, get rid of the lower back pain, help her to be comfortable at parties? These are straightforward research questions appropriate for the process-outcome paradigm.

These questions may be framed a little more carefully. Keeping in mind that the therapy may be different when administered by different therapists, and that the therapy may work differently with different patients, the questions can be rephrased to take into account these fortunate or unfortunate sources of variability. Today the question is more like this: What therapy approaches are more effective with which types of patients in treating what kinds of problems (e.g., Fiske, 1977; Goldstein, Heller & Sechrest, 1966; Kiesler, 1966, 1971a; Strupp, 1963; Strupp & Bergin, 1969)? This standard way of framing research questions includes the standard meaning of outcome as the good changes in the patient's extra-therapy world.

These are the research questions for which extra-therapy outcome measures are much more appropriate than in-therapy outcome measures. Looked at in another way, using extra-therapy outcome measures is fitting for and rather restricted to a particular group of psychotherapy research questions. Scott (1975, p. 118) spells out the more prominent ones:

> Some common purposes for doing efficacy research are to assess the effects of psychotherapy, to test the relative values of competing therapeutic systems, and to determine what kinds of patients are likely to benefit from what kinds of therapeutic approaches. A major long-range goal of efficacy research is to influence clinical decision-makers who must choose among a range of approaches to treatment, and who must adjust their efforts with particular patients according to the best available information about what a therapeutic effort may reasonably be expected to accomplish. A second long-range goal of efficacy research may be to influence the development of psychotherapeutic systems, and perhaps the process by which the development of particular therapeutic systems is encouraged while others may be discouraged.

For those researchers who are drawn toward such questions, the process-outcome paradigm is fitting; for those researchers who follow the process-outcome paradigm, their research is more or less limited to such questions.

What would the researcher or clinician do if the findings seemed to indicate that the approach was not especially effective, did not work as well as some other approach, did not bring about the kinds of changes which were expected? Suppose the researcher did the study to see if the approach worked, and the findings generally were disappointing. Suppose that the researcher liked a particular way of doing family therapy, did a study to see if it worked, and the findings were unfriendly. What consequences and implications would that have? Would the clinician abandon that approach to family therapy? Would the cognitive family therapist convert to experiential family therapy? I think it would be rare indeed that the cognitive family therapist would look at the findings and conclude that the reasonable next action is to start doing some other kind of family therapy. In general, giving up the approach that didn't seem to be too effective is not a likely consequence.

Would the researcher or clinician conclude that the approach is not especially appropriate with those kinds of patients? This is possible if only because it is less threatening; the clinician need only be more selective with whom the approach is used. The problem is how one goes about identifying "those kinds of patients." I doubt very much if clinicians would readily accept the classification used in the research. If a study pointed toward bioenergetic therapy as more effective than client-centered therapy with "neurotics" or middle-aged patients or moderately depressed patients, I doubt if client-centered therapists would send persons whom they describe like that over to bioenergetic therapists. I would expect that the findings would either have no effect on client-centered therapists or that they might tend to redescribe in a client-centered vocabulary the nature of the clients whom they might not be so disposed toward anyway.

If the findings were disappointing, it would be very difficult to modify the component parts of the approach (Mahrer, 1983). Most such designs do not allow the researcher to point out that this concrete technique seemed to work, that one did not, the third did only under these conditions. The process-outcome paradigm is not set up to answer that question, so such fine tuning cannot be done on the basis of efficacy research. Indeed, fine tuning in therapeutic techniques tends overwhelmingly to occur in ways which have essentially nothing to do with the findings of research on the effectiveness of psychotherapy.

So what is likely to be done on the basis of such research? If the findings seemed to indicate that one particular approach is not so effective, what actions would reasonably ensue? The answer depends upon the reason the research was done in the first place. If the research is supported by a funding agency which gives money to a number of treatment agencies, the findings may provide a basis for how to distribute the money. But suppose the researcher liked a particular approach, and the research was designed to see if the approach was effective, no matter how that question was phrased. Then what? What actions might be taken on the basis of glum and disappointing findings? The main action I would foresee is changing the design, the methodology, and especially the outcome measures. In other words, there is a likely answer to the initial question, i.e., what would the researcher or clinician do if the findings seemed to indicate that the approach was not especially effective. The answer is that the clinician or researcher would look about for a friendlier set of outcome measures. Indeed, one main effect of most of these studies is to identify a package of outcome measures favorable to one's approach. Then the researcher or clinician is more justified to say that my approach is effective on the basis of research(!)

The process-outcome paradigm is inappropriate to study actual therapist operations. Orlinsky and Howard (1978) provided a soundly comprehensive review of studies relating "process" characteristics to extra-therapy outcome. The guiding intent across the review and the studies was to identify what it is about the process of psychotherapy that might be related to good and effective outcomes.

They concluded that good and effective extra-therapy outcomes were related to a positive relational interaction between patient and therapist, to patients talking in a meaningfully concrete way about themselves and their lives, and to therapists talking in a genuinely self-congruent manner about patients' inner experiences and feelings. These are not actual therapeutic operations. They are not specific acts or methods carried out by therapists. Indeed, the process-outcome paradigm is not equipped to identify actual, specific therapist acts or operations (Mahrer, 1983). Research done from this paradigm, and this includes most research relating process to extra-therapy outcomes, can shed little or no light on specific concrete acts or operations which the therapist carries out in therapy.

What such research is designed to uncover are the characteristics of psychotherapy in general. Indeed, the net result of the research on the relationship between process and extra-therapy outcome is to confirm a general definition of most psychotherapies. Accordingly, such research confirms that good and effective extra-therapy outcomes are related to psychotherapies which are characterized by a positive patient-therapist relationship in which patients talk meaningfully about themselves and their lives, and in which therapists talk in a genuine and self-congruent manner about the patients' inner experiences and feelings. These are the definitional characteristics of most therapies.

Research following a process-outcome paradigm can perhaps highlight the overall characteristics of those therapies which are tied to whatever they mean by good and effective extra-therapy outcomes. But such research is inappropriate for the study of actual therapist operations.

Indeed, the conceptual basis of the process-outcome paradigm does not equip it to study therapist operations. The good things that therapists do are not expected to produce immediately consequent significant changes in the in-therapy behavior of the patient. There are few if any significant in-therapy moments which are to be the result of particular therapeutic operations. Instead, that paradigm paints a picture of gradually accumulating effects of particular kinds of therapeutic processes. What therapists do is genuinely a process, the gradually unfolding consequences of which will tend to occur over the course of the therapy and especially in the patient's external world. This paradigm is linked to therapeutic processes that yield gradually accumulating, extra-therapy consequences. It is quite understandable that Orlinsky and Howard's summary of such research failed to find actual therapeutic operations of a specific, concrete, when-I-do-this-here-is-what-the-patient-then-does nature. It is quite understandable that their summary of such research illuminates "process operations," that is, characteristics of a therapist working within the process-outcome paradigm: engaging in a positive therapist-patient relation, being genuine and self-congruent in talking about patients' inner experiences and feelings, and getting patients to talk meaningfully about themselves and their lives. Not only is the process-outcome paradigm essentially inappropriate to study actual, concrete therapist operations, but it is designed to confirm general processes which are linked to extra-therapy outcomes.

There is another way of trying to see which therapist operations seem to be effective ones. It consists in comparing lots of therapies in terms of outcomes in order to see which therapies seem to produce in terms of outcomes in order to see which therapies seem to produce the best results. Then the researcher makes some reasonable guesses about what actual therapist operations seem to characterize the one(s) which comes out best. For example, Smith, Glass and Miller (1980) reviewed the reported findings of many studies covering many different kinds of therapies and using various outcome criteria. These therapies were then ranked in terms of which produced the best effects or "effect sizes." On the basis of such a review, it was possible to reason that certain techniques seem to characterize the therapies which have the higher effect sizes:

> The highest average effect size, 2.38, was produced by cognitive therapies that go by such labels as systematic rational restructuring, rational state-directed therapy, cognitive rehearsal, and fixed-role therapy. Techniques used in these therapies include active persuasion and confrontation of dysfunctional ideas and beliefs. (Glass & Kliegl, 1983, p. 29)

Such designs do not come very close to studying actual therapist operations such as "actual persuasion and confrontation of dysfunctional ideas and beliefs." It does not seem reasonable to conclude from such a design that particular techniques are good or useful or effective. It does not even seem reasonable to conclude that when these techniques are used, here are the outcome effects. It almost seems that whatever process-outcome design is used, the findings are inappropriate for the study of actual therapist operations.

What Is the Real Payoff in Psychotherapy?:
The In-Therapy Change Paradigm

The experiential method represents a different paradigm of psychotherapy. It is one in which therapeutic methods are designed to produce changes in the therapy session itself. The methods are designed to enable the patient to be different, to sample what it is like to be a changing person, and these changes occur in the session itself. Therapeutic methods are successful, effective, working to the extent that actual, real, genuine changes occur in the session itself. What is more, these changes constitute the first and foremost meaning of "outcome" from the perspective of an experiential theory of psychotherapy.

It must be underscored that these changes are not the kinds of changes which the process-outcome paradigm labels as "process." In the process-outcome paradigm, insight is a welcomed process change, for example. If the patient acquires insight, that is good, for that paradigm labels insight, rightfully, as a process change, one which may ultimately lead to the real article in the patient's extra-therapy world. But in the in-therapy change paradigm our in-therapy changes do not include insight. Our changes include (a) the actual manifestation of the directions of change available to that individualized patient. Everything discussed under our first meaning of psychotherapeutic change (chapter 2) is to occur in the therapy session itself. Our changes include (b) indices of psychotherapeutic movement. Everything discussed under experiential psychotherapy's meaning of psychotherapeutic change (chapter 3) is to occur in the therapy session itself. Our changes include (c) being and becoming the way which is prescribed in the analysis and study of the therapist statements (chapter 4). Everything discussed under the third meaning of psychotherapeutic change is to occur in the therapy session itself. Our meanings of psychotherapeutic change embrace changes which are to occur in the therapy session itself. This is the difference between our representative of the in-therapy change paradigm as contrasted with the standard process-outcome paradigm.

The two meanings of "outcome": In-therapy and extra-therapy. In the process-outcome paradigm, payoff changes occur outside of therapy and in the patient's extra-therapy world. This makes sense because therapy is treatment; it is process. In the "in-therapy change" paradigm, therapy is a set of operations, a method, designed to bring about real, genuine, payoff changes in the session itself. That is the immediate goal of the methods. Whether or not these actual changes also occur (or transfer or generalize) to the patient's extra-therapy world is a secondary issue. In other words, final, payoff changes — "outcomes" — can occur in therapy (in the in-therapy change paradigm) and they can occur in the patient's extra-therapy world (exclusively so, in the process-outcome paradigm, and also so, in the in-therapy change paradigm). But Kiesler is not speaking for most psychotherapy researchers in legitimizing both meanings of "outcome":

> . . . a distinction is made between two arenas of patient change—that which should be evident in the interview behavior of the patient (in-therapy change) and that which should be apparent in the patient's behavior outside of the interview—with his peers or family, on the job, and so forth (extra-therapy change). (Kiesler, 1971a, pp. 41, 43)

> It seems clear . . . that improvement in the patient manifested in his interview behavior, is just as legitimately outcome as any extra-therapy change . . . to the extent that one is investigating in-therapy patient changes, he is concerned directly with outcome; and to the extent that one is interested in outcome, he needs to be cognizant of in-therapy patient changes. To put this differently, there seem to be two important areas of patient change: that change manifest in the therapy hours themselves, and concomitant changes observed outside the therapy interaction (in situ). (Kiesler, 1971a, p. 46)

If one accepts only the standard process-outcome paradigm, then what Kiesler says cannot make real sense. If one accepts the in-therapy change paradigm or both paradigms, then what Kiesler says makes good sense.

In the process-outcome paradigm, the real change occurs outside, in the patient's extra-therapy world. In our paradigm, the real change occurs in the therapy session itself. That is a main difference between the two. This means that the core problem in psychotherapy research is quite different in the two paradigms. In the process-outcome paradigm, the core problem is studying the relationship between the therapy (process) and the extra-therapy changes (outcome):

> The core problem of psychotherapy research is the determination of causal relations between sets of process and outcome variables. To what extent, and in what ways, are changes in the patient's personality and life the con-

sequences of events that occur in psychotherapy? This link, after all, must be established before psychotherapy can rightfully be given praise or blame for a patient's fate. (Orlinsky & Howard, 1978, p. 319)

This does not hold true for the in-therapy change paradigm. In this paradigm, the pay off change is to occur in the session itself, not in the extra-therapy world. That is where the research problem lies. The analogous statement for the in-therapy change paradigm would be something like this:

> The core problem of psychotherapy research is the determination of causal relations between the operations and methods of the therapist and the changes in the patient during the session, i.e., between in-therapy methods and in-therapy patient consequences. To what extent and in what ways are in-therapy changes in the patient the consequences of therapist operations and methods? This link, after all, must be established before psychotherapy can become a scientific enterprise.

The core problems of psychotherapy research vary according to the paradigm one holds. There are genuine differences between the core problems as seen from the process-outcome paradigm, and from the in-therapy change paradigm.

If the researcher accepts the in-therapy change paradigm, then it is legitimate to look in therapy for the payoff changes. While one may also look outside therapy, it is the in-therapy changes which are highlighted. If, for example, the payoff changes pertain to changes in behaviors involving closeness, behaviors involving fighting, and complaining behaviors, then the place to look for these behavioral changes is within the therapy sessions themselves. In such a study, Horowitz, Marmar and Wilner (1979) observed the changes in these three classes of behavior in a woman seen in over 100 hours of psychotherapy. They looked for in-therapy outcomes.

In-therapy change and the extra-therapy world. In experiential psychotherapy, one of the foremost changes is that of letting oneself be and behave as the new person, and to do so within the context of the external world (chapter 3). This means that the patient, in the therapy session, turns his attention to the world and the life stretching out before him, i.e., the extra-therapy world. The task of this final phase of the session is to live in this world, to exist within its context. The task is to sample, to taste, to undergo the being and the behaving as a new and different person. Now that genuine and substantive change has occurred in the course of the session, the consideration turns to enabling that genuinely and substantively changed person to sample what it is like to be and behave differently in the extra-therapy world.

That is the limit of the threshold between the world of experiential psychotherapy and the external world. There are several reasons why experiential psychotherapy invites the patient to sample new ways of being and behaving in the extra-therapy world but declines to have any investment in getting or forcing or influencing the patient to be any particular way in the extra-therapy world. One is that the therapy process is designed to enable the person to undergo substantive changes in the person that he is; the context is the therapy world, the therapy experience. That is all. Another is that within the existential-humanistic approach, the patient is granted a full measure of choice in every way, including the choice of new ways of being and behaving in the extra-therapy world. Whether or not to talk in that jumbled and illogical way with his grandfather is his choice. By following the experiential method, he enabled himself to be a person who does not talk that way. That felt good. He sampled and considered whether or not to be this new way with his wife and with his children, and even with his grandfather. When he leaves the therapy room, he becomes a person who has his own choice; how he lets himself be and behave with his grandfather is his own choice and responsibility. All in all, the experiential method focuses on in-therapy changes, including that of being and behaving in new ways in the extra-therapy world. Actual changings in the extra-therapy world are secondary, outside our therapeutic domain, and both the responsibility and choice of the patient.

The two meanings of therapist operations: In-therapy change paradigm versus process-outcome paradigm. What is the referent for therapeutic operations? What do we have in mind when we speak of therapeutic methods, techniques, "what the therapist does"? When we answer this question from the perspective of the in-therapy change paradigm, the referents are much more specific, operationable, concrete than in the process-outcome paradigm. We have in mind a verbatim transcript or an audiotape or videotape, and we point to the words and actions of the therapist. Typically there is a framing out of a specific sequence of therapist doings, patient doings, therapist doings, patient doings. Indeed, the referents are so defined, specific, and concrete that what the therapist does lends itself to systems of categorization, classifications of therapist operations, methods, techniques, and statements. We may define a particular therapist operation as self-disclosing, reflecting, restating, confronting, telling the patient to say it again, inquiring about the patient's immediate feeling, asking the patient to "be" (speak as) some significant other, general interpretation, pointing out the relationship between immediate behavior and early themes, simple acknowledgment of what the patient says, initiating an encounter with the patient, and so on. Within the in-therapy change paradigm, the meanings of therapeutic operations are specific, concrete, and objective.

Within the process-outcome paradigm, the meaning of therapist operations can be quite similar. It can refer to specific and concrete operations just as in the in-therapy change paradigm. But the more common meaning is quite different. Therapist operations generally refer to more molar packages such as supportive therapy, vector analysis, systematic desensitization, analysis of the transference, assertion training, relaxation training, bereavement counseling, and so on. This molar meaning of therapist operations has little or no place in the in-therapy change paradigm.

The in-therapy change paradigm allows the researcher to look for antecedent therapist operations which accounted for this defineable significant in-therapy patient change. Once we locate the significant moment, we open the window to one or two or a few more therapist operations. The in-therapy change paradigm invests the research with the distinct possibility of finding what led to that good patient change by studying therapist and patient causal events occurring just a little before the in-therapy significant patient change (e.g., Gervaize, Mahrer, & Markow, in press).

Not so in the process-outcome paradigm. According to that paradigm, the causal determinants typically are highly complex, consist of a gradual accumulation of packages of vague variables occurring over preceding sessions and including everything from the total history of the therapist-patient interactions to whatever is going on now, from the therapist's undefined values to the therapist's formless attitudes toward therapy:

> . . . any therapeutic technique is firmly embedded in and thoroughly intertwined with the therapist's personality and the total history of a particular patient-therapist interaction including its current context. It is supported by the therapist's attitudes, values, personal philosophy, etc., which act like a carrier wave from which techniques are inseparable. (Strupp, 1977, p. 8)

The researchable meaning of therapist operations varies considerably when we frame therapist operations from the perspective of the in-therapy change paradigm versus the process-outcome paradigm.

Advantages of Studying In-Therapy Change

The in-therapy change paradigm focuses on the investigation of in-therapy change, quite independent of extra-therapy outcomes. There are some distinct advantages to such a domain of study.

Hypothesis testing and intensive observation. Cronbach (1975) has called for research to adopt a more even balance between what he calls "hypothesis testing" and what he calls "intensive observation." He refers to psychological research in general and psychotherapy research in particular. In a similar vein, Fiske (1977) strongly urges psychotherapy research to examine the acts, events, effects, and consequences which occur within the psychotherapy context itself. The in-therapy change paradigm is smoothly congruent with these calls. The domain of what occurs in psychotherapy beautifully lends itself to generating and testing hypotheses that, for example, "these operations, carried out under these conditions, lead to these consequences" (e.g., Mahrer, Fellers, Brown, Gervaize & Durak, 1981). The domain of what occurs in psychotherapy lends itself to intensive observation of the acts, events, effects, and consequences which take place within the psychotherapy context. From the perspective of the in-therapy change paradigm, the fitting arena of study, the domain of research, is found in the whole complex of the therapy sessions themselves. If we seek to develop therapeutic operations into a systematic science, it is essential to study what goes on in the therapeutic sessions themselves; " . . . research based on the rigorous observation and measurement of in-therapy conduct is an essential requirement for the growth of psychotherapy research as a science" (Greenberg, 1983, p. 170).

What are the patient consequences of specific therapist operations used under defined conditions? For this question, our focus is on specific therapist operations. We inquire about the patient consequences to specific therapist operations used under defined conditions. To answer this question, one must study concrete events in the therapy session themselves:

> Exactly how does the therapist contribute to the effectiveness of treatment? How do the discrete, minute acts of the therapist affect the next actions of the patient? . . . Although some research has involved judgments about characteristics of whole treatment sessions or of 5-minute segments, almost nothing has been done on moment-to-moment interactions. Is this not where the treating actually takes place? (Fiske et al., 1970, p. 24)

The emphasis is upon the in-therapy patient consequences or effects of designated therapist operations (or verbal behaviors or methods or statements) (Greenberg, 1979; Horowitz, 1979; Rice, 1974; Rice & Greenberg, 1984). A somewhat more careful step is to examine the patient conditions under which the therapist does something, and then to look at the in-therapy patient effects. As Greenberg puts it, the design is one " . . . in which the specific effects of specific interventions applied at specific client moments are investigated" (1983, p. 179).

Our question is answered by starting with selected therapist operations under selected therapeutic conditions, and then seeing what in-therapy patient consequences occur. As framed by Greenberg, " . . . a new approach to process research which studies process in the context of strategic interactions may help illuminate differential effects by specifying what client performance is set in motion by what therapist intervention at what particular point in therapy" (1981, p. 24).

Greenberg is one of the pioneers of this approach to in-therapy research. Mahrer (1983) has referred to this method as the study of conditions-operations-consequences, but the idea is the same. That is, the interest is in studying what the therapist does (operations) under specified conditions in therapy (conditions), and the ensuing consequences in regard to the patient (consequences). Regardless of the vocabulary, no matter how sophisticated the design and the measures, the central point is that these are the kinds of questions practitioners are concerned about. Indeed, these are the matters with which clinicians deal in their actual practice.

In-therapy change, in this regard, refers to the patient consequences. When the patient sinks into heartfelt sobbing, and the therapist murmurs quietly "Go ahead" or the therapist closes her eyes and knows how the patient is feeling, what change occurs in the patient? When the patient suddenly is hurt and frustrated, and blurts out "What's the use? I'll never be any different", and the therapist reflects or self-discloses or interprets or fully agrees with the patient, what happens? What changes occur in the way the patient is? These are the kinds of questions which are asked and answered by the in-therapy change paradigm. They are the questions many practitioners are concerned about, for they come right out of the heart of the clinical psychotherapist. Behind the research vocabulary is the same concern with the same kinds of questions. What is somewhat different is that these questions can be answered by means of careful research investigation within the in-therapy change paradigm.

What therapeutic operations lead to significant patient changes, to psychotherapeutic movement? From our perspective, from the perspective of those who hold to an in-therapy change paradigm, this is perhaps the foremost question for our psychotherapy research. On the basis of research addressed toward this question, developments and improvements can be made in actual therapeutic operations. The underlying proposition is that developments and improvements in actual therapeutic operations can be made much more soundly on the basis of research on in-therapy changes than on the basis of extra-therapy changes.

To answer this key question, at least three components should be included in the research. First, it means that we should define precisely what is meant by in-therapy patient changes and significant psychotherapeutic movement. While the precise defining of in-therapy patient changes and significant psychotherapeutic movement may vary with the therapeutic approach, this first step is essential.

> If we want to learn the therapist's contribution to the effectiveness of psychotherapy, we must sooner or later get down to what goes on, moment by moment, in the interactions between therapist and patient. We must decide what patient actions are indicative of effective treatment. (Fiske, 1977, p. 30)

The second component is the necessity for research tape libraries (Mahrer, 1979, 1983). We need libraries containing the actual tapes, both audiotapes and videotapes, of many therapists with many patients. We need whole complete series of sessions, from initial to final sessions. We need series which contain the good work of fine therapists from all the therapy professions. We need tapes which include all kinds of significant moments of change, process, progress, improvement.

Third, it means that we must study the therapeutic operations which seem to lead to these significant patient changes, indices of psychotherapeutic movement. As Greenberg (1975, 1979, 1981) describes this, it is a matter of studying what characterizes those prized in-therapy patient events, of studying what helped bring it about, how it occurs. Fiske (1977) gets even more precise in showing how to do this. After identifying the in-therapy significant patient changes, the indices of psychotherapeutic movement, the researcher takes a careful look at what occurs just before:

> Then we can examine what actions of the therapist preceded the actions we would like to see maximized. It might prove necessary to consider not only therapist-patient pairings of actions but also triads—patient-therapist-

patient. It will be tedious and laborious work, but such labor seems unavoidable. (p. 30)

There is some research of this nature. For example, Luborsky and his colleagues have studied these in-therapy outcomes, these significant patient changes, these indices of psychotherapeutic movement. They studied what therapists do, the therapeutic conditions, occurrences and events which were related to the rising and falling of such significant patient changes, in-therapy outcomes, as headaches, periods of forgetfulness, stomach pains, and epileptic attacks (Luborsky, 1978; Luborsky & Auerbach, 1969; Luborsky & Mintz, 1975). We need a concerted research attack on this question, a concerted study of therapist operations linked to significant in-therapy changes.

This research question is first and foremost for the in-therapy change paradigm. It can hardly be answered, nor is it a major question, from the process-outcome paradigm. The standard meanings of "outcomes" can tell us precious little, if anything, about the specific operations of the therapist. Strupp puts this rather carefully:

Identical therapeutic outcomes may be achieved by a variety of therapeutic techniques. . . . Since all therapeutic techniques are relatively broad gauged in application as well as effect, therapeutic outcomes—at least in the present state of knowledge and in the foreseeable future—cannot be used to validate a set of theoretical assumptions concerning therapeutic change. (1977, p. 10)

If we want to discover what specific therapeutic operations and methods bring about specific good patient changes, if we want to refine and develop our practice, the process-outcome paradigm is far less equipped to do the job than the in-therapy change paradigm.

Systematic development toward a science of psychotherapeutic operations: In-therapy change paradigm versus process-outcome paradigm. By studying what occurs in psychotherapy itself, changes can be made in what therapists do, when they do it, and how they do it. In order to develop therapeutic operations into a systematically organized science of psychotherapy, it is essential to study what goes on in the therapeutic sessions themselves; " . . . research based on the rigorous observation and measurement of in-therapy conduct is an essential requirement for the growth of psychotherapy research as a science" (Greenberg, 1983, p. 170).

It may seem that the process-outcome paradigm ought to yield research findings, on the basis of which the actual practice of psychotherapy may be altered. I believe, however, that research flowing out of the process-outcome paradigm has little chance of providing findings which tell us how to modify sets of therapeutic operations. What is more, the actual state of affairs seems to be that such psychotherapy research has indeed yielded disappointingly slight effects on psychotherapeutic practice. This seems to hold true both for standard "outcome" research (e.g., Barlow, 1981) and also for "process" research (Elliott, 1983a; Luborsky & Spence, 1978; Orlinsky & Howard, 1978; Strupp, 1980a, 1980b).

There is much more precision and confidence in studying the relation between in-therapy operations and in-therapy consequences or outcomes than there is in studying in-therapy "processes" and later extra-therapy "outcomes." Orlinsky and Howard (1978) identify the core problem in psychotherapy research as " . . . the determination of causal relations between sets of process and outcome variables," but unfortunately, " . . . As of the present moment, such a causal attribution is supported mainly by circumstantial evidence, practical assumptions, and intuition." And the reason is that we cannot do careful experiments. "The usual inductive method for determining the causal dependence of one set of variables on another is the experiment, but clinical psychotherapy has proven a peculiarly difficult subject for true experiments." So we are limited to best hunches and statistically based tendencies. "As a result we are limited to conclusions that certain process variables are associated with certain outcome variables at acceptable levels of statistical significance" (pp. 319–320). The relationships between process and outcome variables are filled with too much noise, distance, confounding variables, lack of rigor and lack of precision to move our crude operations toward a refined art, a respectable craft, or a genuine science.

Not so in the study of in-therapy operations and in-therapy consequences. They are much more closely linked to one another. They are open to much more precision and rigor and carefulness of conclusions. In moving toward a genuine science of psychotherapeutic practice, I submit that the most productive research is generated by the in-therapy change paradigm as compared with the process-outcome paradigm.

To what extent has therapeutic practice changed as a result of psychotherapy research? To what extent does psychotherapy research have direct implications for changes in actual therapeutic practice? In a review of the last decades of psychotherapy research, Greenberg (1981) concludes that the answer is "very little":

> After decades of research the amount of well established knowledge about what affects therapeutic outcomes is disappointingly meagre. Research of the sort done in the last decade, although approaching clinical relevance, still has not offered much to practicing clinicians. (p. 31)

Indeed, psychotherapy research can exert little effect on therapeutic practice when the research looks at extra-therapy outcomes rather than in-therapy outcomes. When research looks at extra-therapy outcomes, the findings can tell us something about behavior therapy or assertion training or depth of experiencing or brief psychotherapy. But we will be able to make few linkages from the findings to what the therapist does right here when the patient is crying or when the patient is losing control or when the patient is being excited about his father's visit. There will be little change in how the therapist starts a session or how termination is handled or what the therapist does when the patient challenges the therapist. In short, the usual emphasis on extra-therapy outcomes will tell us very little about the actual practices of therapists.

In the open marketplace of psychotherapy research, the challenge is this. I submit that the in-therapy change paradigm is superior to the process-outcome paradigm in the systematic modification and development of therapist operations toward a science of psychotherapeutic practice.

CONCLUSIONS

1) Most current meanings and measures of psychotherapy change fall under three classes: changes in the patient's psychopathological condition, changes in the patient's problems, and changes in some pertinent personality dimensions.

2) Researchers who are inclined to accept and use one or more of these common meanings and measures of psychotherapy change tend to take a particular position on four conceptual issues relating to the definition of psychotherapy, the meaning of personality and psychotherapeutic change. If the researcher does not share these positions, if the researcher instead accepts different positions, then the researcher is ready for new meanings and measures of psychotherapeutic change. In short, those who tend to use the three common meanings and measures of psychotherapeutic change share one conceptualization, and those who share an alternative conceptualization would tend to have their own meanings and measures of psychotherapeutic change. An existential-humanistic theory of human beings and its experiential theory of psychotherapy are ready for their own meanings and measures of psychotherapeutic change.

3) Here are the meanings of psychotherapeutic change from an experiential theory of psychotherapy: (a) Researchable statements about the individualized patient's potential directions of change. (b) Researchable indices of psychotherapeutic movement and change. (c) Researchable statements about how the patient is to be or become, from a reconceptualization of therapist statements as prescriptions-for-change. These are different from the three common meanings of psychotherapeutic change given in the first conclusion. Each of the three proposed meanings of psychotherapeutic change is described with the aim of their being useable by psychotherapy researchers.

4) In order to measure psychotherapeutic change using the three proposed meanings, the best data are in-therapy data rather than the standard extra-therapy data. The researcher will tend to use in-therapy data if the researcher holds to what is proposed as the "in-therapy change" paradigm of psychotherapy. However, the researcher will tend to use extra-therapy data if the researcher holds to what is described as the "process-outcome" paradigm of psychotherapy. Most researchers follow this process-outcome paradigm of psychotherapy. This may change.

REFERENCES

Adams, H. E. & Frye, R. L. Psychotherapeutic techniques as conditioned reinforcers in a structured interview. *Psychological Reports*, 1964, 4, 163–166.

Assum, A. L. & Levy, S. J. Analysis of a nondirective case with follow up interview. *Journal of Abnormal and Social Psychology*, 1948, 43, 78–89.

Auld, F. A., Jr. & Murray, E. J. Content-analysis studies of psychotherapy. *Psychological Bulletin*, 1955, 52, 377–395.

Auerbach, H. H. & Luborsky, L. Accuracy of judgements of psychotherapy and the nature of the "good hour". In J. Shlien, H. F. Hunt, J. P. Matarazzo, & C. Savage (Eds.) *Research on Psychotherapy. Volume 3.* Washington, D.C.: American Psychological Association, 1968.

Auerswald, M. C. Differential reinforcing power of restatement and interpretation on client production of affect. *Journal of Counseling Psychology*, 1974, 21, 9–14.

Barlow, D. H. Empirical practice and realistic research: New opportunities for clinicians. *Journal of Consulting and Clinical Psychology*, 1981, 49, 147–219.

Barnabei, F., Cormier, W. H., & Nye, S. L. Determining the effects of three counselor verbal responses on client verbal behavior. *Journal of Counseling Psychology*, 1974, 21, 355–359.

Battle, C., Imber, S., Hoehn-Saric, R., Stone, A., Nash, E., & Frank, J. Target complaints as criteria of improvement. *American Journal of Psychotherapy*, 1966, 20, 184–192.

Bergin, A. E., & Lambert, M. S. The evaluation of therapeutic outcomes. In S. L. Garfield & A. E. Bergin (Eds.) *Handbook of psychotherapy and behavior change*, 2nd ed. New York: John Wiley, 1978. Pp. 134–189.

Bergman, D. V. Counseling method and client response. *Journal of Consulting Psychology*, 1951, 15, 216–224.

Bereiter, C. Some persisting dilemmas in measuring change. In C. Harris (Ed.) *Problems in measuring change*. Madison: University of Wisconsin Press, 1963.

Berzins, J. I., Bednar, R. L., & Severy, L. J. The problem of intersource consensus in measuring therapeutic outcomes: New data and multivariate perspectives. *Journal of Abnormal Psychology*, 1975, 84, 10–19.

Braaten, L. J. The movement from non-self to self in client-centered psychotherapy. *Journal of Counseling Psychology*, 1961, 8, 20–24.

Budge, S. A critical look at the psychotherapeutic outcome research paradigm. *Psychotherapy: Theory, Research and Practice*, 1983, 20, 294–306.

Bugental, J. F. T. The person who is the psychotherapist. *Journal of Consulting Psychology*, 1964, 28, 272–277.

Burton, A. (Ed.) *What makes behavior change possible?* New York: Brunner/Mazel, 1976.

Butler, J. M. The iconic mode in psychotherapy. In D. A. Wexler & L. N. Rice (Eds.) *Innovation in Client-Centered Therapy*. New York: Wiley-Interscience, 1974.

Butler, J. M., Rice, L. N. & Wagstaff, A. K. On the naturalistic definition of variables: An analogue of clinical analysis. In H. Strupp & L. Luborsky (Eds.) *Research in psychotherapy*, Vol. 2. Washington, D.C.: American Psychological Association, 1962.

Campbell, D. T. From description to experimentation: Interpreting trends as quasi-experiments. In C. Harris (Ed.) *Problems in measuring change*. Madison: University of Wisconsin Press, 1963.

Campbell, D. T. & Stanley, J. C. Experimental and quasi-experimental designs for research on teaching. In N. L. Gage (Ed.) *Handbook of research on teaching*. Chicago: Rand McNally, 1963.

Carkhuff, R. R. *Helping and human relations*. Vol. 2. New York: Holt, Rinehart and Winston, 1969.

Carkhuff, R. R. & Berenson, B. G. *Beyond counseling and therapy*. New York: Holt, Rinehart and Winston, 1967.

Cartwright, D. S. Patient self-report measures. In I. E. Waskow and M. B. Parloff (Eds.) *Psychotherapy change measures*. Rockville, Maryland: National Institute of Mental Health, 1975. Pp. 48–64.

Claiborn, C. D. Interpretation and change in counseling. *Journal of Counseling Psychology*, 1982, *29*, 439–454.

Cofer, C. N. & Chance, J. The discomfort-relief quotient in published cases of counseling and psychotherapy. *Journal of Psychology*, 1950, *29*, 219–224.

Cook, J. J. Silence in psychotherapy. *Journal of Counseling Psychology*, 1964, *11*, 42–46.

Cronbach, L. J. Beyond the two disciplines of scientific psychology. *American Psychologist*, 1975, *30*, 116–127.

Dahlstrom, W. G. Recommendations for patient measures evaluating psychotherapy: Test batteries and inventories. In I. E. Waskow and M. B. Parloff (Eds.) *Psychotherapy change measures*. Rockville, Maryland: National Institute of Mental Health, 1975. Pp. 14–31.

Derogatis, L. R., Lipman, R. S., Rickels, K., Uhlenhuth, E. H., & Covi, L. The Hopkins Symptom Checklist: A measure of primary symptom dimensions. In P. Pichot (Ed.) *Psychological Measurements in psychopharmacology: Modern problems in pharmacopsychiatry. Vol. 7.* Basil, Switzerland: S. Karger, 1974. Pp. 79–110.

Dittman, T. The interpersonal process in psychotherapy: Development of a research method. *Journal of Abnormal and Social Psychology*, 1952, *47*, 236–244.

Dollard, J. & Miller, N. E. *Personality and psychotherapy*. New York: McGraw-Hill, 1950.

Dollard, J. & Mowrer, O. H. A method of measuring tension in written documentation. *Journal of Abnormal and Social Psychology*, 1947, *42*, 3–32.

DuBois, P. H. & Manning, W. H. (Eds.) *Methods of research in technical training*. St. Louis: Washington University, 1961.

Duncan, S., Jr., Rice, L. N. & Butler, J. M. Therapists' paralanguage in peak and poor psychotherapy hours. *Journal of Abnormal Psychology*, 1968, *73*, 566–570.

Elliott, R. Fitting process research to the practicing psychotherapist. *Psychotherapy: Theory Research and Practice*, 1983a, *20*, 47–55.

Elliott, R. Significant events in brief counseling interviews: An empirical taxonomy. Unpublished manuscript, Department of Psychology, University of Toledo, 1983b.

Elliott, R. "That in your hands": A comprehensive process analysis of a significant event in psychotherapy. *Psychiatry*, 1983c, *46*, 113–129.

Elliott, R. A discovery-oriented approach to significant events in psychotherapy: Interpersonal Process Recall and Comprehensive Process Analysis. In L. N. Rice & L. S. Greenberg, (Eds.) *Patterns of change.* New York: Guilford, 1984a. Pp. 249–286.

Elliott, R. Significant events and the analysis of therapeutic impacts. Paper presented at the Society for Psychotherapy Research, Banff, Alberta, June, 1984b.

Elliott, R., Cline, J., & Shulman, R. Effective processes in psychotherapy: A single case study using four evaluative paradigms. Paper presented at meeting of the Society for Psychotherapy Research, Sheffield, England, June, 1983.

Elliott, R. & Feinstein, L. Helping intention rating procedures: Overview and uses. Unpublished manuscript. University of Toledo, 1978.

Fagan, J. Three sessions with Iris. *Counseling Psychologist,* 1974, *4,* 42–60.

Fiske, D. W. Methodological issues in research on the psychotherapist. In A. S. Gurman & A. M. Razin (Eds.) *Effective psychotherapy,* Elmsford, New York: Pergamon, 1977.

Fiske, D. W., Hunt, H. H., Luborsky, L., Orne, M. T., Parloff, M. B., Rieser, M. F., & Tuma, A. H. Planning of research on effectiveness of psychotherapy. *Archives of General Psychiatry,* 1970, *22,* 22–32.

Frank, G. H. & Sweetland, A. A study of the process of psychotherapy: The verbal interaction. *Journal of Consulting Psychology,* 1962, *26,* 135–138.

Frank, J. D. *Persuasion and healing.* 2nd ed. New York: Schocken, 1974.

Frank, J. D. The present status of outcome research. In M. R. Goldfried (Ed.) *Converging themes in psychotherapy.* New York: Springer, 1982, Pp. 281–290.

Gassner, S., Sampson, H., Weiss, J., & Brumer, S. The emergence of warded-off contents. *Psychoanalysis and Contemporary Thought,* 1982, *5,* 55–75.

Gendlin, E. T., Beebe, J., Cassens, J., Klein, M., & Oberlander, M. Focusing ability in psychotherapy, personality and creativity. In J. M. Shlien, H. F. Hunt, J. D. Matarazzo, & C. Savage (Eds.). *Research in Psychotherapy.* Vol. 3. Washington, D.C. American Psychological Association, 1968.

Gervaize, P. A., Mahrer, A. R., & Markow, R. Therapeutic laughter: What therapists do to promote strong laughter in patients. *Psychotherapy in Private Practice,* in press.

Glass, G. V. & Kliegl, R. M. An apology for research integration in the study of psychotherapy. *Journal of Consulting and Clinical Psychology,* 1983, *51,* 28–41.

Gleser, G. O. Evaluation of psychotherapy outcome by psychological tests. In I. E. Waskow and M. B. Parloff (Eds.) *Psychotherapy change measures.* Rockville, Maryland: National Institute of Mental Health, 1975. Pp. 32–34.

Goldfried, M. R. Toward the delineation of therapeutic change principles. *American Psychologist,* 1980, *35,* 991–999.

Goldfried, M. R. (Ed.) *Converging themes in psychotherapy.* New York: Springer, 1982.

Goldstein, A. P., Heller, K., & Sechrest, L. B. *Psychotherapy and the psychology of behavior change.* New York: Wiley, 1966.

Gomes-Schwartz, B. Effective ingredients in psychotherapy: Prediction of outcome from process variables. *Journal of Consulting and Clinical Psychology,* 1978, *46,* 1023–1035.

Gottman, J. M. & Markman, H. J. Experimental designs in psychotherapy research. In S. L. Garfield & A. E. Bergin (Eds.) *Handbook of psychotherapy and behavior change.* New York: Wiley, 1978.

Gottman, J. M., Markman, H. J. & Notarius, C. The topography of marital conflict: A sequential analysis of verbal and nonverbal behavior. *Journal of Marriage and the Family*, 1977, August, 461–477.

Gough, H. G. *Manual for the California Psychological Inventory*. Palo Alto: Consulting Psychologists Press, 1957.

Graff, H. & Luborsky L. Long term trends in transference and resistance: A report on a quantitative-analytic method applied to four psychoanalyses. *Journal of the American Psychoanalytic Association*, 1977, 25, 471–490.

Greenberg, L. *A task analytic approach to the events of psychotherapy*. Unpublished doctoral dissertation, York University, Toronto, 1975.

Greenberg, L. S. Resolving splits: Use of the two-chair technique. *Psychotherapy: Theory, Research and Practice*, 1979, 16, 310–318.

Greenberg, L. S. Advances in clinical intervention research: A decade review. *Canadian Psychology*, 1981, 22, 25–34.

Greenberg, L. S. Psychotherapy process research. In E. Walker (Ed.) *Handbook of clinical psychology*. New York: Dorsey, 1983.

Greenberg, L. S. A task analysis of interpersonal conflict resolution. In L. N. Rice & L. S. Greenberg (Eds.) *Patterns of change: Intensive analysis of psychotherapy process*. New York: Guilford, 1984.

Greenberg, L. S. & Pinsof, W. *Psychotherapeutic process: A research handbook*. New York: Guilford, in press.

Gruen, W. Fool's gold? *APA Monitor*, December, 1980, 34.

Haigh, G. Defensive behavior in client-centered therapy. *Journal of Consulting Psychology*, 1949, 13, 181–189.

Harvey, O. J., Hunt, D. E., & Shroeder, H. M. *Conceptual systems and personality organization*. New York: Wiley, 1961.

Hayes, S. C., Hussian, R. A., Turner, A. E., Anderson, K. B. & Grub, T. D. The effect of coping statements on progress through a desensitization hierarchy. *Journal of Behavior Therapy and Experimental Psychiatry*, 1983, 14, 117–129.

Hekmat, H. Reinforcing values of interpretations and reflections. *Journal of Abnormal Psychology*, 1971, 77, 25–31.

Highlen, P. S. & Baccus, G. K. Effects of reflection of feeling and probe on client self-referenced affect. *Journal of Counseling Psychology*, 1977, 24, 440–443.

Hill, C. E. & Gormally, J. Effects of reflection, restatement, probe, and nonverbal behaviors on client affect. *Journal of Counseling Psychology*, 1977, 24, 92–97.

Hill, C. E. & O'Grady, R. E. A list of therapist intentions: Illustrated in a single case and with therapists of varying theoretical intentions. *Journal of Counseling Psychology*, in press.

Hoehn-Saric, R., Frank, J. D., & Gurland, B. J. Focused attitude change in neurotic patients. *Journal of Nervous and Mental Diseases*, 1968, 147, 124–133.

Hoehn-Saric, R., Frank, J. D., Imber, S. D., Nash, E. H., Stone, A. R., & Battle, C. C. Systemic preparation of patients for psychotherapy: I. Effects on therapy behavior and outcome. *Journal of Psychiatric Research*, 1964, 2, 267–281.

Hoehn-Saric, R., Liberman, B., Imber, S. D., Stone, A. R., Frank, J. D. & Ribich, F. D. Attitude change and attribution of arousal in psychotherapy. *Journal of Nervous and Mental Diseases*, 1974, 159, 234–243.

Hoehn-Saric, R., Liberman, B., Imber, S. D., Stone, A. R., Pande, S. K. & Frank, J. D. Arousal and attitude change in neurotic patients. *Archives of General Psychiatry*, 1972, 26, 51–56.

Hoffnung, R. J. Conditioning and transfer of affective self-references in a role-playing counseling interview. *Journal of Consulting and Clinical Psychology*, 1969, 33, 527–531.

Holt, R. R. & Luborsky, L. *Personality patterns of psychiatrists: A study in selection techniques.* Vol. 2. Topeka, Kansas: Menninger Foundation, 1958.

Holzman, P. S. Cognitive and perceptual tests for evaluating psychotherapy outcome. In J. E. Waskow and M. B. Parloff (Eds.) *Psychotherapy change measures.* Rockville, Maryland: National Institute of Mental Health, 1975. Pp. 129–142.

Horowitz, C. M., Sampson, H., Siegelman, E. Y., Weiss, J., & Goodfriend, S. Cohesive and dispersal behaviors: Two classes of concomitant change in psychotherapy. *Journal of Consulting and Clinical Psychology,* 1978, *46,* 556–564.

Horowitz, L. M., Sampson, H., Siegelman, E. Y., Wolfson, A., & Weiss, J. On the identification of warded off mental contents. *Journal of Abnormal Psychology,* 1975, *84,* 454–458.

Horowitz, M. J. *States of mind.* New York: Plenum, 1979.

Horowitz, M. J., Marmar, C., & Wilner, N. Analysis of patient states and trait transitions. *Journal of Nervous and Mental Diseases,* 1979, *167,* 97–99.

Hoyt, M. F. Therapist and patient actions in "good" psychotherapy sessions. *Archives of General Psychiatry,* 1980, *37,* 159–170.

Hoyt, M. F., Marmar, C. R., Horowitz, M. J. & Alvarez, W. F. The therapist action scale and the patient action scale: Instruments for the assessment of activities during dynamic psychotherapy. *Psychotherapy: Theory, Research and Practice,* 1981, *18,* 109–116.

Hunt, J. McV. Measuring the effects of social casework. *Transactions of the New York Academy of Science,* 1947, *9,* 78–88.

Hunt, J. McV. A social agency as a setting for research—The Institute of Welfare Research. *Journal of Consulting Psychology,* 1949, *13,* 69–81.

Hunt, J. McV. & Kogan, L. S. *Measuring results in social casework.* New York: Family Service Association of America, 1950.

Imber, S. D. Patient direct self-report techniques. In I. E. Waskow and M. B. Parloff (Eds.) *Psychotherapy change measures.* Rockville, Maryland: National Institute of Mental Health, 1975. Pp. 40–47.

Isaacs, K. S. & Haggard, E. A. Some methods used in the study of affect in psychotherapy. In L. A. Gottschalk and A. H. Auerbach (Eds.) *Methods of research in psychotherapy.* New York: Appleton-Century-Crofts, 1966.

Jacobs, D., Charles, E., Jacobs, T., Weinstein, H., & Mann, D. Preparation for psychotherapy of the disadvantaged patient. *American Journal of Orthopsychiatry,* 1972, *42,* 666–674.

Kagan, N. Interpersonal process recall: a method of influencing human interaction, 1975. (Available from N. Kagan, 434 Erickson Hall, College of Education, Michigan State University, East Lansing, Michigan 48824.)

Kanfer, F. H. Report on outcome measures in behavior therapy. In I. E. Waskow and M. B. Parloff (Eds.) *Psychotherapy change measures.* Rockville, Maryland: National Institute of Mental Health, 1975. Pp. 75–87.

Kanfer, F. H. & Phillips, J. S. *Learning foundations of behavior therapy.* New York: Wiley, 1970.

Kanfer, F. H., Phillips, J. S., Matarazzo, J. D. & Saslow, G. Experimental modification of interviewer content in standardized interviews. *Journal of Consulting Psychology,* 1960, *24,* 528–536.

Kauffman, P. E. & Raimy, V. C. Two methods of assessing therapeutic progress. *Journal of Abnormal and Social Psychology,* 1949, *44,* 379–385.

Kennedy, J. J. & Zimmer, J. M. Reinforcing value of five stimulus conditions in a quasi-counseling situation. *Journal of Counseling Psychology,* 1968, *15,* 357–362.

Kiesler, D. J. Some myths of psychotherapy research and the search for a paradigm. *Psychological Bulletin*, 1966, *65*, 110–136.

Kiesler, D. J. Experimental designs in psychotherapy research. In A. E. Bergin and S. L. Garfield (Eds.) *Handbook of psychotherapy and behavior change: An empirical analysis*. New York: John Wiley, 1971a. Pp. 36–74.

Kiesler, D. J. Patient experiencing and successful outcome in individual psychotherapy of schizophrenics and psychoneurotics. *Journal of Consulting and Clinical Psychology*, 1971b, *37*, 370–385.

Kiesler, D. J. *The process of psychotherapy: Empirical foundations and systems of analysis*. Hawthorne, New York: Aldine, 1973.

Kiesler, D. J., Mathieu, P. L., & Klein, M. M. Sampling from the recorded therapy interview: A comparative study of different segment lengths. *Journal of Consulting Psychology*, 1964, *28*, 349–357.

Kirtner, W. L. & Cartwright, D. S. Success and failure in client-centered therapy as a function of initial in-therapy behavior. *Journal of Consulting Psychology*, 1958, *22*, 329–333.

Kiresuk, T. J. & Sherman, R. E. Goal attainment scaling: A general method for evaluating comprehensive community mental health programs. *Community Mental Health Journal*, 1968, *4*, 443–453.

Klein, M. H., Mathieu, P. L., Gendlin, E. T., & Kiesler, D. J. *The Experiencing Scale: A research and training manual*. Madison: Wisconsin Psychiatric Institute, 1970.

Klonoff, H. & Cox, B. A. Problem-oriented approach to analysis of treatment outcome. *American Journal of Psychiatry*, 1975, *132*, 836–841.

Krasner, L. Techniques of assessment in behavior therapy. In I. E. Waskow and M. B. Parloff (Eds.) *Psychotherapy change measures*. Rockville, Maryland: National Institute of Mental Health, 1975. Pp. 65–74.

Kurz, R. R. & Grummon, D. L. Different approaches to the measurement of therapist empathy and their relationship to therapy outcomes. *Journal of Consulting and Clinical Psychology*, 1972, *39*, 106–119.

Labov, W. *Sociolinguistic patterns*. Philadelphia: University of Pennsylvania Press, 1972.

Labov, W. & Fanshel, D. *Therapeutic discourse: Psychotherapy as conversation*. New York: Academic Press, 1977.

Laing, R. D. *Sanity, madness and the family*. Harmondsworth, Middlesex: Penguin Books, 1970.

Laing, R. D. *The voice of experience*. New York: Pantheon Books, 1982.

Lawton, G. Neurotic interaction between counselor and counselee. *Journal of Consulting Psychology*, 1958, *5*, 28–33.

Leitenberg, H., Gross, J., Peterson, J. & Rosen, J. C. Analysis of an anxiety model and the process of change during exposure plus response prevention treatment of bulimia nervosa. *Behavior Therapy*, 1984, *15*, 3–20.

Lennard, H. L. & Bernstein, A. *The anatomy of psychotherapy: Systems of communication and expectation*. New York: Columbia University Press, 1960.

Lifshitz, K., & Blair, J. H. The polygraphic recording of a repeated hypnotic abreaction with comments on abreactive psychotherapy. *Journal of Nervous and Mental Diseases*, 1960, *130*, 246–253.

Loevinger, J. & Wessler, R. *Measuring ego development: Construction and use of a sentence completion test*. Vol. 1. San Francisco: Jossey-Bass, 1970.

Loevinger, J., Wessler, R., & Redmore, C. *Measuring ego development: Scoring manual for women and girls*. San Francisco: Jossey-Bass, 1970.

Lord, F. M. Elementary models for measuring change. In C. Harris (Ed.) *Problems in measuring change*. Madison: University of Wisconsin Press, 1963.

Lower, R. B., Escoll, P. S., Little, R. B. & Ottenberg, P. An experimental examination of transference. *Archives of General Psychiatry*, 1973, 29, 738–741.

Luborsky, L. The patient's personality and psychotherapeutic change. In H. Strupp & L. Luborsky (Eds.) *Research in psychotherapy*. Vol. 2. Washington, D.C. American Psychological Association, 1962. Pp. 115–133.

Luborsky, L. Momentary forgetting during psychotherapy and psychoanalysis: A theory and research method. In R. Holt (Ed.) Motives and thought: Psychoanalytic essays in honor of David Rapaport. *Psychological Issues*, 1964, 5, 177–217.

Luborsky, L. Quantitative research on psychoanalytic therapy. In S. L. Garfield & A. E. Bergin (Eds.) *Handbook of psychotherapy and behavior change*. New York: Wiley, 1978.

Luborsky, L. & Auerbach, A. H. The symptom-context method: Quantitative studies of symptom formation in psychotherapy. *Journal of the American Psychoanalytic Association*, 1969, 17, 68–99.

Luborsky, L., Graff, H., Pulver, S., & Curtis, H. A clinical-quantitative examination of consensus on the concept of tranference. *Archives of General Psychiatry*, 1973, 29, 69–75.

Luborsky, L. & Mintz, J. Momentary forgetting during a psychoanalysis: Investigations of symptom-onset conditions. *Psychoanalysis and Contemporary Science*, 1975, 3, 233–268.

Luborsky, L. & Spence, D. Quantitative research on psychoanalytic therapy. In S. L. Garfield & A. E. Bergin (Eds.) *Handbook of Psychotherapy and Behavior Change: An Empirical Analysis* (2nd ed.) New York: Wiley, 1978.

Mahrer, A. R. Some known effects of psychotherapy and a reinterpretation. In A. G. Banet, Jr. (Ed.) *Creative psychotherapies: A source book*. La Jolla: University Associates, 1976. Pp. 334–344.

Mahrer, A. R. *Experiencing: A humanistic theory of psychology and psychiatry*. New York: Brunner/Mazel, 1978a.

Mahrer, A. R. The therapist-patient relationship: Conceptual analysis and a proposal for a paradigm-shift. *Psychotherapy: Theory, Research and Practice*, 1978b, 15, 201–215.

Mahrer, A. R. Sequence and consequence in experiential psychotherapies. In C. L. Cooper and C. Alderfer (Eds.) *Advances in experiential social processes*. New York: John Wiley and Sons, 1978c. Pp. 39–65.

Mahrer, A. R. An invitation to theoreticians and researchers from an applied experiential practitioner. *Psychotherapy: Theory, Research and Practice*, 1979, 16, 406–418.

Mahrer, A. R. Research on theoretical concepts of psychotherapy. In W. de Moor & A. R. Wijngaarten (Eds.) *Psychotherapy: Research and training*. Amsterdam: Elsevier/North Holland Biomedical Press, 1980.

Mahrer, A. R. *Experiential psychotherapy: Basic practices*. New York: Brunner/Mazel, 1983.

Mahrer, A. R., Brown, S. D., Gervaize, P. A., & Fellers, G. Reflection, self-exploration, and client-centered communication: Some unexpected in-therapy consequences. *Journal of Communication Therapy*, 1983, 2, 1–13.

Mahrer, A. R., Clark, E. L., Comeau, L., & Brunette, A. Therapist statements as prescriptions-for-change. *Journal of Communication Therapy*, in press.

Mahrer, A. R., Durak, G. M., Lawson, K. C. & Nifakis, D. J. Interpretation as a means of enhancing the role of the therapist. *Journal of Communication Therapy*, in press.

Mahrer, A. R., Edwards, H. P., Durak, G. M. & Sterner, I. The psychotherapy patient and the initial session: What to do with the emotional state. *The Psychotherapy Patient*, in press.

Mahrer, A. R., Fellers, G. L., Brown, S. D., Gervaize, P. A., & Durak, G. M. When does the counselor self-disclose and what are the in-therapy consequences? *Canadian Counsellor*, 1981, *15*, 175–179.

Mahrer, A. R. & Gervaize, P. A. Impossible roles therapists must play. *Canadian Psychology*, 1983, *24*, 81–87.

Mahrer, A. R. & Gervaize, P. A. An integrative review of strong laughter in psychotherapy. *Psychotherapy*, 1984, *21*, 510–516.

Mahrer, A. R., Nifakis, D. J., Abhukara, L., & Sterner, I. Microstrategies in psychotherapy: The patterning of sequential therapist statements. *Psychotherapy*, 1984, *21*, 465–472.

McNair, D. M., Lorr, M., & Droppleman, L. F. *FITS Manual for the profile of mood states*. San Diego, California: Educational and Industrial Testing Service, 1971.

Merbaum, M. The conditioning of affective self-references by three classes of generalized reinforcers. *Journal of Personality*, 1963, *31*, 179–191.

Merbaum, M. & Southwell, E. A. Conditioning of affective self-references as a function of the discriminative characteristics of experimenter intervention. *Journal of Abnormal Psychology*, 1965, *76*, 180–187.

Mintz, J., Auerbach, A. H., Luborsky, L. & Johnson, M. Patients', therapists' and observers' views of psychotherapy: A "Rashomon" experience or a reasonable consensus? *British Journal of Medical Psychology*, 1973, *46*, 83–89.

Mintz, J., Luborsky, L. & Christoph, P. Measuring the outcomes of psychotherapy: Findings of the Penn psychotherapy project. *Journal of Consulting and Clinical Psychology*, 1979, *47*, 319–334.

Mischel, W. *Personality and assessment*. New York: Wiley, 1968.

Mowrer, O. H., Hunt, J. McV., & Kogan, L. S. Further studies utilizing the Discomfort—Relief Quotient. In O. H. Mowrer (Ed.) *Psychotherapy: Theory and research*. New York: Ronald, 1953. Pp. 257–295.

Mowrer, O. H., Light, B. H., Luria, A., & Zeleny, M. P. Tension changes during psychotherapy with special reference to resistance. In O. H. Mowrer (Ed.) *Psychotherapy: Theory and research*. New York: Ronald, 1953. Pp. 546–640.

Murray, E. J. A case study in a behavioral analysis of psychotherapy. *Journal of Abnormal and Social Psychotherapy*, 1954, *49*, 305–310.

Murray, E. J. Interview measures and psychotherapy outcome. In I. E. Waskow and M. B. Parloff (Eds.) *Psychotherapy change measures*. Rockville, Maryland: National Institute of Mental Health, 1975, Pp. 116–117.

Murray, E. J., Auld, F., Jr., & White, A. M. A psychotherapy case showing progress but no decrease in the discomfort-relief quotient. *Journal of Consulting Psychology*, 1954, *18*, 349–353.

Nichols, M. P. Outcome of brief cathartic therapy. *Journal of Consulting and Clinical Psychology*, 1974, *42*, 403–410.

Nichols, M. P. & Zax, M. *Catharsis in psychotherapy*. New York: Gardner, 1977.

Orlinsky, D. E. & Howard, K. I. The good therapy hour. *Archives of General Psychiatry*, 1967, *16*, 621–632.

Orlinsky, D. E. & Howard, K. I. *Varieties of psychotherapeutic experience*. New York: Teacher's College Press, 1975.

Orlinsky, D. E. & Howard, K. I. The therapists' experience of psychotherapy. In A. S. Gurman & A. M. Razin (Eds.) *Effective psychotherapy: A handbook of research*. Oxford, England: Pergamon Press, 1977.

Orlinsky, D. E. & Howard, K. I. The relation of process to outcome in psychotherapy. In S. L. Garfield & A. E. Bergin (Eds.) *Handbook of psychotherapy and behavior change*. New York: Wiley, 1978, Pp. 283–329.

Parloff, M. B. Can psychotherapy research guide the policy-maker? A little knowledge may be a dangerous thing. *American Psychologist*, 1979, *34*, 296–306.

Paul, G. L. Behavior modification research: Design and tactics. In C. M. Franks (Ed.) *Assessment and status of the behavior therapies and associated developments*. New York: McGraw-Hill, 1969.

Pentony, P. *Models of influence in psychotherapy*. New York: Free Press, 1981.

Pope, B. Research on therapeutic style. In A. S. Gurman & A. M. Razin (Eds.) *Effective psychotherapy*. Elmsford, New York: Pergamon, 1977.

Pope, B. *The mental health interview*. Elmsford, New York: Pergamon, 1979.

Powell, W. J. Differential effectiveness of interviewer interventions in an experimental interview. *Journal of Consulting and Clinical Psychology*, 1968, *32*, 210–215.

Prochaska, S. A. *Systems of psychotherapy: A transtheoretical analysis*. Homewood, Ill.: Dorsey Press, 1979.

Raimy, V. C. Self reference in counseling interviews. *Journal of Consulting Psychology*, 1948, *12*, 153–163.

Raskin, N. J. An analysis of six parallel studies of the therapeutic process. *Journal of Consulting Psychology*, 1949, *13*, 206–220.

Raskin, N. J. The psychotherapy research project of the American Academy of Psychotherapists. *American Psychologist*, 1965, *20*, 597 (Abstract).

Rice, L. N. Client behavior as a function of therapist style and client resources. *Journal of Counseling Psychology*, 1973, *26*, 306–311.

Rice, L. N. The evocative function of the therapist. In D. Wexler & L. N. Rice (Eds.) *Innovations in client-centered therapy*. New York: Wiley, 1974.

Rice, L. N. & Greenberg, L. S. A method for studying the active ingredients in psychotherapy: Applications to client-centered and Gestalt therapy. Paper presented to the Society for Psychotherapy Research, Denver, 1974.

Rice, L. N. & Greenberg, L. S. *Patterns of change: An intensive analysis of psychotherapeutic process*. New York: Guilford, 1984.

Rice, L. N., Koke, C. J., Greenberg, L. S., & Wagstaff, A. K. *Manual for client vocal quality*. Toronto, Ontario: Counselling Development Centre, York University, 1979.

Rice, L. N. & Wagstaff, A. K. Client voice quality and expressive style as indices of productive psychotherapy. *Journal of Consulting Psychology*, 1967, *31*, 557–563.

Robbins, L. & Wallerstein, R. S. The research strategy and tactics of the psychotherapy research project of the Menninger Foundation and the problem of controls. In E. A. Rubenstein and M. B. Parloff (Eds.) *Research in psychotherapy*. Vol 1. Washington, D.C. American Psychological Association, 1959. Pp. 27–43.

Rogers, C. R. The necessary and sufficient conditions of therapeutic personality change. *Journal of Consulting Psychology*, 1957, *21*, 95–103.

Rogers, C. R. A process conception of psychotherapy. *American Psychologist*, 1958, *13*, 142–149.

Rogers, C. R. *On becoming a person*. Boston: Houghton Mifflin, 1970.

Schauble, P. G. & Pierce, R. M. Client in-therapy behavior: A therapist's guide to progress. *Psychotherapy: Theory, Research and Practice*, 1974, *11*, 229–234.

Scheff, T. J. *Catharsis in healing, ritual, and drama*. Berkeley: University of California Press, 1979.

Schonfield, J., Stone, A. R., Hoehn-Saric, R., Imber, S. D., & Pande, S. K. Patient therapist convergence and measures of improvement in short-term psychotherapy. *Psychotherapy: Theory, Research, and Practice*, 1969, *6*, 267–271.

Scott, W. H. Measures of perceptual and cognitive tendencies in psychotherapy research. In I. E. Waskow and M. B. Parloff (Eds.) *Psychotherapy change measures*. Rockville, Maryland: National Institute of Mental Health, 1975. Pp. 118–128.

Searle, J. R. A classification of illocutionary acts. *Language in Society*, 1976, *5*, 1–23.

Shapiro, T. *Clinical psycholinguistics*. New York and London: Plenum, 1979.

Sloane, R. B., Cristol, A. H., Pepernik, L., & Staples, F. R. Role preparation and expectation of improvement in psychotherapy. *Journal of Nervous and Mental Diseases*, 1970, *150*, 18–26.

Smith, M. L., Glass, G. V. & Miller, T. I. *The benefits of psychotherapy*. Baltimore, Maryland: Johns Hopkins University Press, 1980.

Speisman, J. C. Depth of interpretation and verbal resistance in psychotherapy. *Journal of Consulting Psychology*, 1959, *23*, 93–99.

Stiles, W. B. Measurement of the impact of psychotherapy sessions. *Journal of Consulting and Clinical psychology*, 1980, *2*, 176–185.

Strong, S. R., Wambach, C. A., Lopez, F. G. & Cooper, R. K. Motivational and equipping functions of interpretation in counseling. *Journal of Counseling Psychology*, 1979, *26*, 98–107.

Strupp, H. H. The outcome problem in psychotherapy revisited. *Psychotherapy: Theory, Research and Practice*, 1963, *1*, 1–13.

Strupp, H. H. On the basic ingredients of psychotherapy. *Journal of Consulting and Clinical Psychology*, 1973, *41*, 1–8.

Strupp, H. H. A reformulation of the dynamics of the therapist's contribution. In A. S. Gurman and A. M. Razin (Eds.) *Effective psychotherapy: A handbook of research*. Oxford: Pergamon, 1977. Pp. 3–22.

Strupp, H. H. Success and failure in time-limited psychotherapy. *Archives of General Psychiatry*, 1980a, *37*, 595–603.

Strupp, H. H. Review of Horowitz, M. J., States of mind: Analysis of change in psychotherapy. *Contemporary Psychology*, 1980b, *25*, 6–8.

Strupp, H. H., & Bergin, A. E. Some empirical and conceptual bases for coordinated research in psychotherapy. *International Journal of Psychiatry*, 1969, *7*, 18–90.

Strupp, H. H., & Bloxom, A. L. Preparation of lower class patients for group psychotherapy. *Journal of Consulting and Clinical Psychology*, 1973, *41*, 373–384.

Strupp, H. H., & Bloxom, A. L. Therapists' assessment of outcome. In I. E. Waskow and M. B. Parloff (Eds.) *Psychotherapy change measures*. Rockville, Maryland: National Institute of Mental Health, 1975. Pp. 170–180.

Strupp, H. H., Chasson, J. B., & Ewing, J. A. Toward the longitudinal study of the psychotherapeutic process. In L. A. Gottschalk & A. H. Auerbach (Eds.) *Methods of research in psychotherapy*. New York: Appleton-Century-Crofts, 1966.

Strupp, H. H., Chasson, J. B., & Ewing, J. A. Longitudinal study of psychotherapy: Problems of methodology and quantification. In H. H. Strupp (Ed.) *Psychotherapy: Clinical, research, and theoretical issues*. New York: Jason Aronson, 1973. Pp. 424–476.

Strupp, H. H. & Hadley, S. W. A tripartite model of mental health and therapeutic outcomes: With special reference to negative effects in psychotherapy. *American Psychologist*, 1977, 32, 187–196.

Truax, C. B., & Carkhuff, R. R. The experimental manipulation of therapeutic conditions. *Journal of Consulting Psychology*, 1965, 29, 119–124.

Truax, C. B., & Carkhuff, R. R. *Toward effective counseling and psychotherapy.* Chicago: Aldine, 1967.

Truax, C. B., & Wargo, D. G. Effects of vicarious therapy pre-training and alternate sessions on outcome in group therapy with outpatients. *Journal of Consulting and Clinical Psychology*, 1969, 33, 440–447.

Tucker, L. R., Damarin, F., & Messick, S. A base-free measure of change. *Psychometrika*, 1966, 31, 457–473.

Walker, A. M., Rablen, R. A. & Rogers, C. R. Development of a scale to measure process changes in psychotherapy. *Journal of Clinical Psychology*, 1960, 16, 79–85.

Wallerstein, R. S. The psychotherapy research project of the Menninger Foundation: An overview at the midway point. In L. A. Gottschalk and A. H. Auerbach (Eds.) *Methods of research in psychotherapy.* New York: Appleton-Century-Crofts, 1966. Pp. 500–516.

Wallerstein, R. S. The psychotherapy research project of the Menninger Foundation: A semifinal view. In J. M. Shlien (Ed.) *Research in psychotherapy*, Vol. 3. Washington, D.C.: American Psychological Association, 1968. Pp. 584–605.

Wallerstein, R. S., Robbins, L., Sargent, H., & Luborsky, L. The psychotherapy research project of the Menninger Foundation. *Bulletin of the Menninger Clinic*, 1956, 20, 221–280.

Warren, N. C., & Rice, L. N. Structuring and stabilizing psychotherapy for low-prognosis clients. *Journal of Consulting and Clinical Psychology*, 1972, 39, 173–181.

Waskow, I. E. Reinforcement in a therapy-life situation through selected responding to feelings of content. *Journal of Consulting Psychology*, 1962, 26, 11–19.

Waskow, I. E. & Parloff, N. B. (Eds.) *Psychotherapy change measures.* Rockville, Maryland: National Institute of Mental Health, 1975.

Watzlawick, P. *The language of change: Elements of therapeutic communication.* New York: Basic Books, 1978.

Weed, L. L. Medical records that guide and teach. *New England Journal of Medicine*, 1968, 278, 593–657.

Wexler, D. A. A scale for the measurement of client and therapist expressiveness. *Journal of Clinical Psychology*, 1975, 31, 486–489.

Wexler, D. A. Self-actualization and cognitive processes. *Journal of Consulting and Clinical Psychology*, 1974, 42, 47–53.

Yalom, I. D. *The theory and practice of group psychotherapy.* (2nd ed.) New York: Basic Books, 1975.

NAME INDEX

Adams, H. E., 103
Alvarez, W. F., 106, 107
Assum, A. L., 101
Auerbach, H. H., 89, 94, 96, 105, 182
Auerswald, M. C., 103
Auld, F., Jr., 101, 137–38

Baccus, G. K., 103
Barlow, D. H., 183
Barnabei, F., 103
Battle, C., 147
Bednar, R. L., 3, 22
Beebe, J., 100, 103
Bereiter, C., 150
Berenson, B. G., 99
Bergin, A. E., xiv, 3, 22, 25, 167
Bergman, D. V., 103
Bernstein, A., 143–44, 146–47
Berzins, J. I., 3, 22
Blair, J. H., 103
Bloxom, A. L., xiv, 147
Braaten, L. J., 101
Brown, S. D., 103, 178
Brumer, S., 105
Brunette, A., 141, 156, 157, 163
Budge, S., 18
Bugental, J. F. T., 142
Burton, A., xiv
Butler, J. M., 99, 106–7

Campbell, D. T., 150
Carkhuff, R. R., 99, 108, 147
Cartwright, D. S., 30
Cassens, J., 100, 103
Chance, J., 101
Charles, E., 147
Chasson, J. B., 104
Christoph, P., 3
Claiborn, C. D., 143
Clark, E. L., 141, 156, 157, 163

Cline, J., 106, 107
Cofer, C. N., 101
Comeau, L., 141, 156, 157, 163
Cook, J. J., 104
Cormier, W. H., 103
Cox, B. A., 25
Cristol, A. H., 147
Cronbach, L. J., 178
Curtis, H., 104

Dahlstrom, W. G., 150
Damarin, F., 150
Derogatis, L. R., 28
Dittman, T., 102
Dollard, J., 96, 101
Droppleman, L. F., 28
DuBois, P. H., 150
Duncan, S., Jr., 106–7
Durak, G. M., 143, 144, 163, 178

Edwards, H. P., 143
Elliott, R., 94, 95, 104, 106, 107, 146, 183
Escoll, P. S., 104
Ewing, J. A., 104

Fagan, J., 157
Fanshel, D., 143, 145
Feinstein, L., 146
Fellers, G., 103, 178
Fenichel, O., 102
Fiske, D. W., xiv, 26, 150, 167, 178, 179, 181–82
Frank, G. H., 103
Frank, J. D., xiv, 106, 147
Frye, R. L., 103

Gassner, S., 105
Gendlin, E. T., 100, 103, 108
Gervaize, P. A., xvi, 13, 103, 132, 142, 163, 177, 178

199

SUBJECT INDEX

abreaction, 103
actualization, 36, 63–64, 66
. bodily sensations of, 39–40
of good form of operating domain,
  36–45, 72
aloneness, externalization of, 51–52
anger:
  experiencing of, 71
  externalized and internalized forms
    of, 47–48, 50
attacking, disintegrative vs. integrative
  form of, 38–39
autonomy:
  good integrated form of, 37, 65
  situational context of, 42, 44

behavioral therapies, 7, 10–11, 18
  indices of psychotherapeutic
    movement in, 105–6, 129, 130
behaviors, 32–33
  disintegrative, 53–58
  extinguishing of, 80–82
  for good form of operating
    domain, 40–45
  integrative, 58–63
  monitored by bodily sensations,
    58–59
  new, in extra-therapy world, 109,
    114–15, 176
  for new operating potentials,
    67–71
  risking changes in, 123–24
  target, 124–25, 128, 130
being, new ways of:
  new experiencing as outcome of,
    70–71
  new external situations for, 68–69
  for new operating potentials,
    67–71
  risking of, 123–24

bodily movements, in strong
  experiencing, 110–11, 112
bodily phenomena:
  extinguishing of, 82–83
  internalized deeper potentials as,
    49
bodily sensations:
  of actualization, 39–40
  behavior monitored by, 58–59
  disintegrative vs. integrative feel-
    ings and, 46–47
  as internalized forms of deeper
    potentials, 48, 49
  in strong experiencing, 110, 111,
    112

California Personality Inventory, 29
cancers, 49
catharsis, 103
change, see psychotherapeutic change
chaos, disintegrative vs. integrative
  form of, 38
childlike experiencing, 71
choice, in existential-humanistic
  approach, 176
client-centered therapies, xi, 27, 28,
  35
  indices of psychotherapeutic move-
    ment in, 99–100, 102–3, 136
clinical literature, on indices of psychotherapeutic movement,
  90–92
clinical researchers, new role for,
  34–36, 44–45, 84–85, 109
cognitive therapies, 29, 35, 172
cohesive behaviors, 129
coldness, externalizations of, 48, 50,
  57
communication, expressive, 119
communications theory, 27